IMAGES
of America

THE PRAIRIE CLUB OF CHICAGO

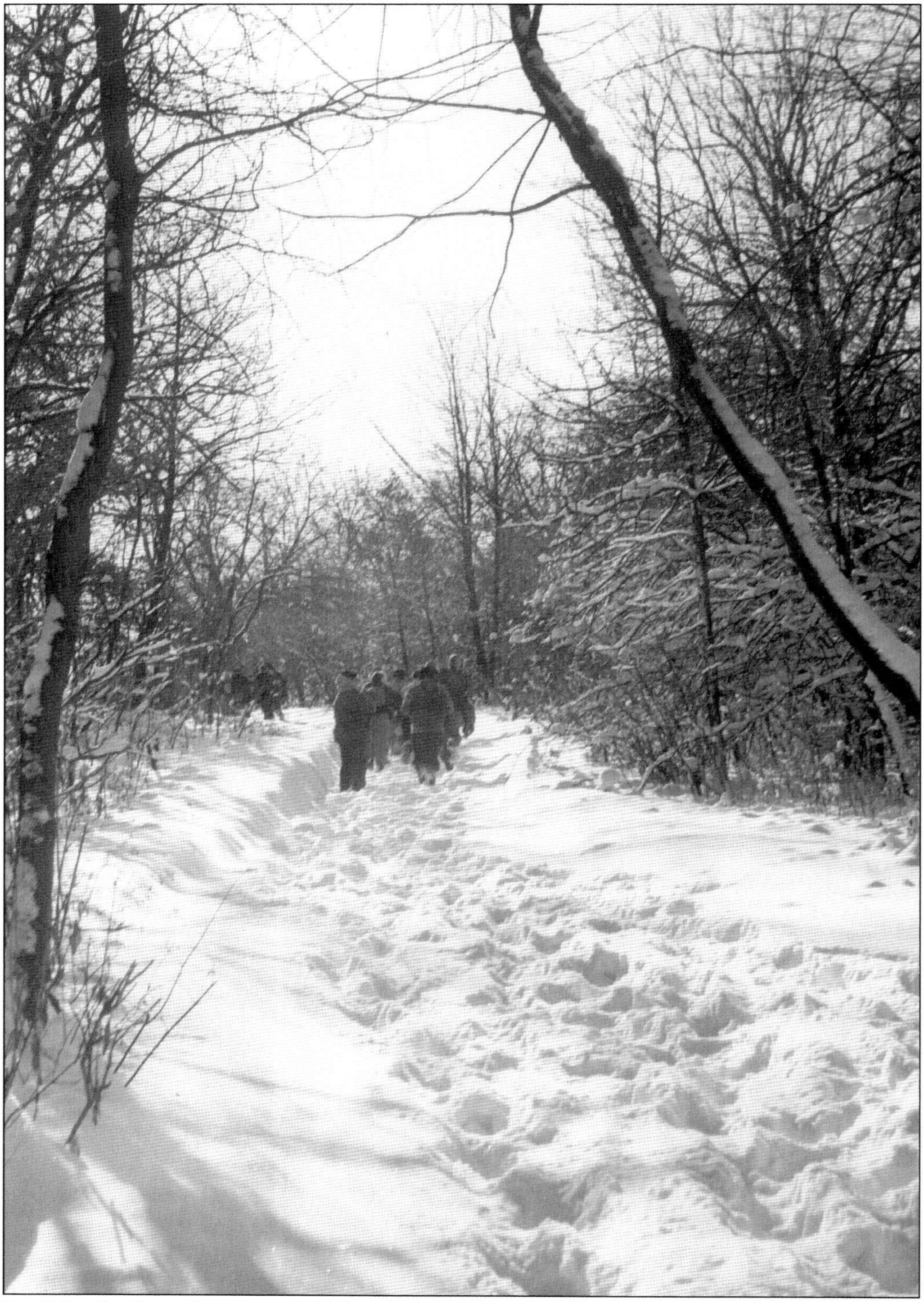

In all kinds of weather, Prairie Club members enjoyed walks out-of-doors. True nature lovers, they left only footprints and memories behind. (Photo courtesy of Jo Wilson.)

IMAGES
of America

THE PRAIRIE CLUB OF CHICAGO

Cathy Jean Maloney

ARCADIA
PUBLISHING

ISBN 978-0-7385-1921-0

Published by Arcadia Publishing
Charleston, South Carolina

Printed in the United States of America

Library of Congress Catalog Card Number: 2001093303

For all general information contact Arcadia Publishing at:
Telephone 843-853-2070
Fax 843-853-0044
E-mail sales@arcadiapublishing.com
For customer service and orders:
Toll-Free 1-888-313-2665

Visit us on the Internet at www.arcadiapublishing.com

Contents

Acknowledgments

I would like to thank the members of the Prairie Club, past and present, for their love and reverence of the outdoors. Had early Prairie Club members not actively protected the wonders of nature, many of our treasured natural landscapes would not exist. Today's Prairie Club members remain true to the ideals of charter members, and I thank them for sharing their thoughts, memories, and hospitality.

Loretta (Lorry) Davies, Executive Director of the Prairie Club, championed this project from the outset. Her enthusiasm and positive attitude have been an enormous help. Most of the contemporary pictures of the Prairie Club are from Lorry. I thank her and the Prairie Club Board of Directors for their support.

Richard (Dick) Spurgin, who, in his words, was "born into the Prairie Club," generously gave his time and input in reviewing drafts for accuracy. Any errors in the book fall squarely on my shoulders.

From the earliest times, Prairie Club members have enjoyed photography. The wonderful images in this book are drawn from such early photographers as Arthur E. Ormes, C.S. Van Wart, A.L. Fitch, Clarence Dudley, Arthur Anderson, Clara Jacobson, and others. Dan Bruhn, a professional photographer in Chesterton, Indiana, was invaluable in reproducing these early pictures from original scrapbooks and archives.

The archives of the Prairie Club are held at the Westchester Public Library in Chesterton, Indiana. Jane Walsh-Brown, Assistant Library Director / Museum Curator, was unbelievably helpful in organizing the archives and making me feel most welcome.

Long overdue and heartfelt thanks go to my Dad, whose "Saturday Afternoon Walks" in Palos inspired a lifetime love of the outdoors in our family. Mom, who nurtured us indoors and out, deserves a bouquet of hugs from her carbon copy. For Mike and Thomas, the "wind beneath my wings," all my love.

INTRODUCTION

Let's take a walk! In today's supersonic, upwardly mobile, moving-at-e-speed world, isn't it nice to downshift to a more pedestrian pace? Whether it's a leisurely stroll through a cool, wooded glen, or a hearty hike through hill and dale, walking in tune with nature clears the mind and calms the soul.

Thanks to the trailblazing efforts of the Prairie Club, Chicagoans are blessed not only with a rich tradition of walking, but also with abundant natural vistas and venues to explore. Formed in 1908, as an outgrowth of the Playground Association of Chicago, and incorporated as a separate entity in 1911, men and women of the Prairie Club literally broke new ground as they sponsored walking trips around Chicago's countryside.

By exposing Chicagoans to the surrounding beauty of nature, the Prairie Club helped build an important constituency for preserving the forests, fields, and prairies. As lovers of nature, the club's mission has always emphasized outdoor recreation and stewardship of the environment.

Through the images in this book, you can follow the footsteps of early Prairie Club members as they looked to nature for relief from societal ills. Like many large American cities in the early 1900s, Chicago's industrialization and waves of immigration spawned crowded, unhealthy urban conditions. Meanwhile, just outside of the city, great swaths of pastoral countryside were being consumed by so-called "Improvement Companies," wherein speculative developers built suburbs first along the railways, then everywhere in between. Neither the city nor its immediate environs seemed safe from the perils of progress.

Reformers of this period, the Progressive Era, emphasized outdoor activities in everything from revised education curricula to sponsored day trips for the urban poor. It was believed that unhealthy living conditions could be alleviated through the creation of small neighborhood parks and greater accessibility to the outdoors.

The national climate favored a back-to-nature movement. President Theodore Roosevelt, in office from 1901 to 1909, made conservation a key campaign crusade. The burgeoning "back to basics" Arts and Crafts movement dovetailed nicely with Chicago's own emerging Prairie School of architecture and landscape. America, and Chicago, were ready to return to their grassroots.

The newly formed Playground Association of America (PAA) held its second annual meeting in Chicago in June 1907. This group, whose leadership included Theodore Roosevelt as honorary president and Chicago's Jane Addams as vice-president, espoused outdoor recreation as a means of social reform. Most of the Prairie Club's charter members were part of the PAA.

About one year later, a subcommittee of the Playground Association of Chicago, headed by Prairie School architect Dwight H. Perkins, issued its first circular. Dated April 14, 1908, the brochure was an open invitation to the premiere series of "Saturday Afternoon Walking Trips" in the "Forests, Fields, Hills and Valleys about the City." These walking trips were co-sponsored by sixteen other kindred organizations, including the City Club, Geographic Society of Chicago, Woman's Outdoor Art League, Art Institute Instructors, Illinois Audubon Society,

The Cliff Dwellers, settlement house leaders, and more.

The first walk on Saturday, April 18, 1908, was led by Dwight Perkins and Alexander M. Wilson, a member of the Appalachian Mountain Club who was instrumental in bringing the Playground Association ideas to Chicago. A total of 128 people joined these pioneer hikers on a 3-mile walk around the Mount Forest District near Willow Springs.

The walks were quite popular, and the upstart group rambled about the Chicago area for three years, growing in numbers and enthusiasm. In the May 4, 1911 bulletin, the new name of the Prairie Club was introduced with the explanation, "to secure a more formal organization and to provide for its increasing activities." Jens Jensen, renowned landscape architect and one of the club's first presidents, is credited with giving the club its new name.

Although weekend walks were a mainstay, the menu of the Prairie Club's outdoor activities had indeed expanded. Weekend trips to scenic areas like Starved Rock and Grand Detour were conducted. Joint trips with the Geographic Society to Yellowstone Park were held. Longer summer trips to Upper Michigan, the western states, and other nature spots were chartered. As early as June 1910, discussions ensued about a proposed camp at the Indiana Dunes. The young hiking club began to spread its wings.

Under those protective wings, many treasures of Chicago's history and environment were preserved. With the early leadership of charismatic and influential Chicagoans and the diversity of talents in its general membership, the Prairie Club left its footprint on many a page in history. Local and national conservation efforts were supported, outdoor camps were built, trails were marked and paths paved, rivers were paddled, dramatic masques performed, and, perhaps most importantly, lifelong friendships were built.

For over 90 years, the Prairie Club has taken the high road in conservation and the love of the outdoors. You are cordially invited to follow in their footsteps, and take a walk with the Prairie Club.

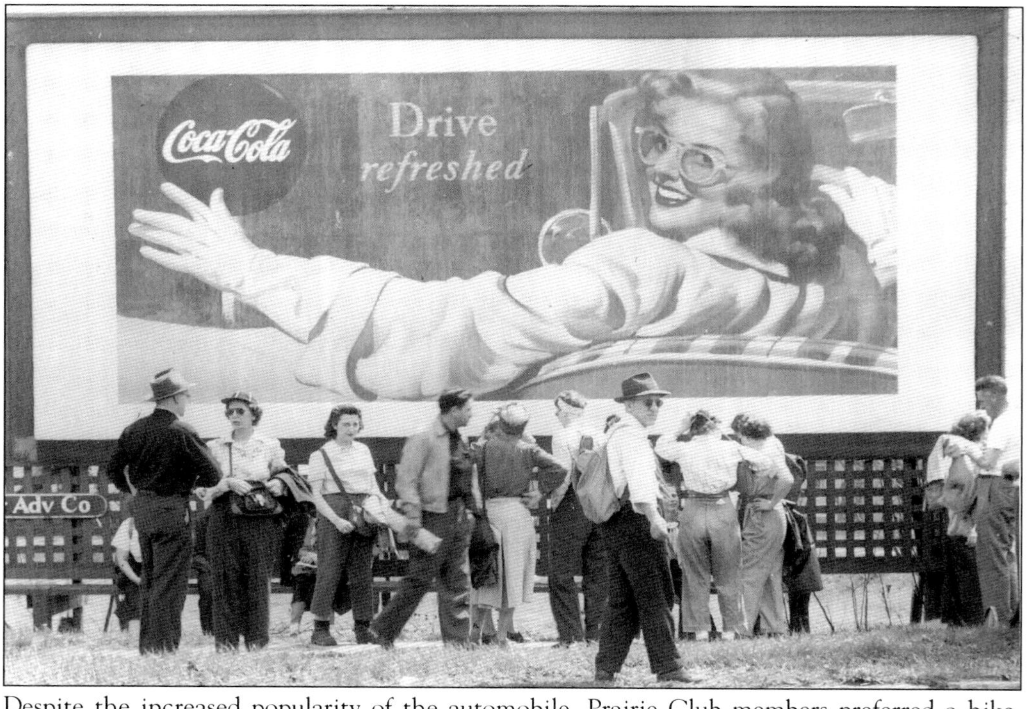

Despite the increased popularity of the automobile, Prairie Club members preferred a hike. Here, a photographer captures the irony as hikers wait under a billboard glorifying the joys of motoring. (Photo courtesy of Jo Wilson.)

One

THE FIRST STEP

If the longest journey begins with a single step, the Prairie Club got off on the right foot. Their first series of five walks in 1908, under the auspices of the Playground Association of Chicago, included Palos Park, Riverside, The Sag, the Mount Forest District, and the North Shore. By 1984, the Prairie Club had sponsored its 3,000th walk, with the Brookfield Zoo chosen as the venue. Club lore has it that, weather notwithstanding, not a single walk has ever been canceled.

The walks served not only as healthful exercise but also to acquaint Chicagoans with their valuable natural resources. With each walk, support grew for what ultimately became impassioned and victorious efforts to establish the Forest Preserves, Indiana Dunes, and other natural sites.

Imagine the challenges of walking in the early 1900s. Women's dresses swept the ground and barbed wire fences, the bane of all hikers, had to be negotiated at every turn. If weather became inclement, there was no turning back. Preparation was the key to a successful walk, and the club soon developed a standard regimen. Scouting parties were sent out to identify the best trails. Walk leaders and rear guides were appointed to keep hikers in line. Rest and refreshment spots were identified well in advance.

Walks often followed water routes around Chicago and outlying areas. The Salt Creek, Chicago River, Thorn Creek, and Sag Valley were popular spots. Hikers would board a designated train or trolley and begin their walks at the destination train depot. Six-mile hikes became the preferred length for Saturday Afternoon Walks, but longer all-day hikes soon became popular.

The impact of the automobile on America was just being felt. In 1902, the American Automobile Association (AAA) was formed in Chicago. By 1908, Henry Ford's Model T was a more common sight on the road. Despite the increasing popularity of the car, or perhaps because of it, the Prairie Club kept walking. Writing in the 1920s, Prairie Club member Samuel Harper penned these words, which still ring true today:

This jazz age demands its amusements on a high key. Walking is commonplace, and produces no thrills. Men seek extraordinary and unusual excitements, and are no longer sensitive to mere beauty. . . The hiker enjoys all the wonderful minutiae of Nature as he saunters by, while the passenger in the automobile only glimpses a wide panorama of hills and dales as he plunges along. . . An automobile keeps you to the paved road, in the construction of which all the beauties of the way have been ruthlessly destroyed. . . Whereas, the foot traveler may be tired but never weary, and his mind is charmed with the details of beauty which marked his every step on the day's journey."

A Hoosier Tramp, by Samuel Harper. The Prairie Club, 1928.

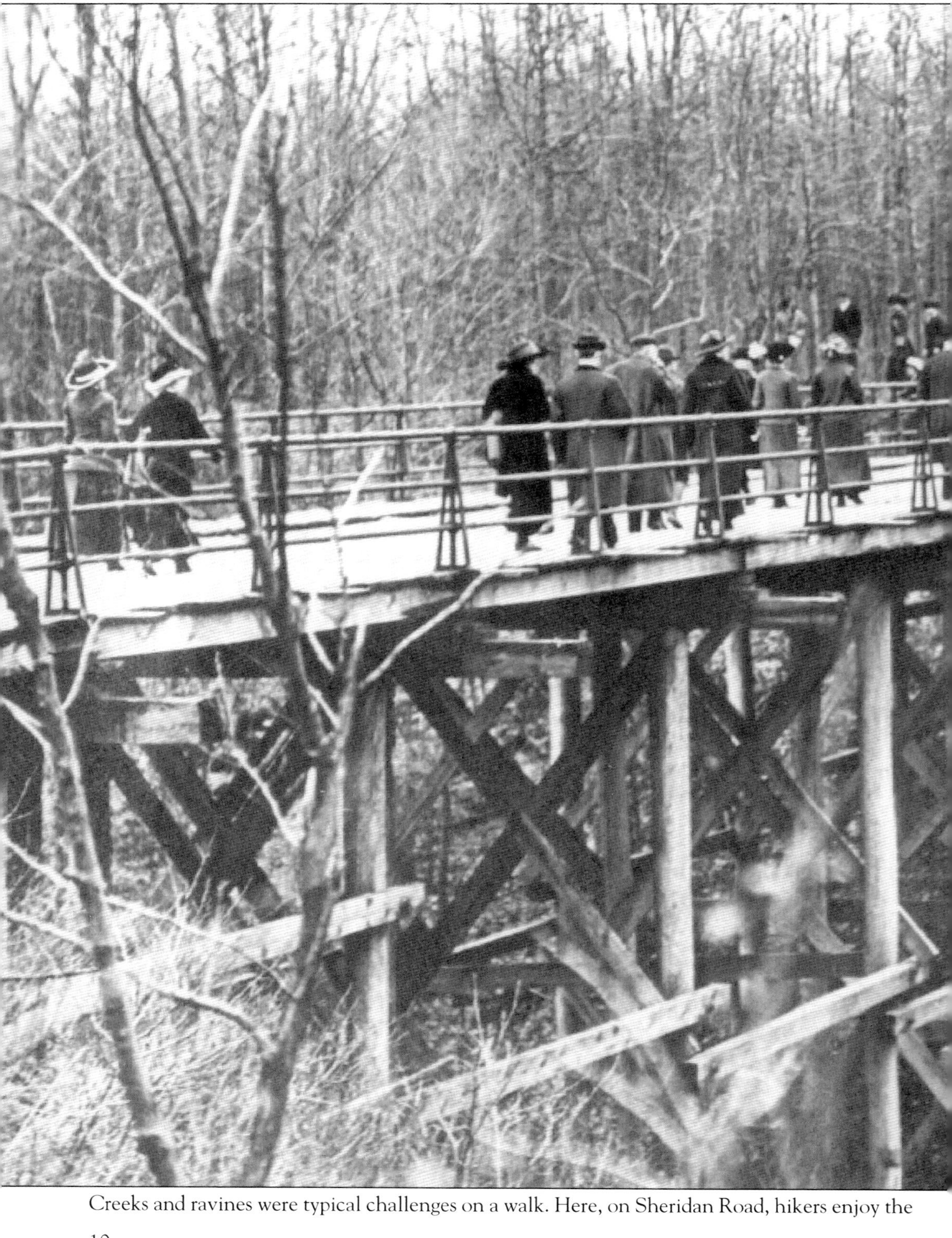

Creeks and ravines were typical challenges on a walk. Here, on Sheridan Road, hikers enjoy the

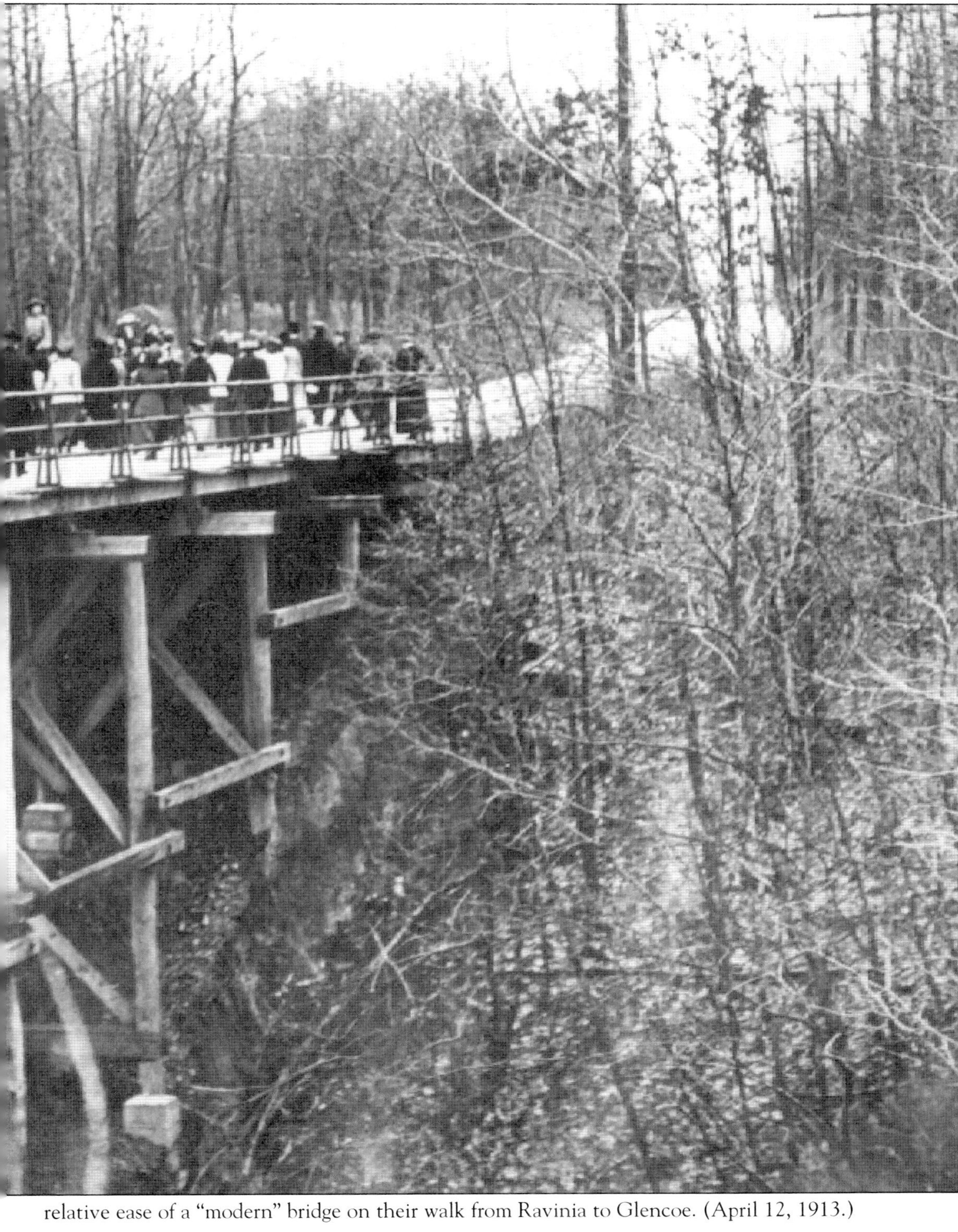

relative ease of a "modern" bridge on their walk from Ravinia to Glencoe. (April 12, 1913.)

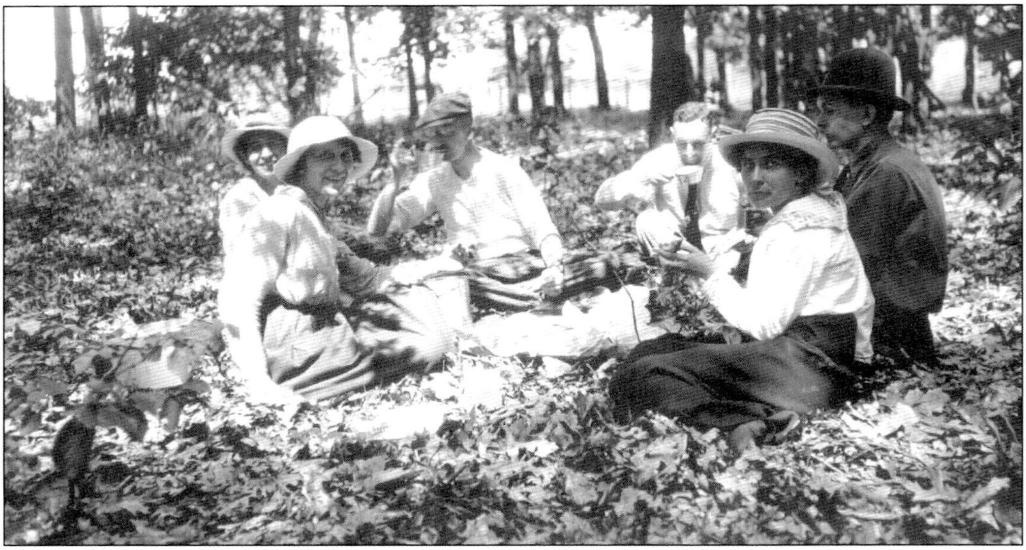

A critical ingredient for a successful walk was the scouting party. These intrepid souls would find the best trails and get permissions from property owners before the troops arrived. Of course, finding a nice picnic spot was also required—as did these pathfinders near Kankakee. (June 1915.)

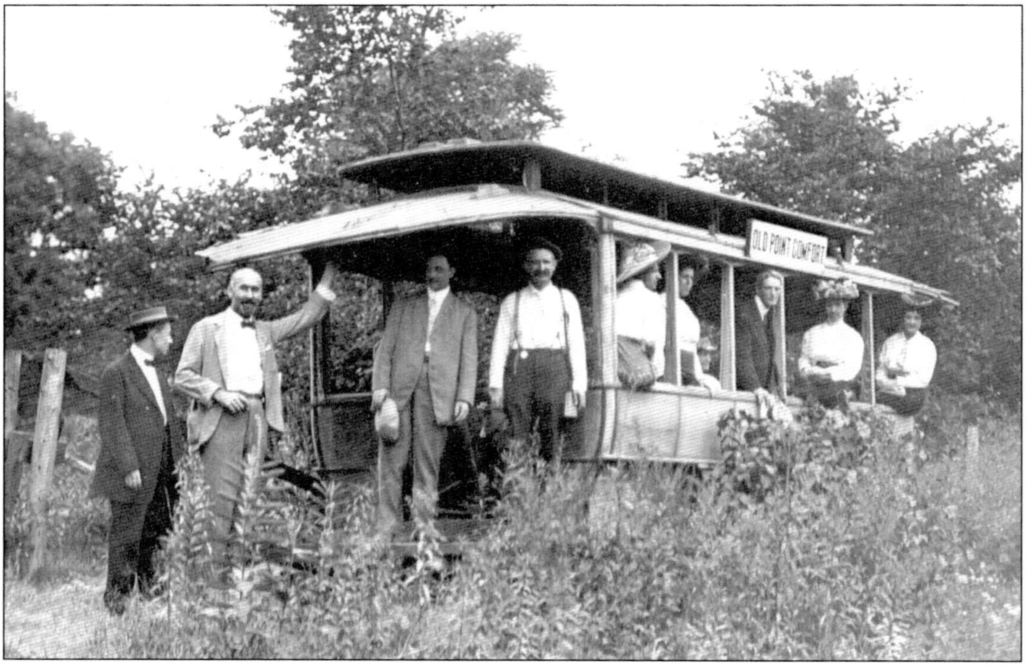

"Old Point Comfort," read the sign on this trolley car near Yorkville. Although this car doesn't appear mobile, the Prairie Club's Transportation Committee was another important group whose job was to find convenient conveyance to each trailhead. (August 1910.)

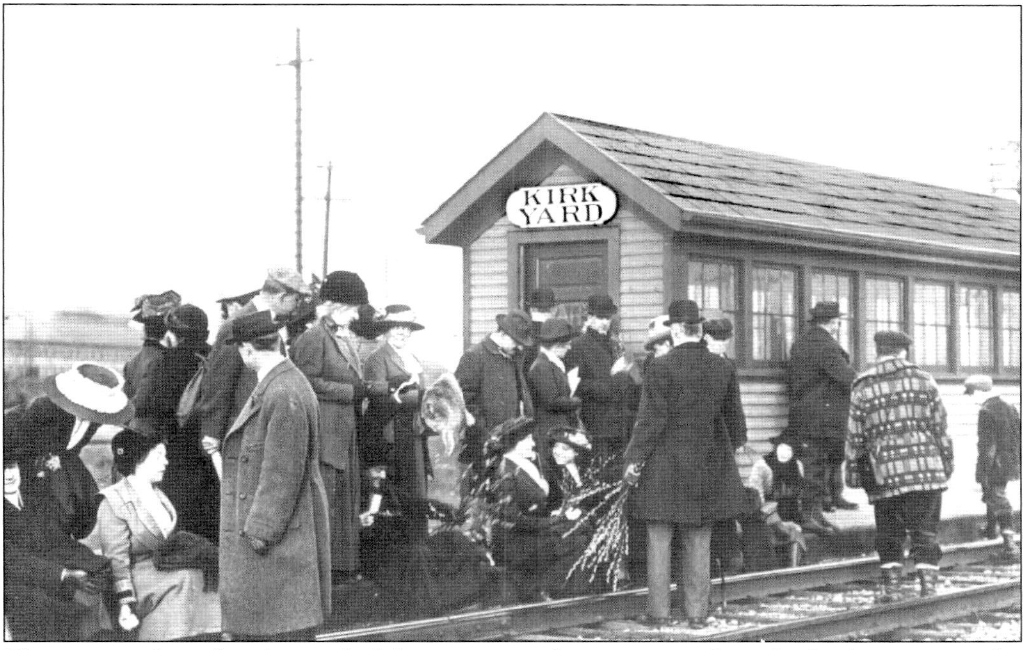

Chicago was the railroad capital of the country, and commuter rail was by far the most popular way to reach the hiking sites. Prairie Club members would board in the Loop and present a coupon to the conductor. Here, the group waits at the Kirk yard after their trip from Clarke. (March 22, 1913.)

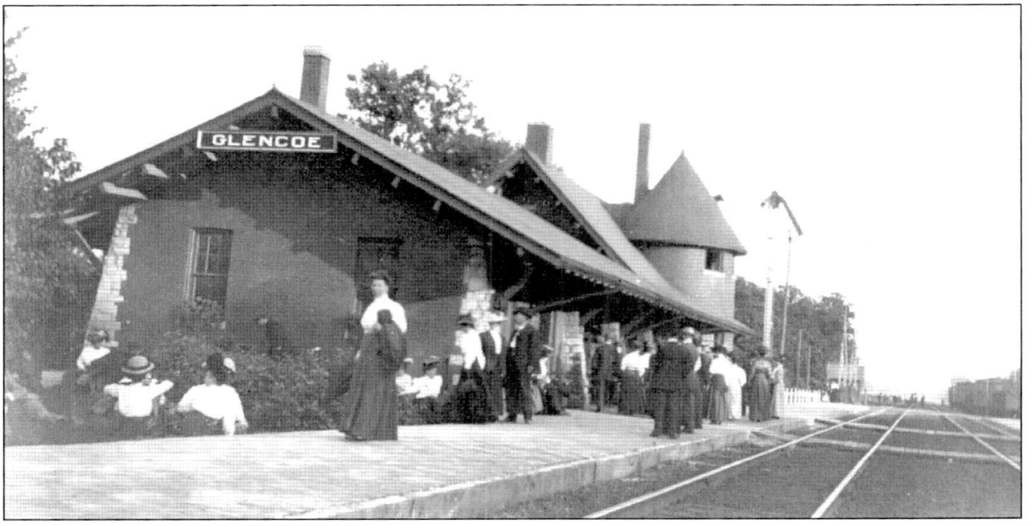

"Waiting for the return train," is handwritten on this photo documenting the Prairie Club's trip along the Skokie, culminating at Glencoe. (September 18, 1909.)

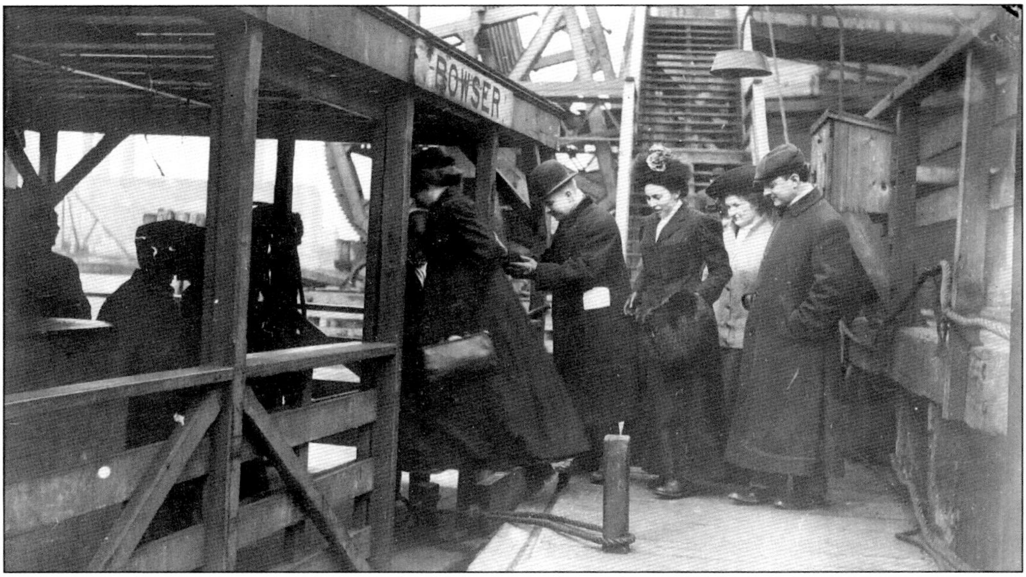

This Salt Creek trip began with a short jaunt on the city's ferryboat at Polk Street. Gertrude Simonds, daughter of landscape gardener Ossian Cole Simonds, is among those Prairie Club members embarking (second from right, according to a handwritten note on the photo). (January 29, 1910.)

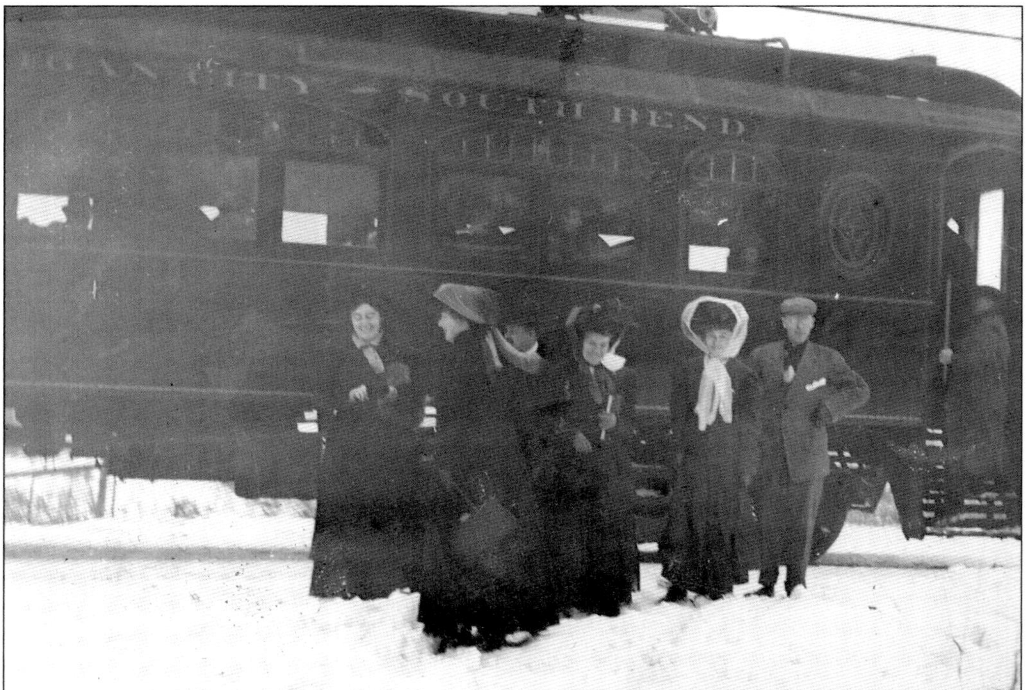

The South Shore Railroad was the main mode of transportation to the Indiana Dunes. Here, Prairie Clubbers disembark on their trip from Dune Park to Mineral Springs. (December 11, 1909.)

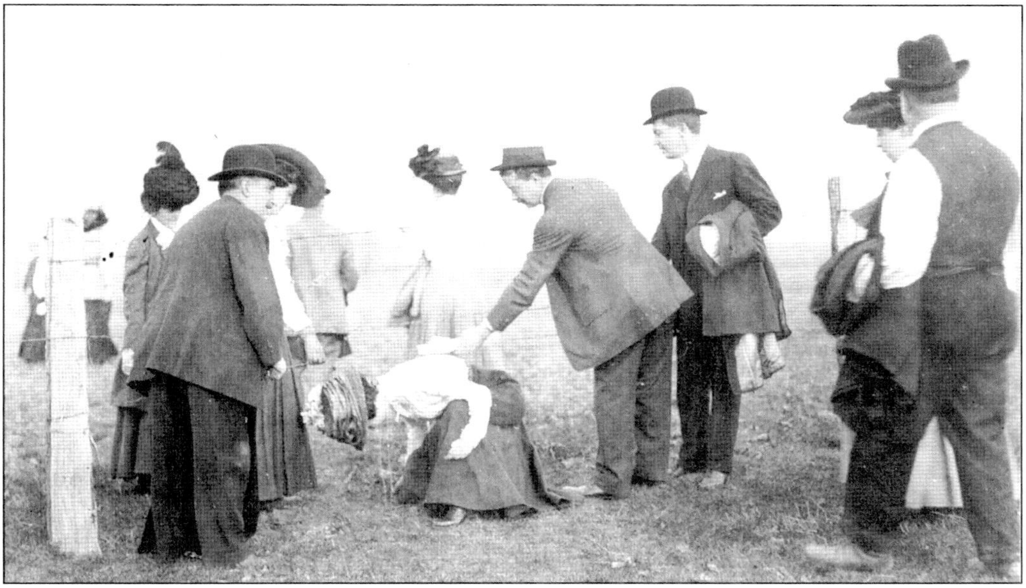

Barbed wire, that marvelous invention for farmers and ranchers, was a dreaded obstacle on every walk. Women found every imaginative way to "skirt" around these fences. (November 1909.)

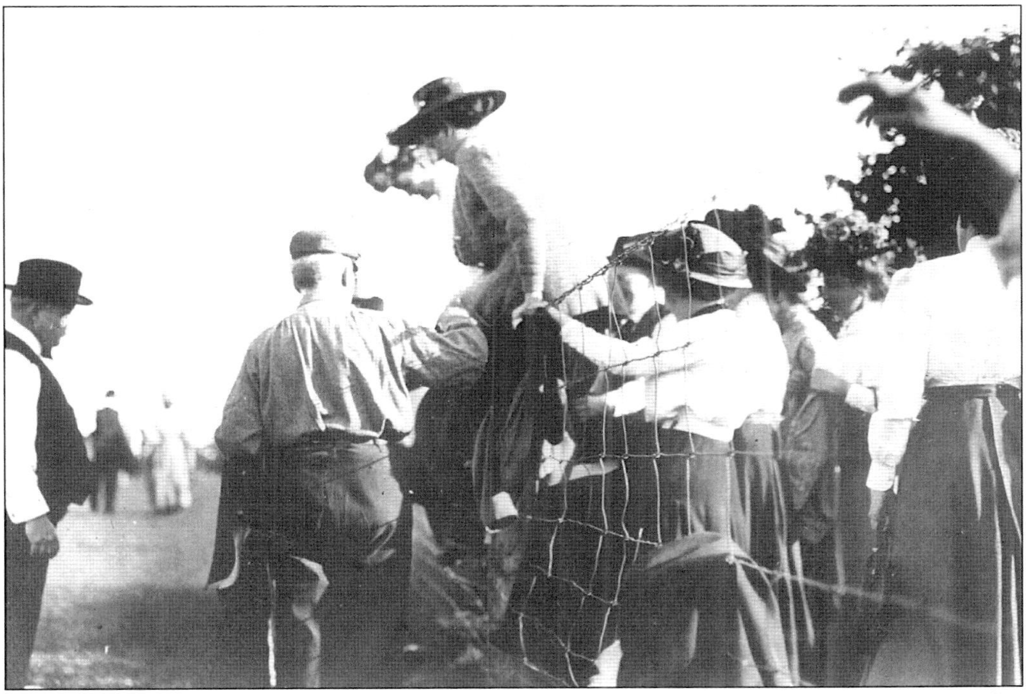

When all else failed, the helping hands of fellow hikers helped members go over the top on this fence in Lisle. (June 19, 1909.)

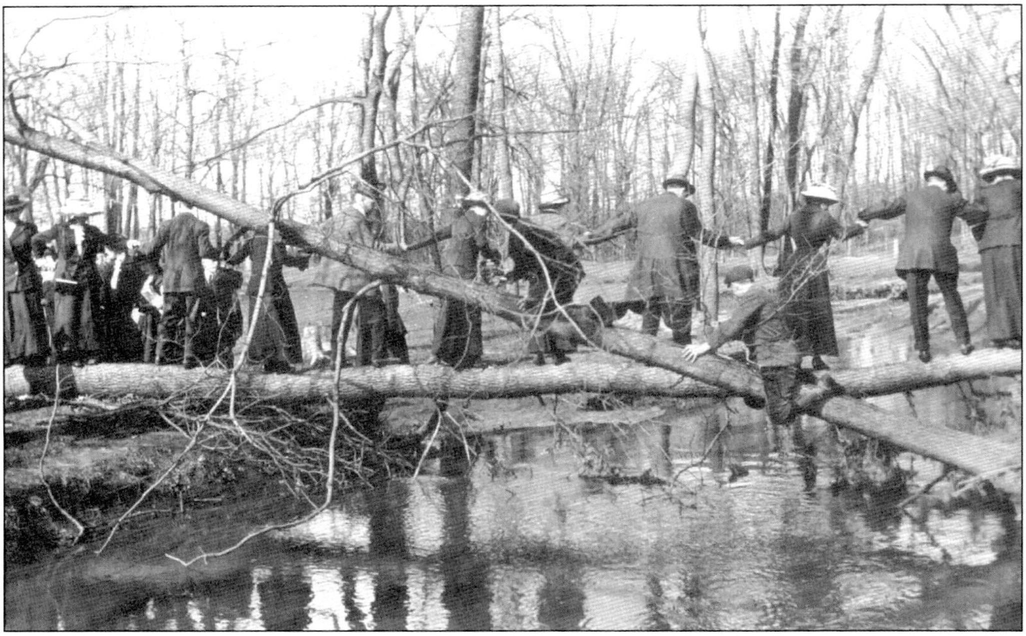

Besides barbed wire fences, hikers were also confronted with streams, creeks, and rivers to ford. Here, a human chain is formed to cross Salt Creek. (April 5, 1913.)

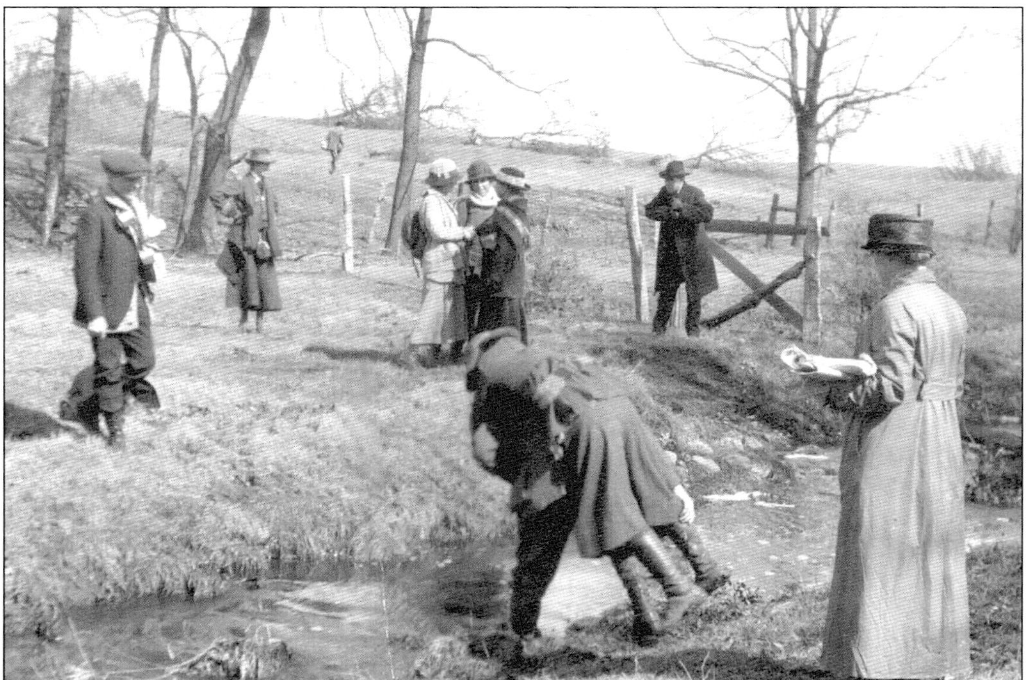

This lady relies on the strong back of a fellow hiker to cross this countryside stream. (1916.)

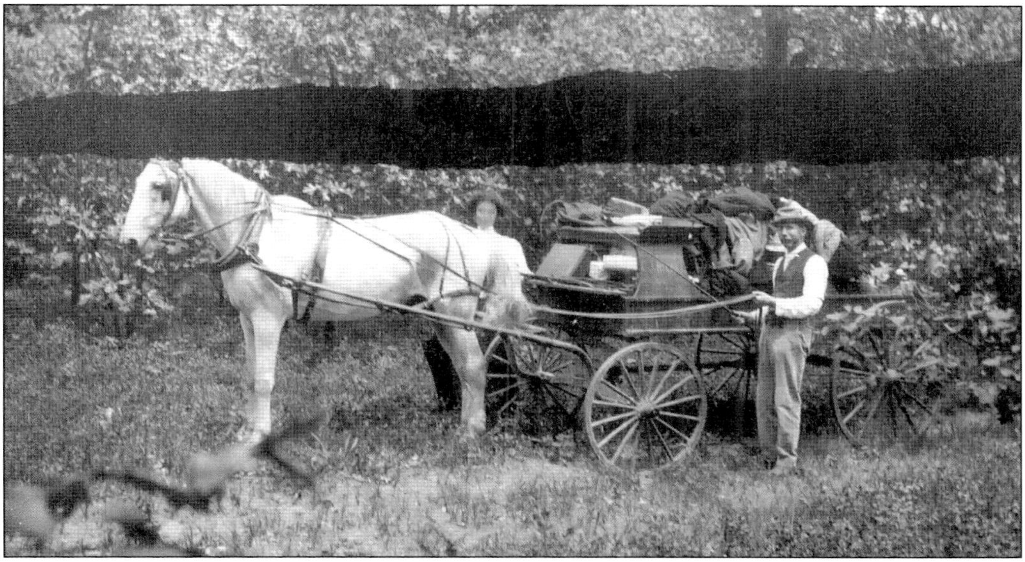

Hikers worked up a good appetite and provisions had to be made for refreshments. In some cases, like this all-day hike in the Dunes, a commissary wagon was hired to bring lunch baskets. (July 4, 1910.)

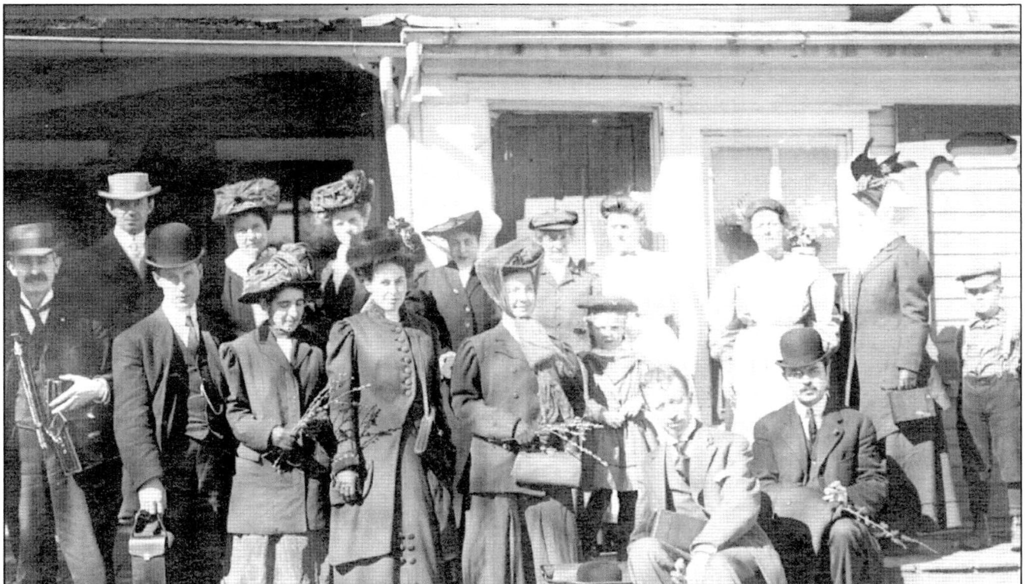

Proper clothing was essential. A 1911 Prairie Club Bulletin recommended sturdy shoes with broad soles, a small cap, and, "In this day of short skirts it should be almost needless to suggest that they are just the thing for cross country walks." Perhaps some of the ladies on this trip to Wheaton needed this advice. (March 20, 1910.)

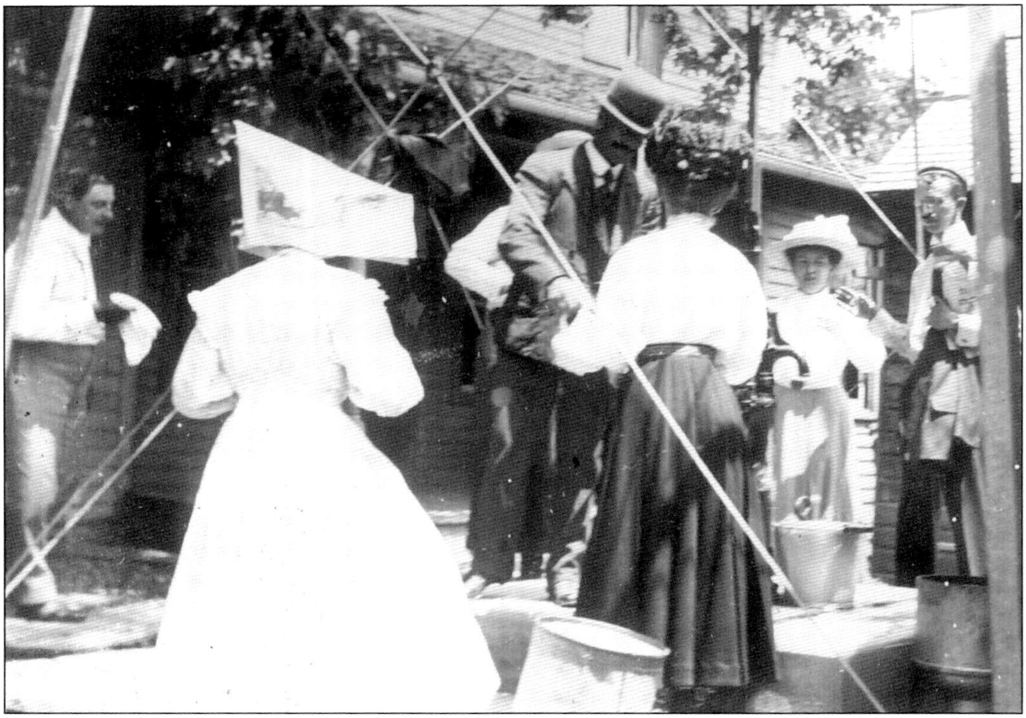

Improvisation was the key. If the weather outsmarted hikers, individual fashion statements were devised. On a trip to Power's Lake, this lady with the newspaper hat, identified only as "Helen," is undoubtedly warding off a too-hot sun. (June 26, 1910.)

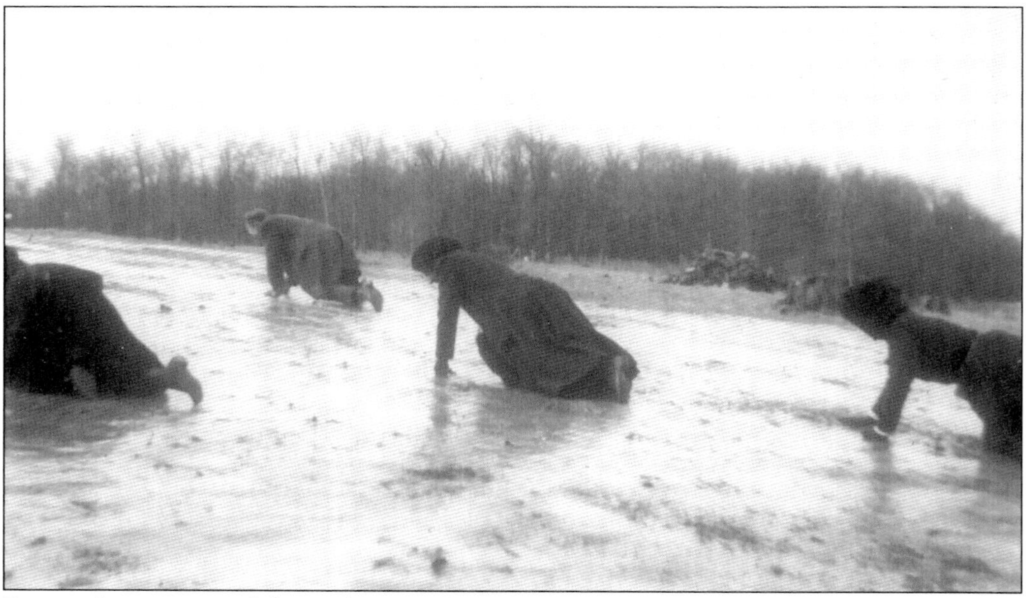

Despite freezing rain, club members crawled across the icy dunes. (No date.)

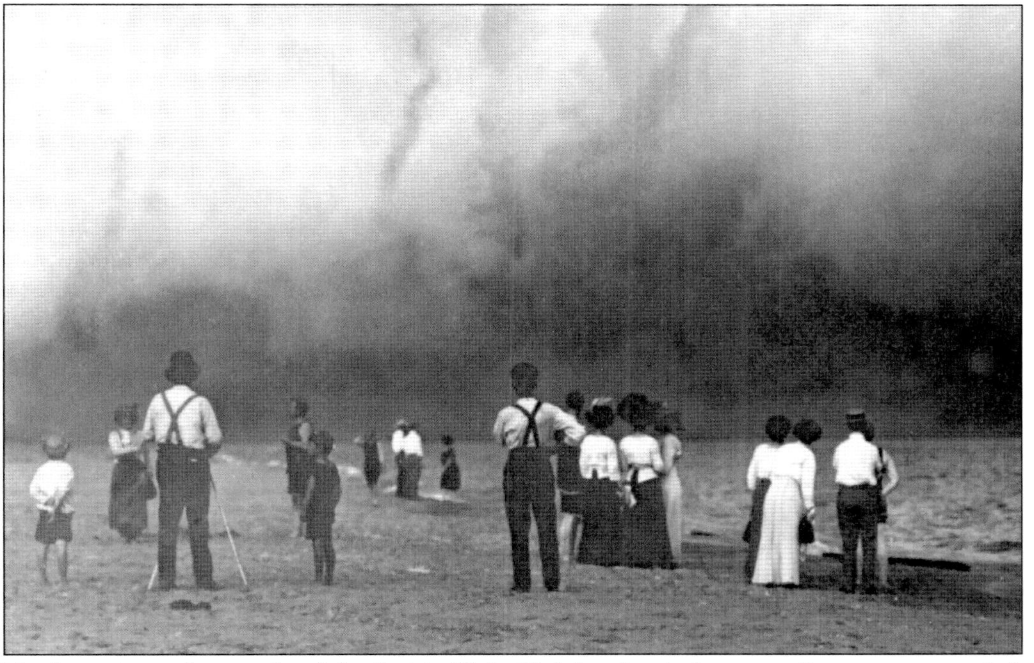

Neither rain nor hot sun fazed the Prairie Club. Club lore has it that no walk was ever canceled. Here, members brace for an approaching storm off Lake Michigan. (September 2, 1912.)

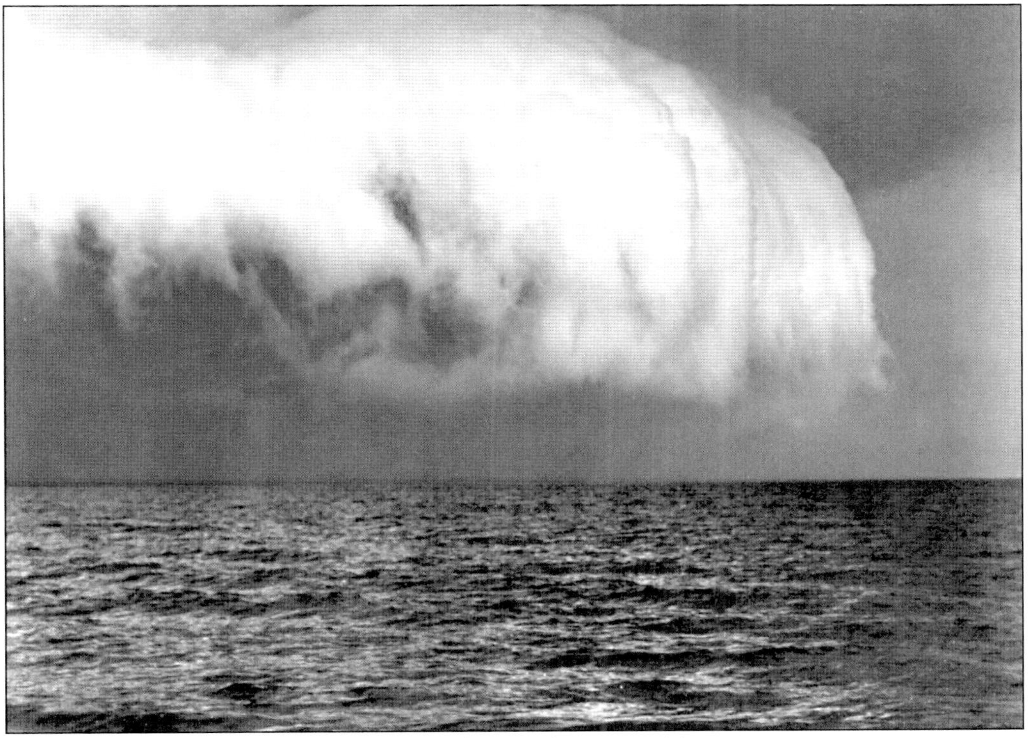

The beach is cleared as the storm arrives. (September 2, 1912.)

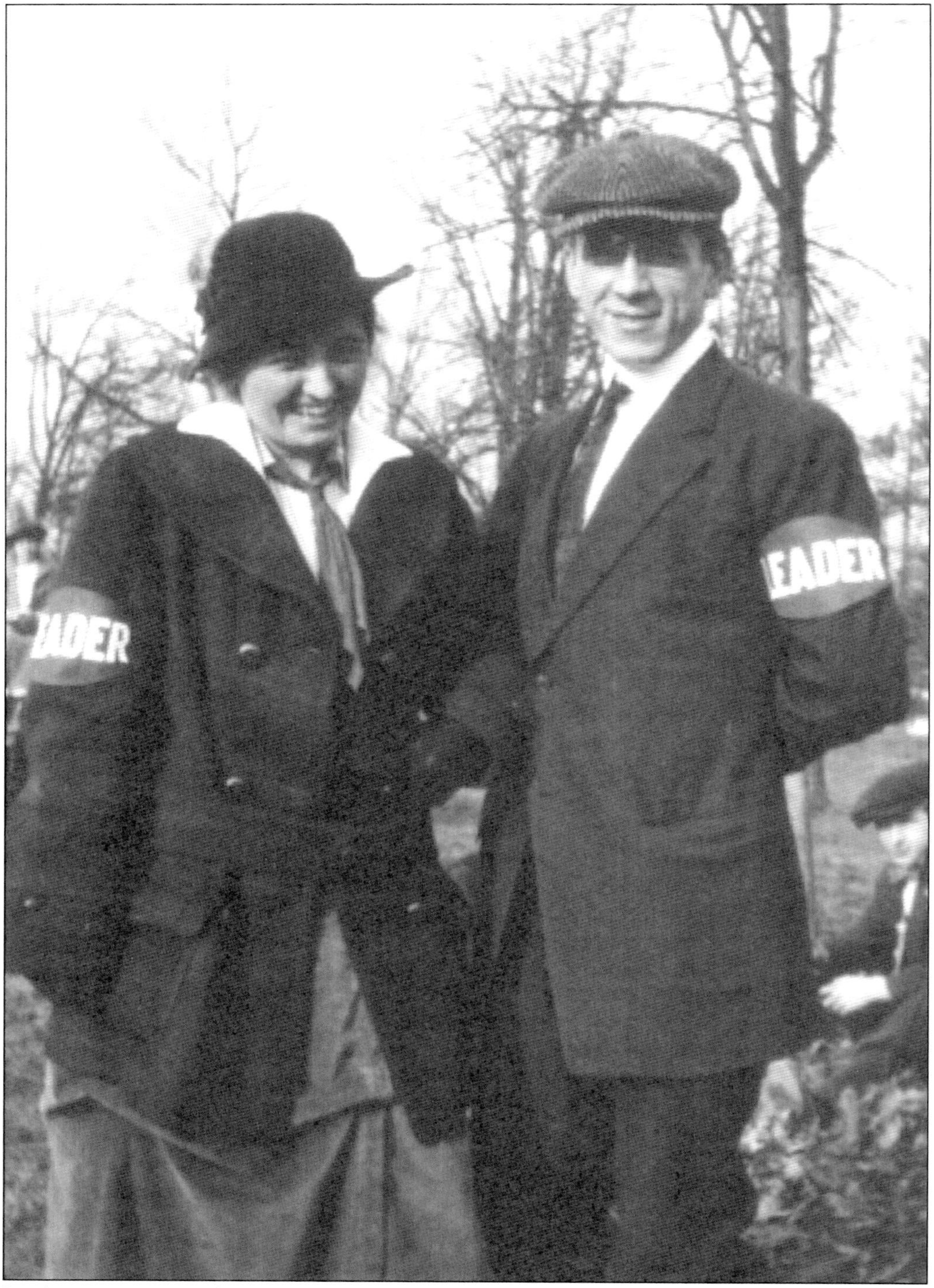

Leaders were essential to a good hike. Members would take turns and often share the dubious honor, like these two leaders from the hike from Elmhurst to Hinsdale along Salt Creek. (March 13, 1915.)

Two

SOUTHERN STROLLS

Some of the earliest walks explored the countryside around Chicago's near and far South Side. The Sag Valley, forested, hilly terrain along the I&M Canal, was a favorite spot. The forest preserves near Palos Park were also popular Prairie Club tramping grounds, and the club created a permanent camp in the area. Longer outings were also sponsored near Kankakee, New Lenox, and other scenic spots.

The train was taken to Palos and Tinley in the early days. Later, automobiles were used to reach the hiking trails. In these sparsely populated areas, wildlife and native plants were plentiful.

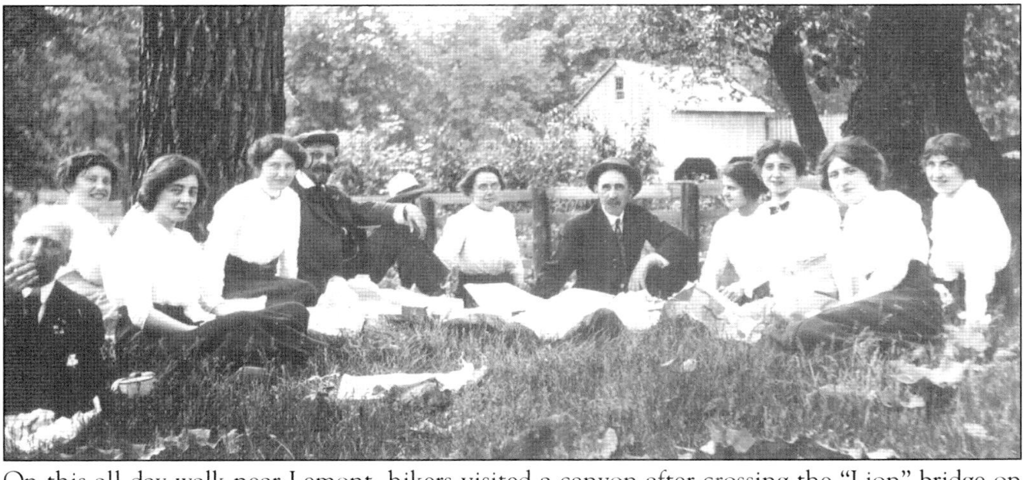

On this all-day walk near Lemont, hikers visited a canyon after crossing the "Lion" bridge on the Des Plaines River. Dinner was eaten near a small quarry "containing a spring and fossils for the keen-eyed," as per the Prairie Club Bulletin. (May 30, 1913.)

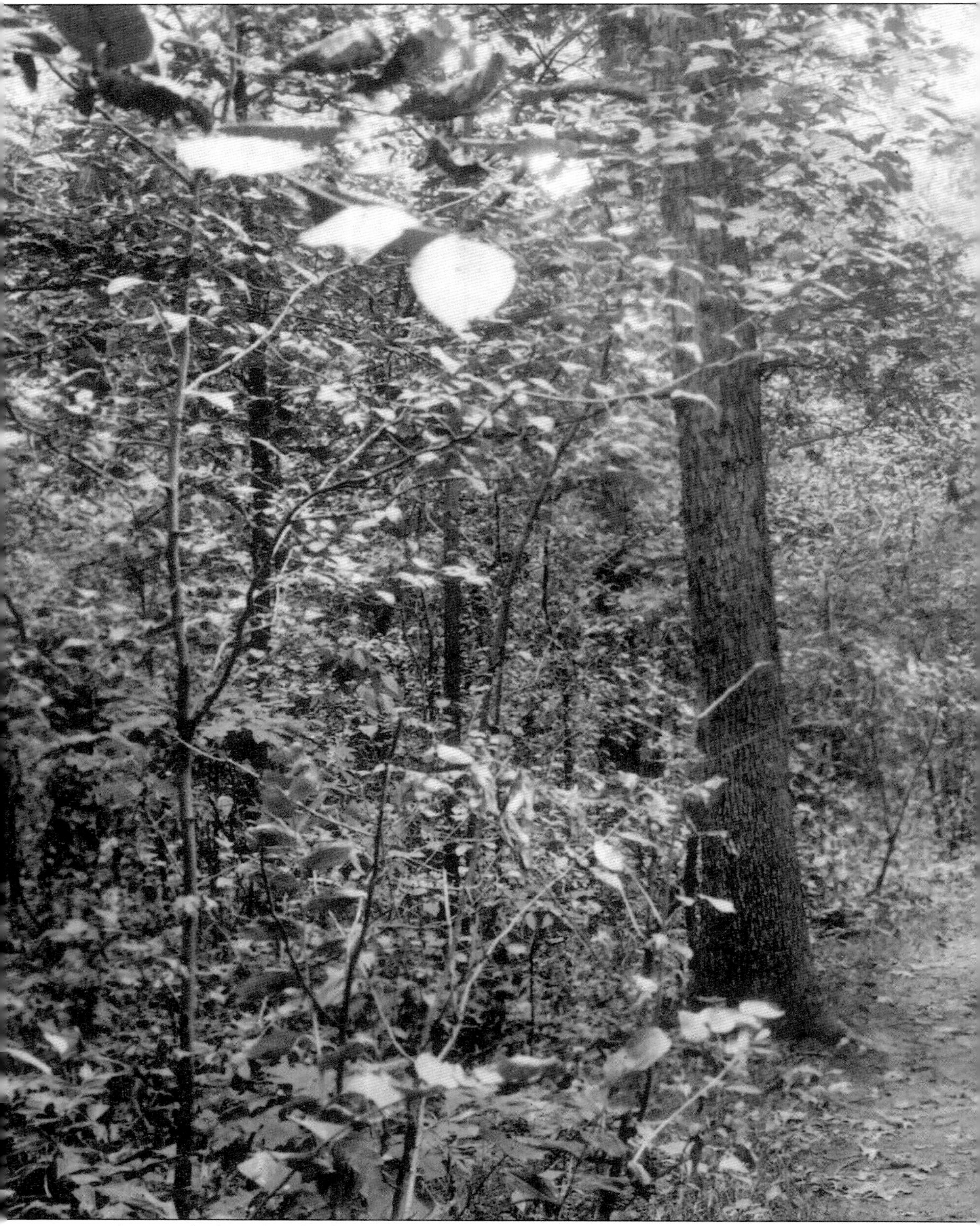

"The Crooked Trail," which wound through the forests and ravines, was a favorite path in Palos.

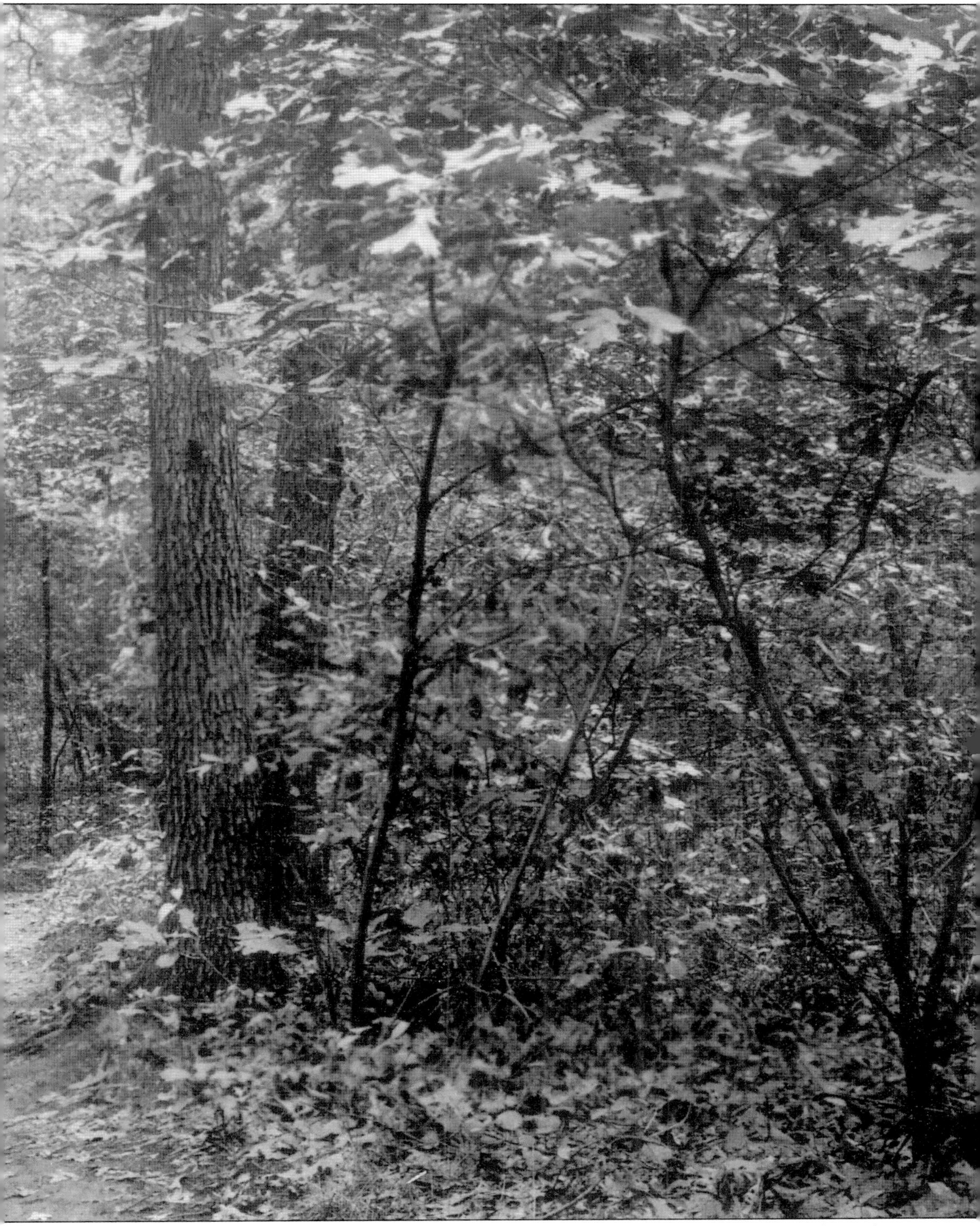
Many of the hiking trails favored by the Prairie Club became part of the forest preserves. (1923.)

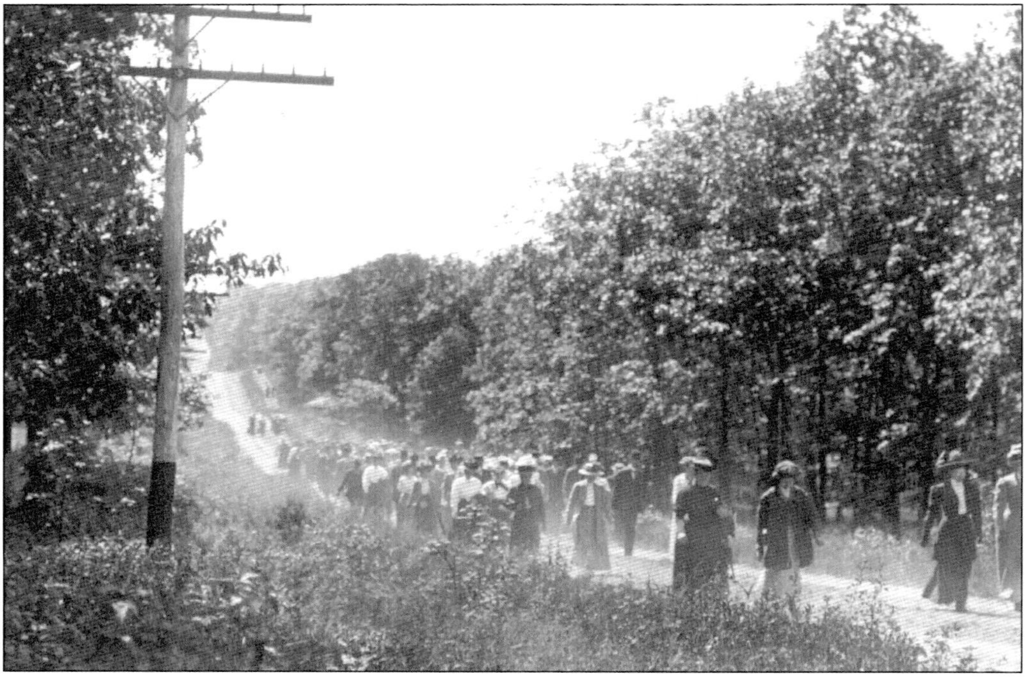

With its many hills, ravines, streams, and forests, Palos Park was a favorite destination for Prairie Club hikes. Here, a veritable parade of hikers walked through the hilly forest. (June 11, 1910.)

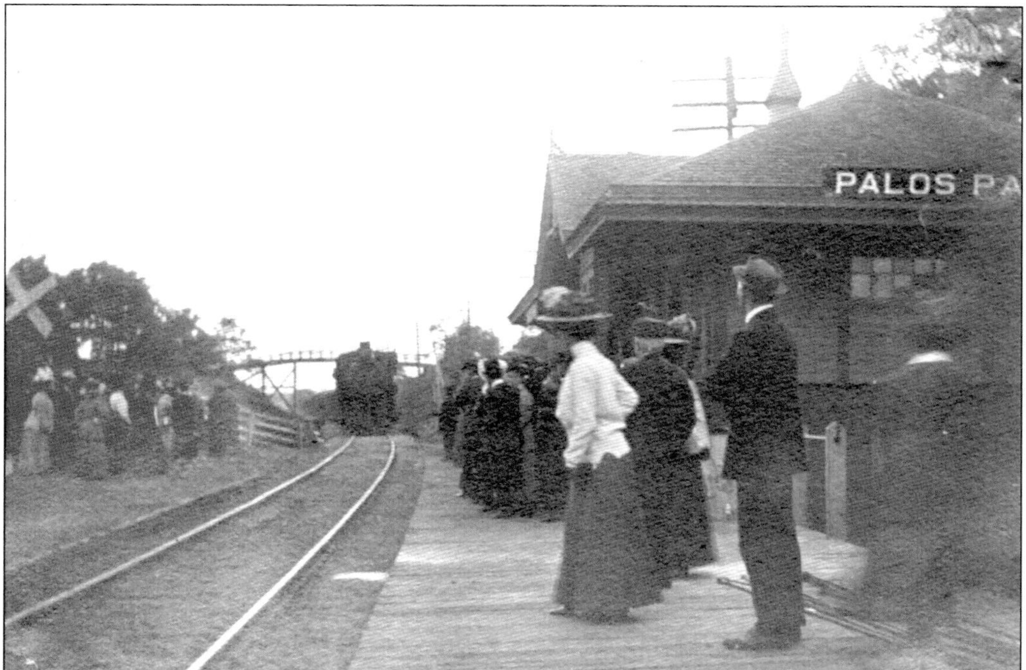

The handwritten caption on this photo says, "not our train." Surely it was a disappointment to weary homebound hikers who had just tramped all over Palos Park. (1908.)

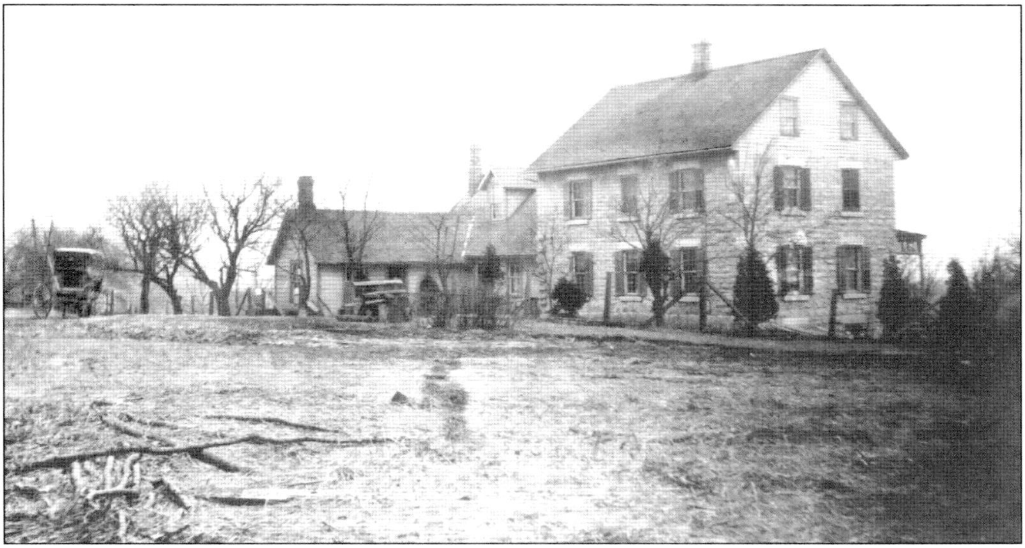

The Preller farm was a favorite rest stop on the Palos hikes because Mrs. Preller was famous for her chicken dinners. Sadly, the Prairie Club bulletin noted, Mrs. Preller could no longer accommodate the crowds and closed her doors. (March 15, 1913.)

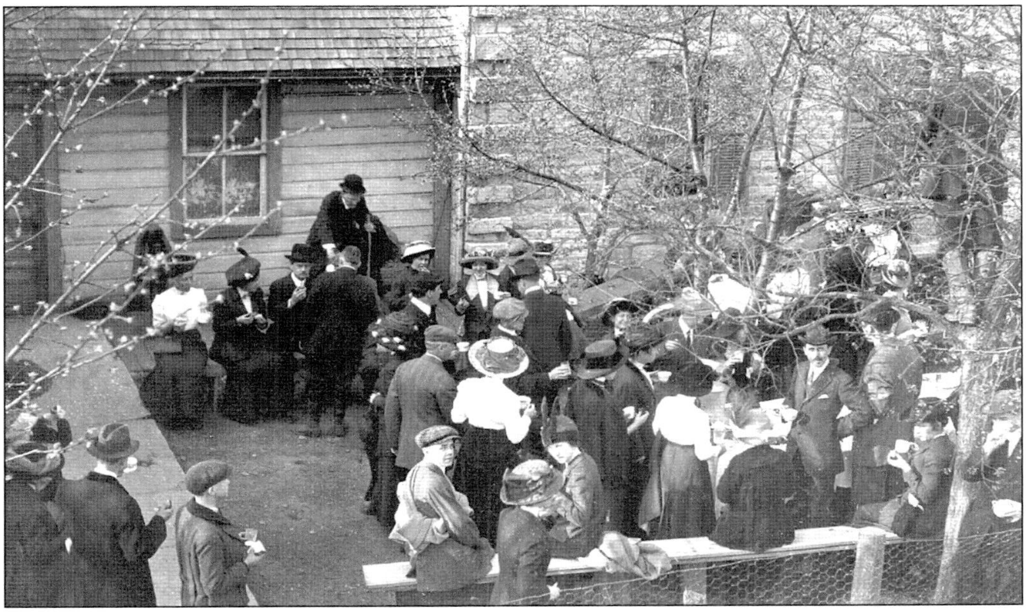

The club enjoyed Mrs. Preller's cooking on this hike between Mount Forest and Palos Park. A 5-mile walk along the north side of Mount Forest Island stopped at Willow Springs and returned to Chicago via Archer Avenue street car. An optional 10-mile walk proceeded to Palos Park. (April 26, 1913.)

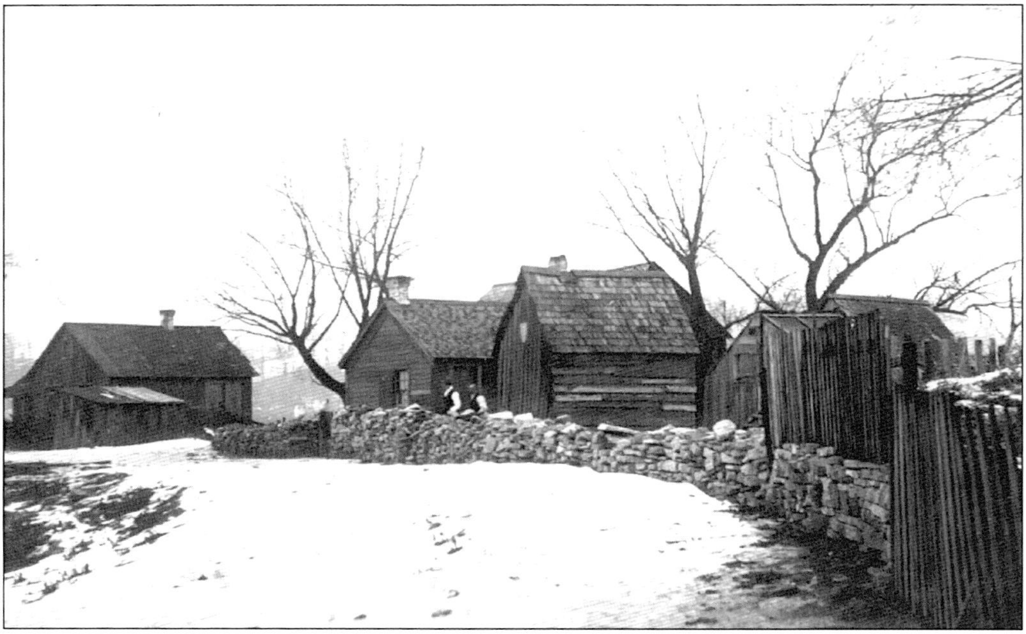

A New Year's walk was sponsored to the Sag, once an actual town near the I&M Canal and Des Plaines River. Here, several old shanties still stood in the Sag valley. (1911.)

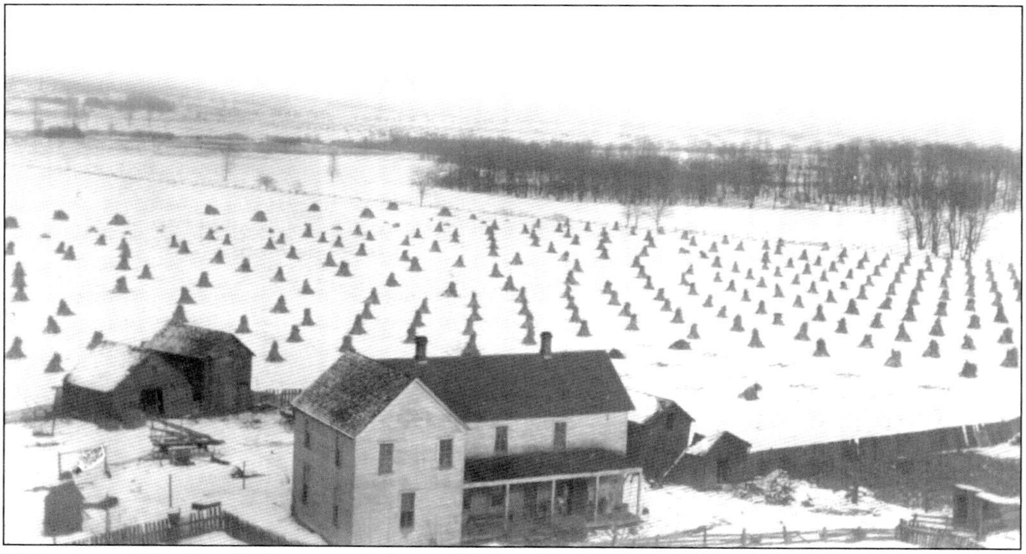

This view of the Sag Valley on a Palos to Willow Springs hike shows a quiet winter scene after the harvest. A handwritten note accompanying the photo says, "Across the Sag from Carrarha's Hill." (1909.)

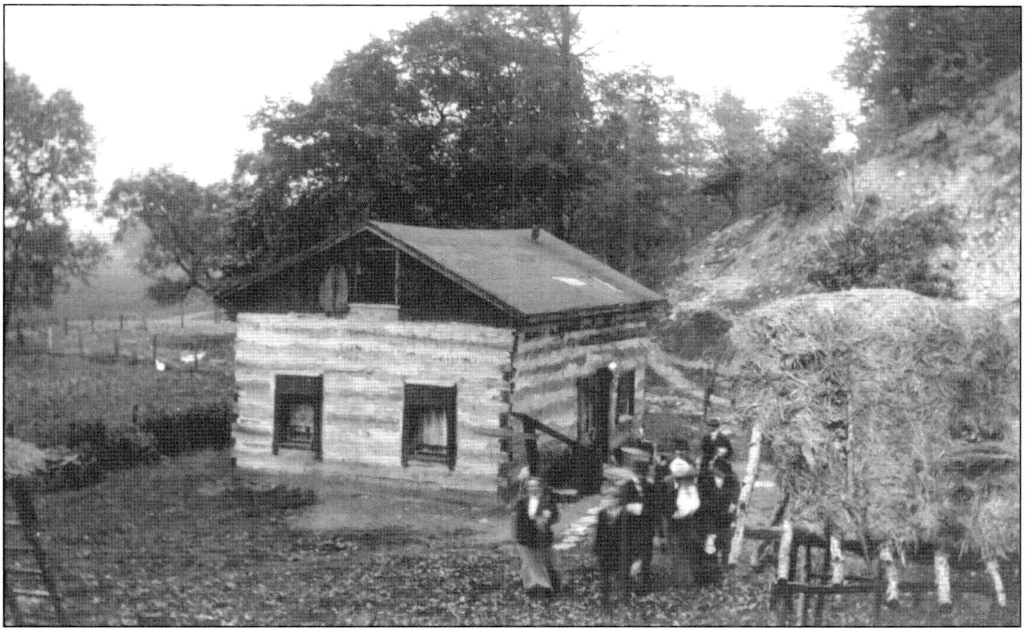

Log cabins like these were seen in the Sag area on Prairie Club walking trips and may have been originally built by workers on the I&M Canal. (June 5, 1909.)

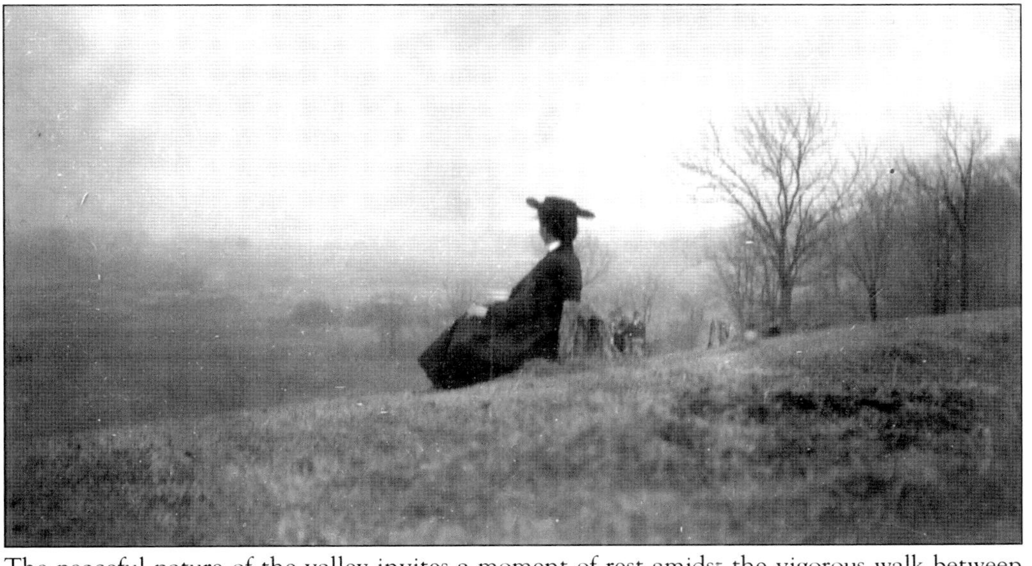

The peaceful nature of the valley invites a moment of rest amidst the vigorous walk between Palos and Willow Springs. A handwritten note on the photo says, "Reverie by Miss Patterson." (April 16, 1910.)

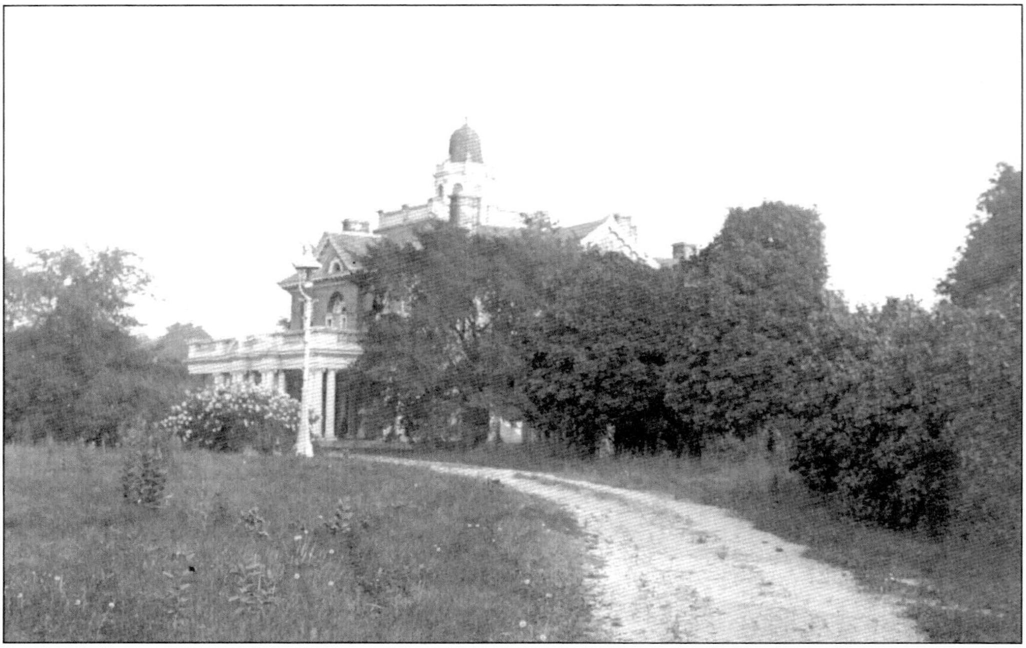

Harlow N. Higginbotham, early Chicago leader, opened up his estate to Prairie Club hikers. A 400-acre tract said to contain all the trees of Northern Illinois surrounded his house, shown here. It is now Pilcher Arboretum in Joliet. (No date.)

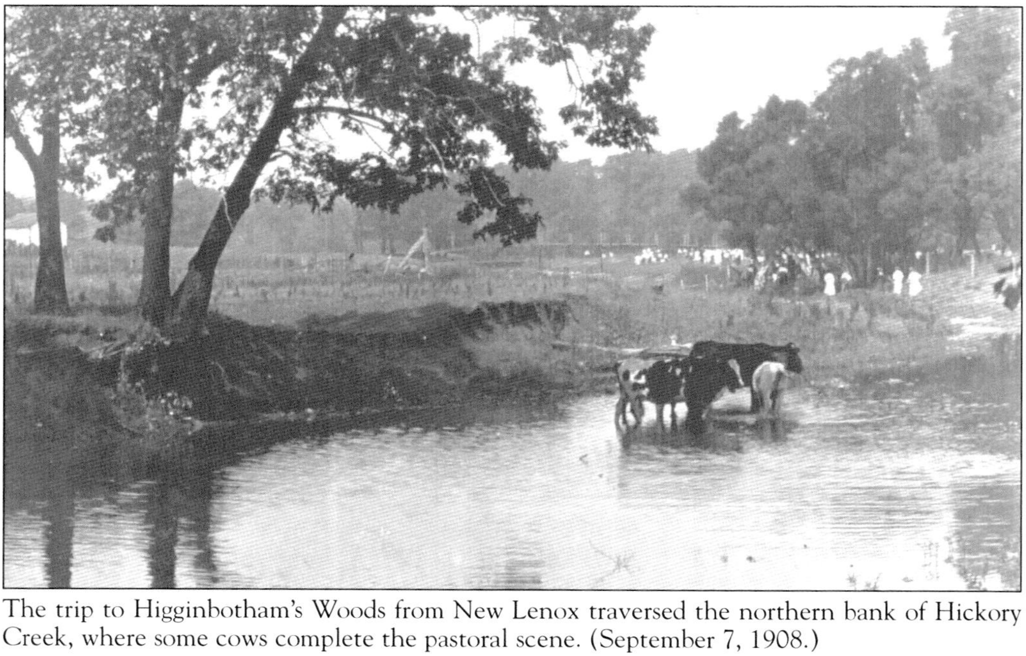

The trip to Higginbotham's Woods from New Lenox traversed the northern bank of Hickory Creek, where some cows complete the pastoral scene. (September 7, 1908.)

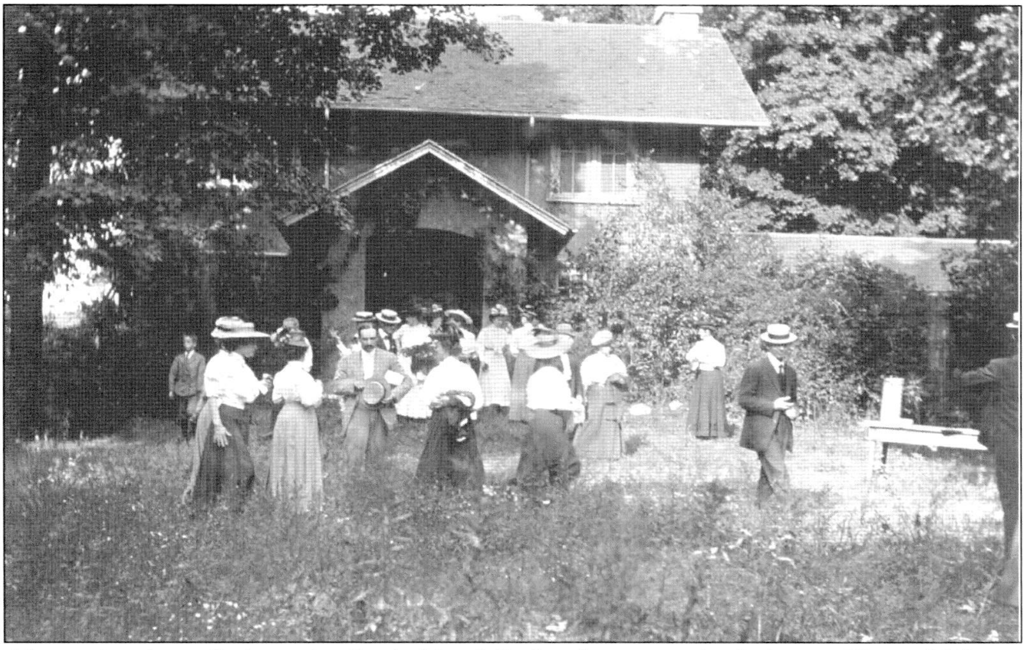

After a 3-mile walk from the Rock Island Railroad station, the lodge at Cherry Hill was a favorite lunch spot for hikers en route from New Lenox to Higginbotham's Woods. (September 7, 1908.)

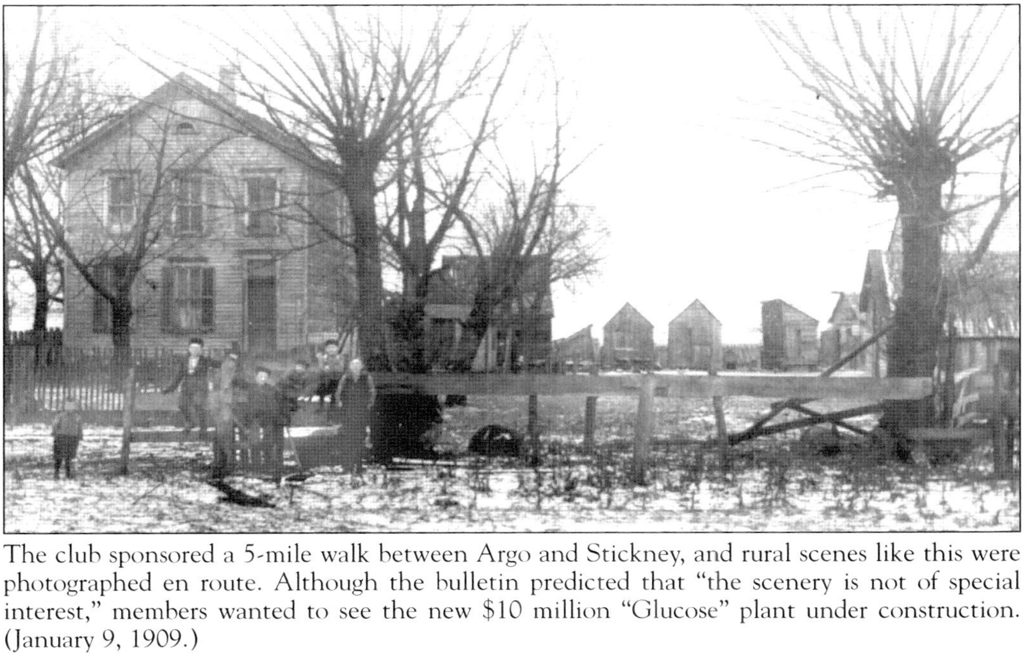

The club sponsored a 5-mile walk between Argo and Stickney, and rural scenes like this were photographed en route. Although the bulletin predicted that "the scenery is not of special interest," members wanted to see the new $10 million "Glucose" plant under construction. (January 9, 1909.)

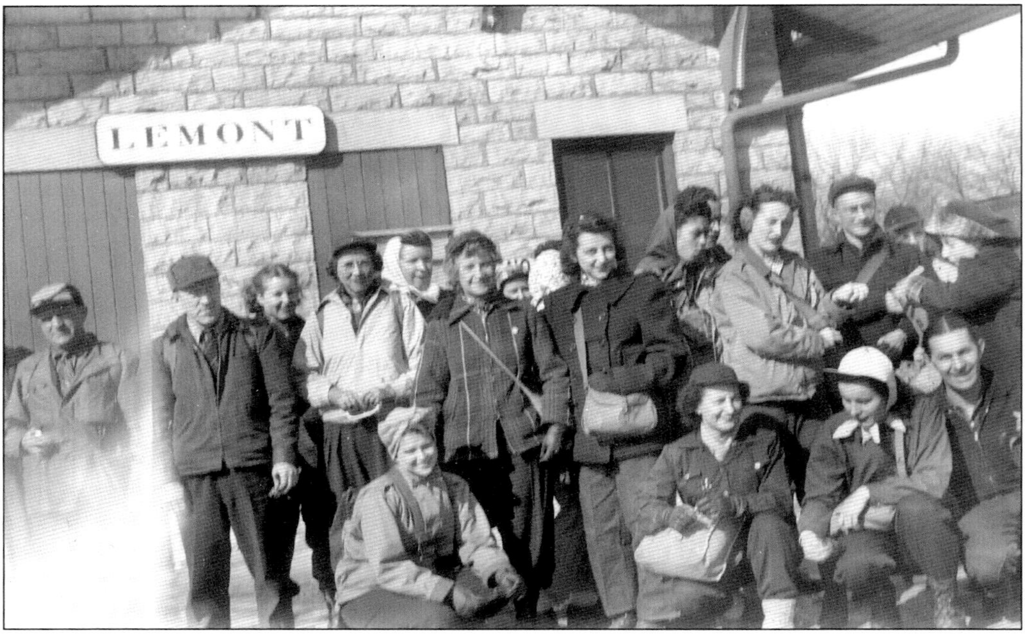

Longer hikes included this 20-mile hike from Lemont to Riverside. (March 14, 1948.)

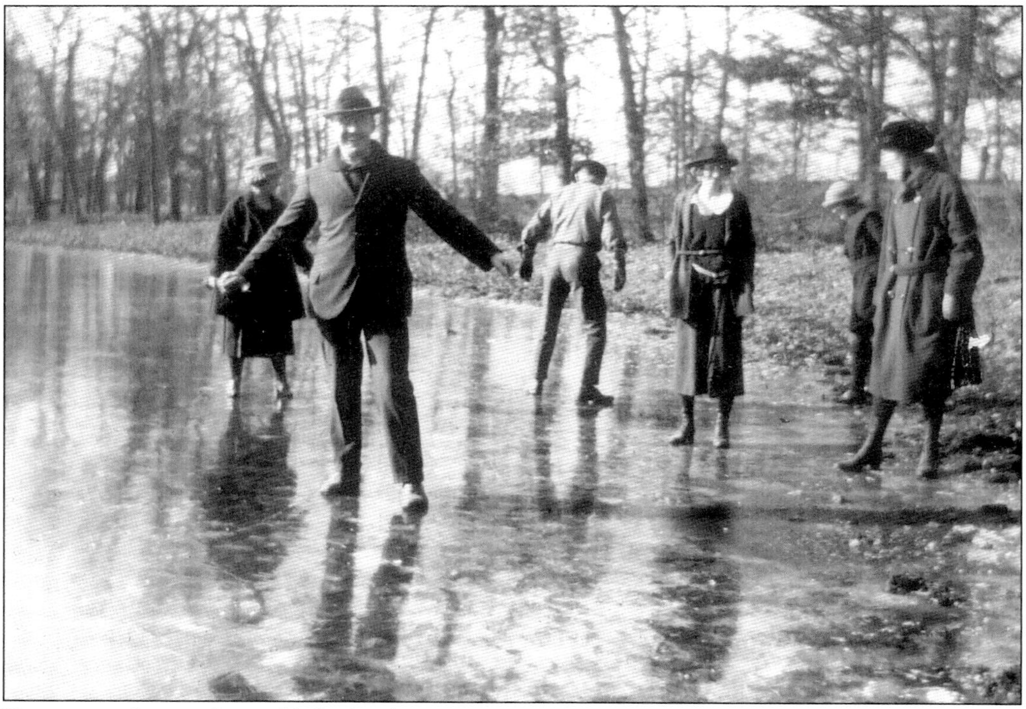
Here, near the newly established Palos Camp, members test the ice. (c. 1923.)

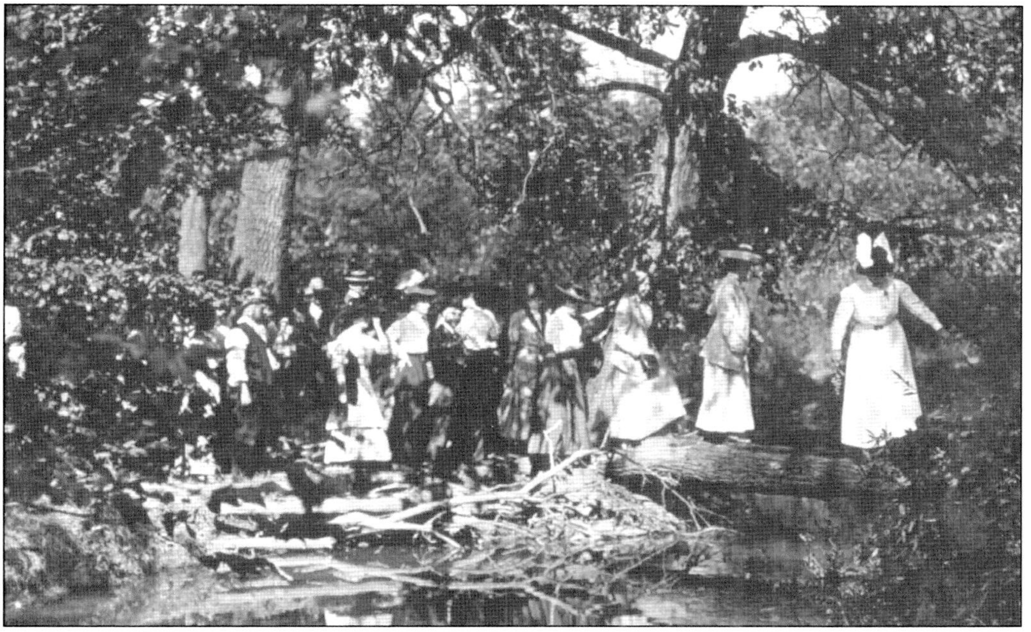

A 6-mile walk along the winding Thorn Creek began in Chicago Heights and ended in Steger. (September 23, 1911.)

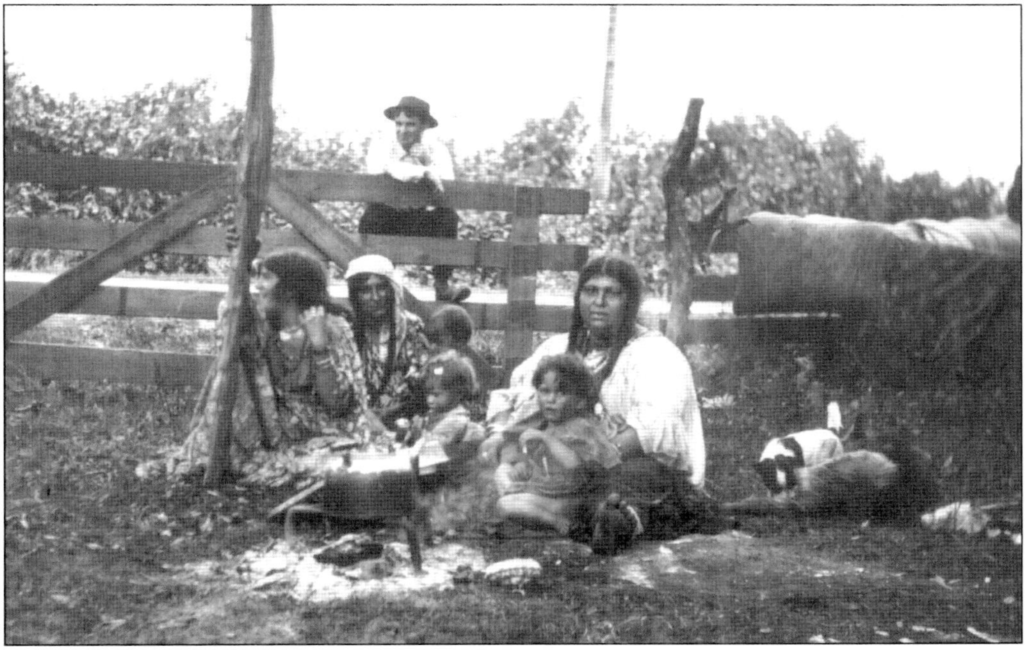

On the weekend trip from Waldron to Wilmington along the Kankakee River, hikers stopped in Bourbonnais and swam in Rock Creek. "We passed a gypsy camp," was the handwritten notation on this photo. (September 4–6, 1915.)

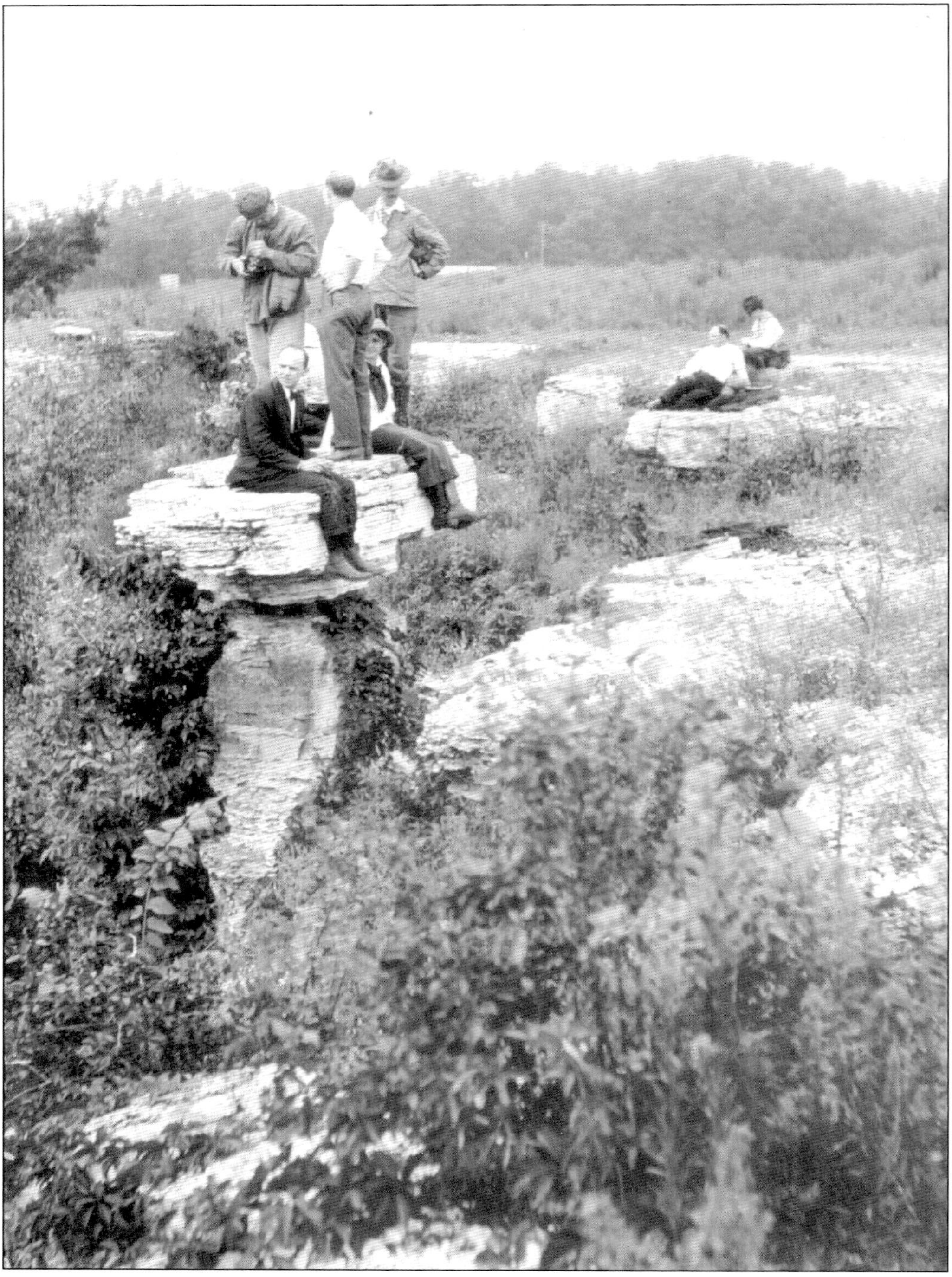

Twenty-seven hikers enjoyed this weekend outing along the banks of the Kankakee River. Here, hikers rest on "Mushroom Rock." (September 4–6, 1915.)

Three

WESTERLY WALKS

The CB&Q Railroad offered ready access to many of the Prairie Club's favorite sites. Trails surrounding the prairies and forests near Downers Grove, Hinsdale, Lisle, Elmhurst, Bensenville, and other points west were joyfully explored.

Many of the walks traced the path of the Salt Creek, Du Page River, or Des Plaines River Valleys. The waterways also provided winter entertainment including ice boating and sailing.

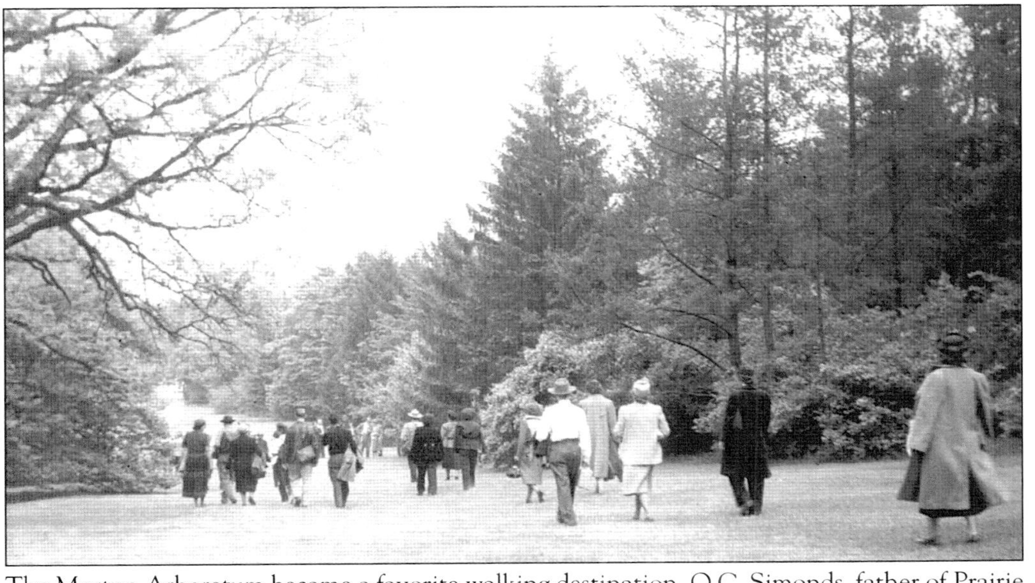

The Morton Arboretum became a favorite walking destination. O.C. Simonds, father of Prairie Club member Gertrude Simonds, and partner of J. Roy West, charter member of the club, landscaped the grounds. (No date.)

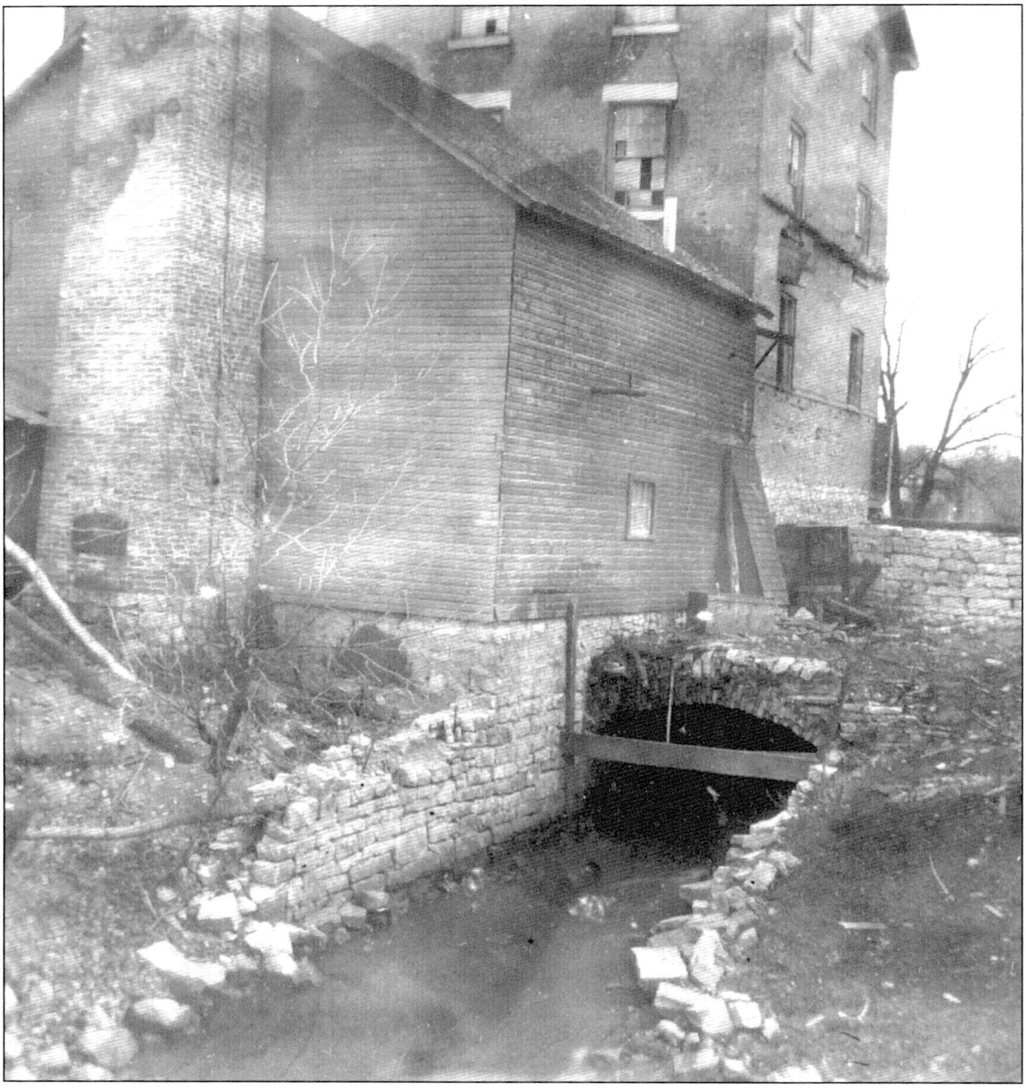

The walk along the Salt Creek passed this old mill at Fullersburg (now the restored Graue Mill). (November 7, 1908.)

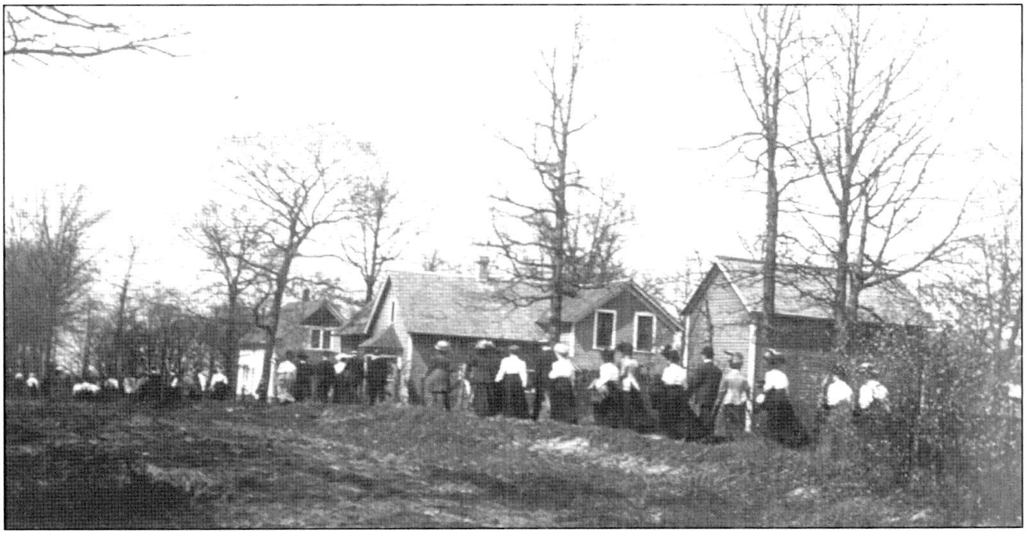

Hinsdale was a popular walking destination. The 5-mile walk went along the Salt Creek from the Hinsdale train station to the station in La Grange. (May 15, 1909.)

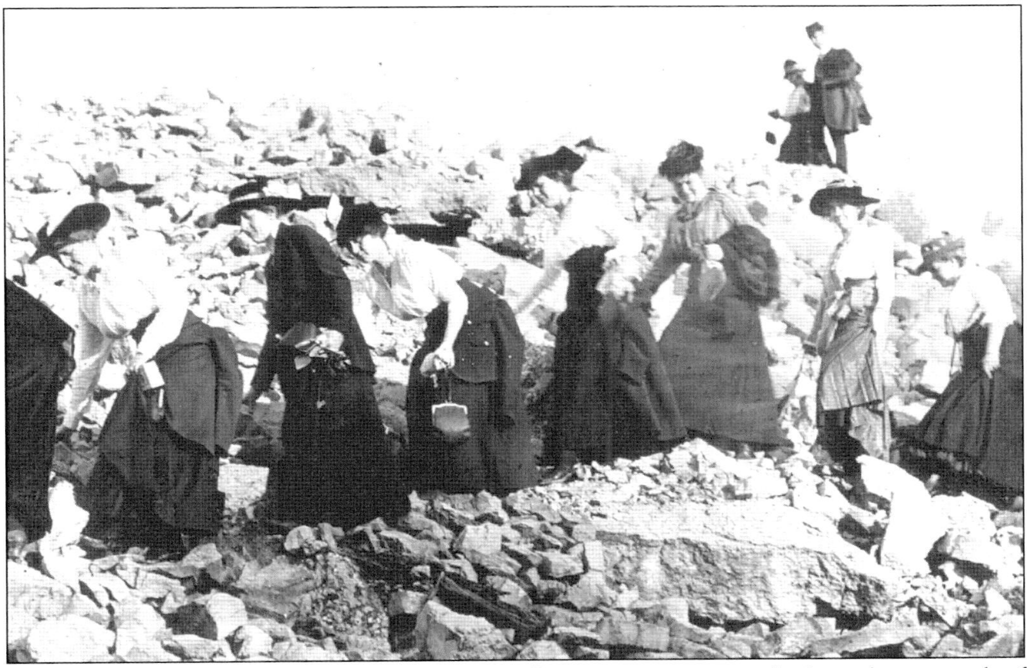

This new walk in the Des Plaines valley near Willow Springs went south along the tow path of the old I&M Canal, then back along the Sanitary & Ship Canal. (October 30, 1915.)

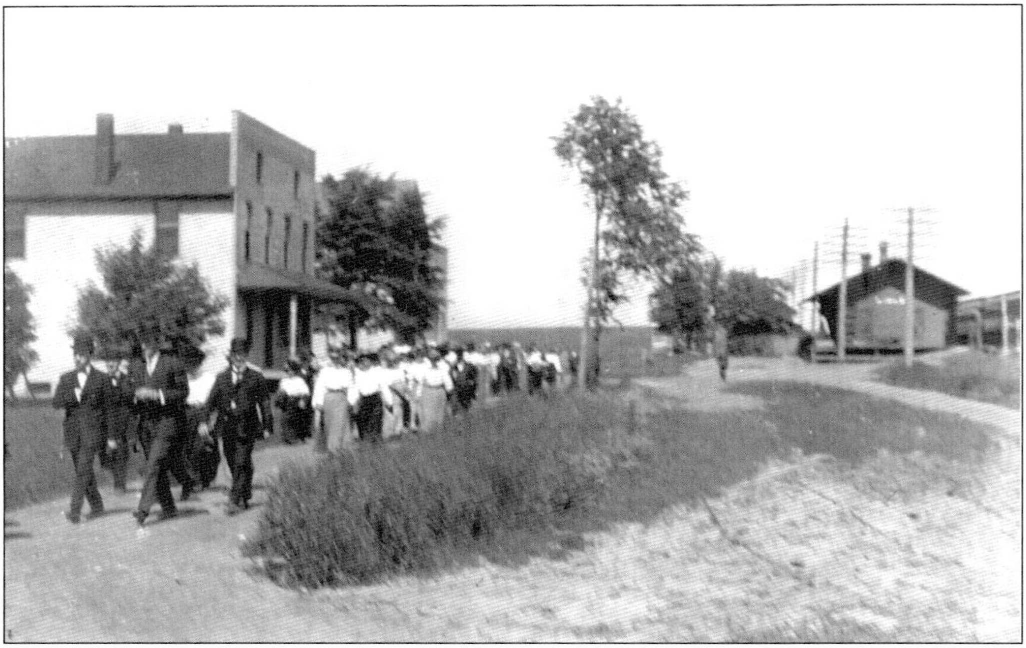

Leaving the train station at Lisle, hikers walked along the Du Page River to Downers Grove. (June 19, 1909.)

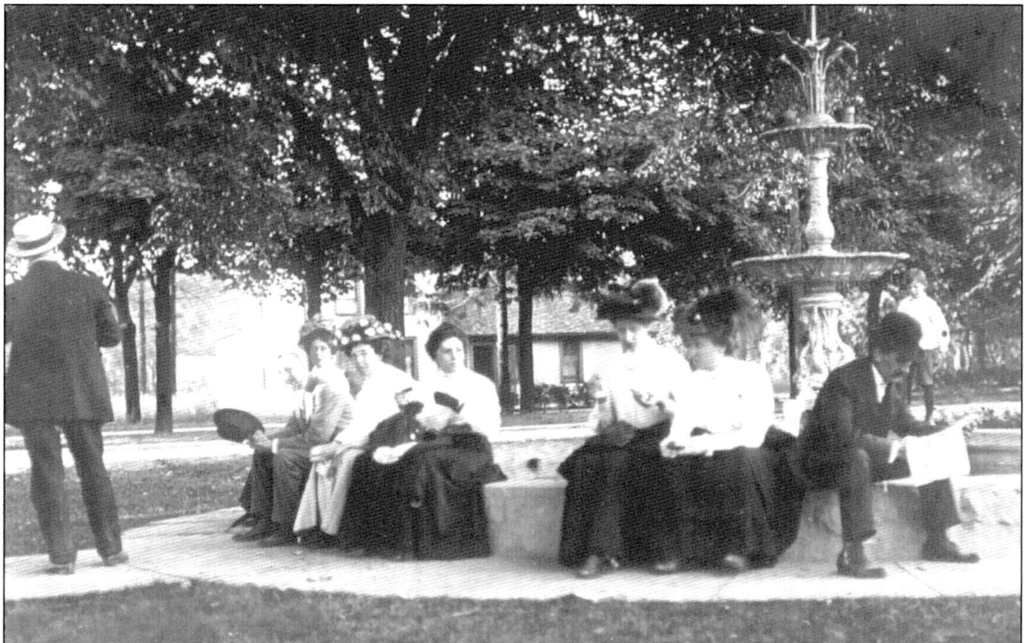

At the end of the hilly and wooded 5-mile walk, hikers rest while they await the train at Downers Grove. Cost of this trip was 80¢. (June 19, 1909.)

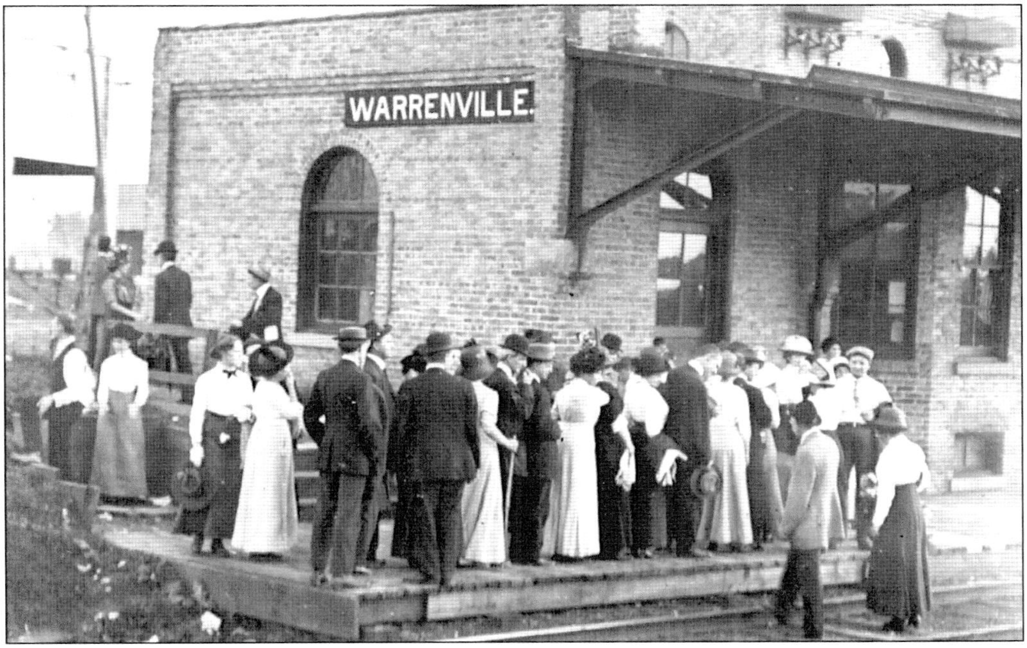

On the Winfield to Warrenville walk, the course followed the east bank of the Du Page River. One of the walk leaders was Miss Catharine Mitchell, a Riverside resident and avid conservationist. Here, hikers await the train at Warrenville. (October 5, 1912.)

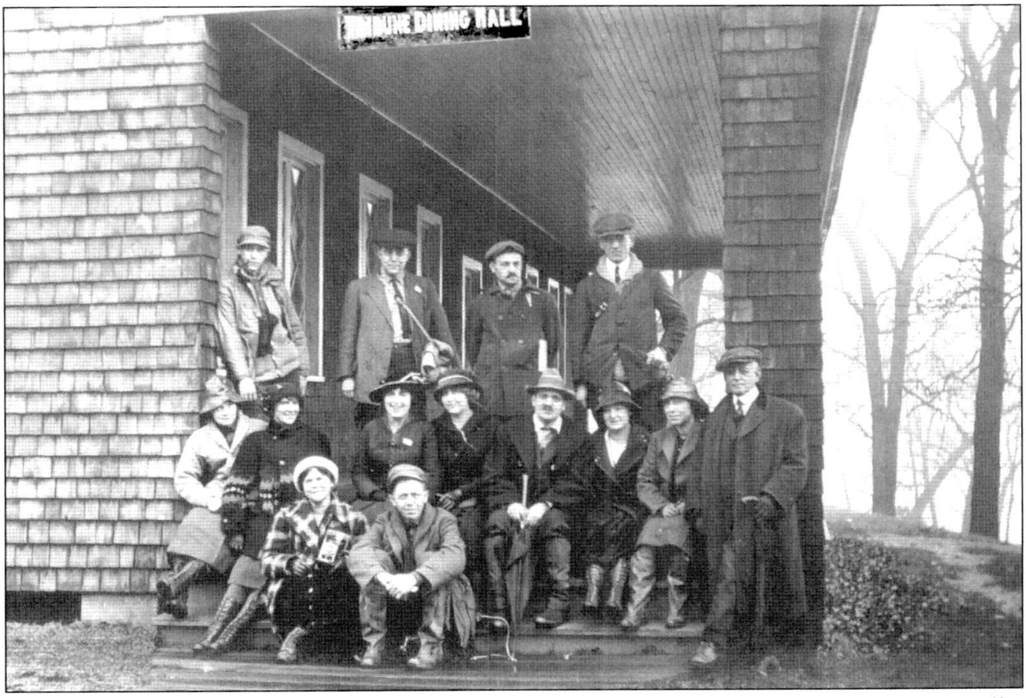

The group paused at the Tribune Camp on the Fox River on their hike to Carpentersville. (February 20–22, 1915.)

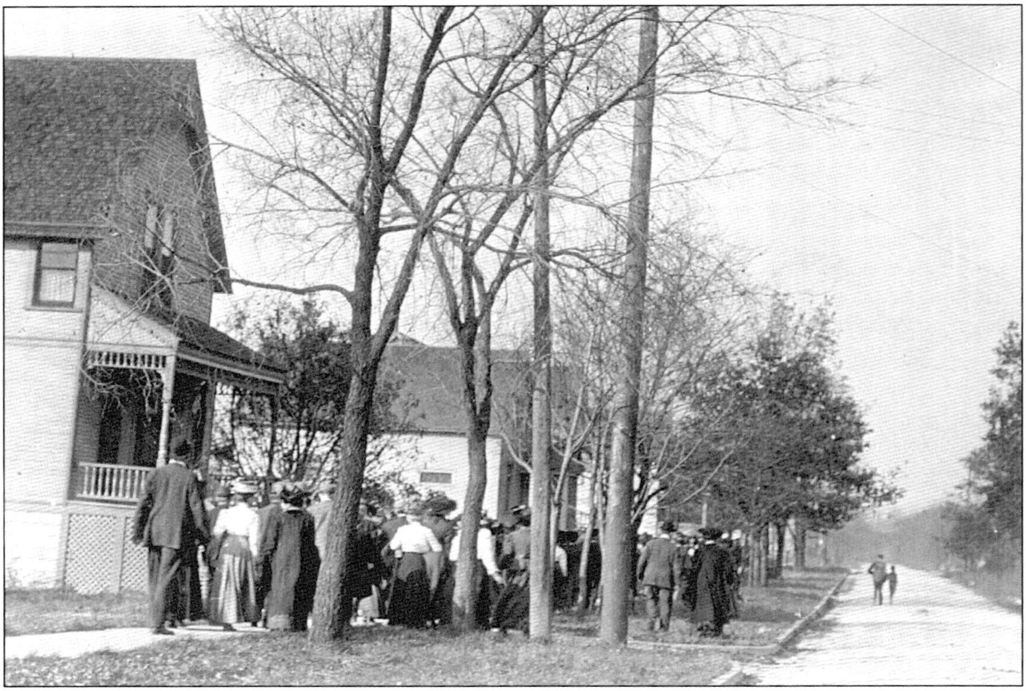

In the autumn, a walk from Brookfield to La Grange was scheduled. Here, the streets of Brookfield are quiet and deserted save for the hikers. (October 30, 1909.)

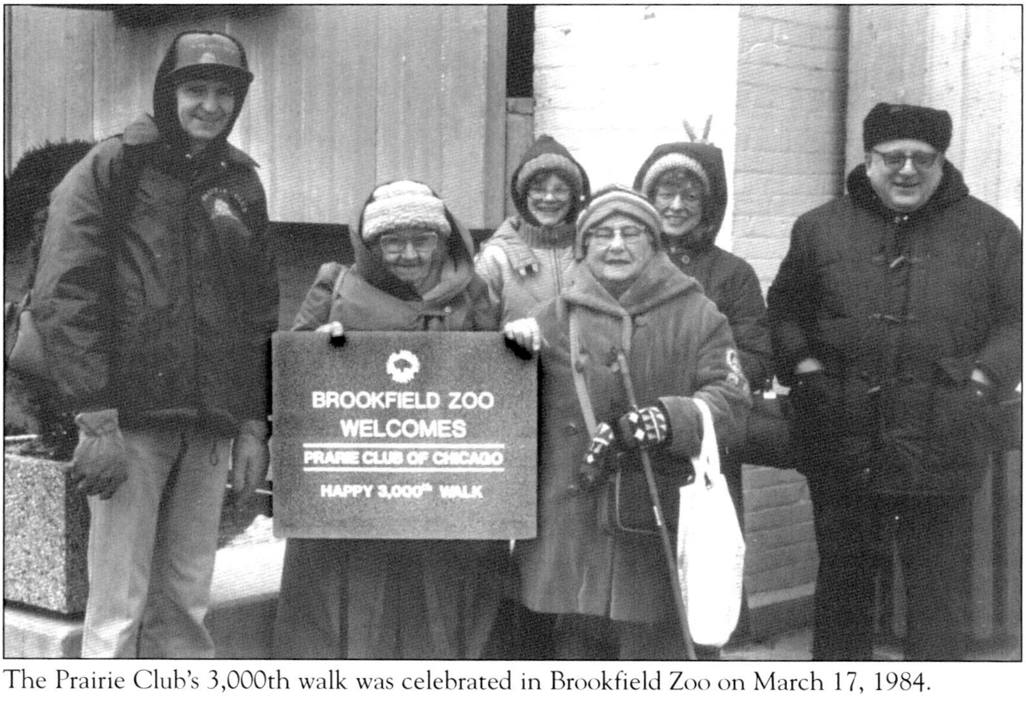

The Prairie Club's 3,000th walk was celebrated in Brookfield Zoo on March 17, 1984.

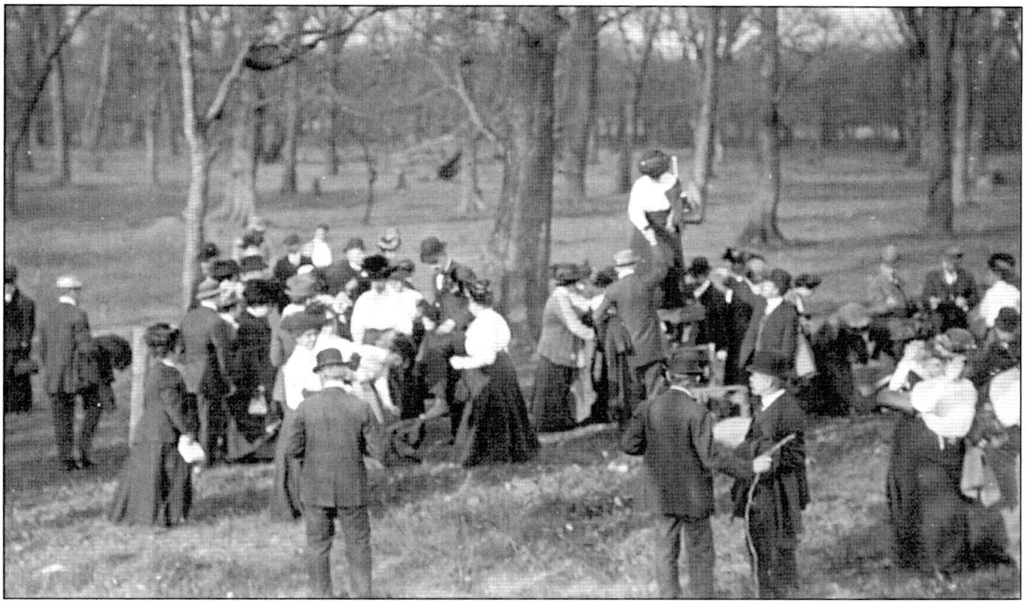

Although Riverside was among the first walks ever scheduled, this route, from Harlem Avenue south to the Ogden ditch and drainage canal, then west to the Des Plaines River, was a new walk. (November 13, 1909.)

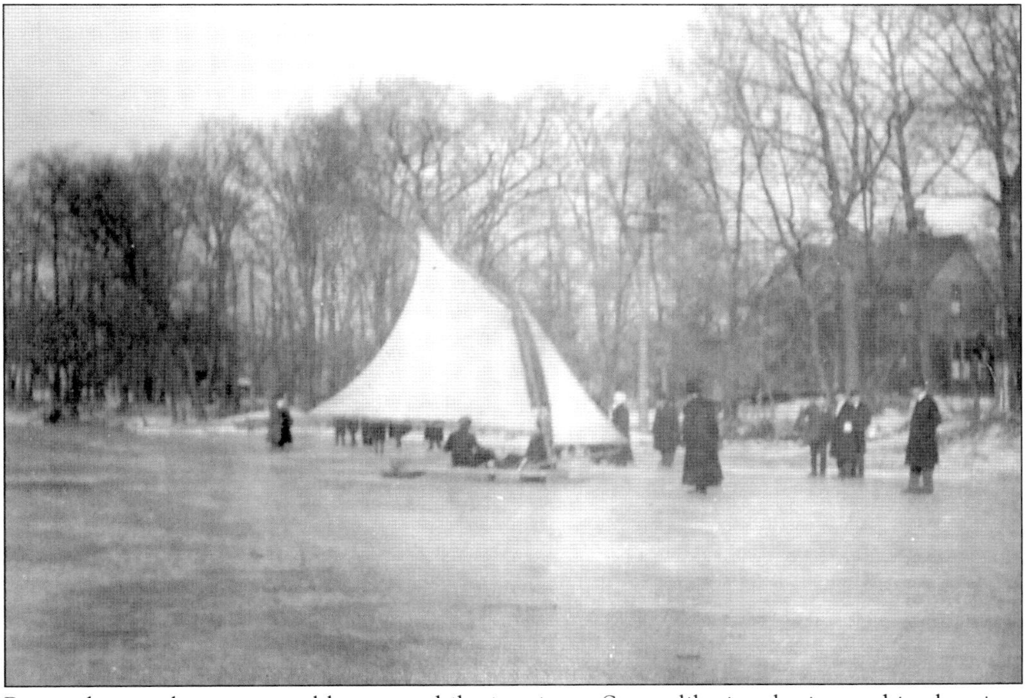

Riverside was also an enjoyable spot to hike in winter. Sports like ice skating and ice boating, shown here, were popular on the Des Plaines River. (February 19, 1910.)

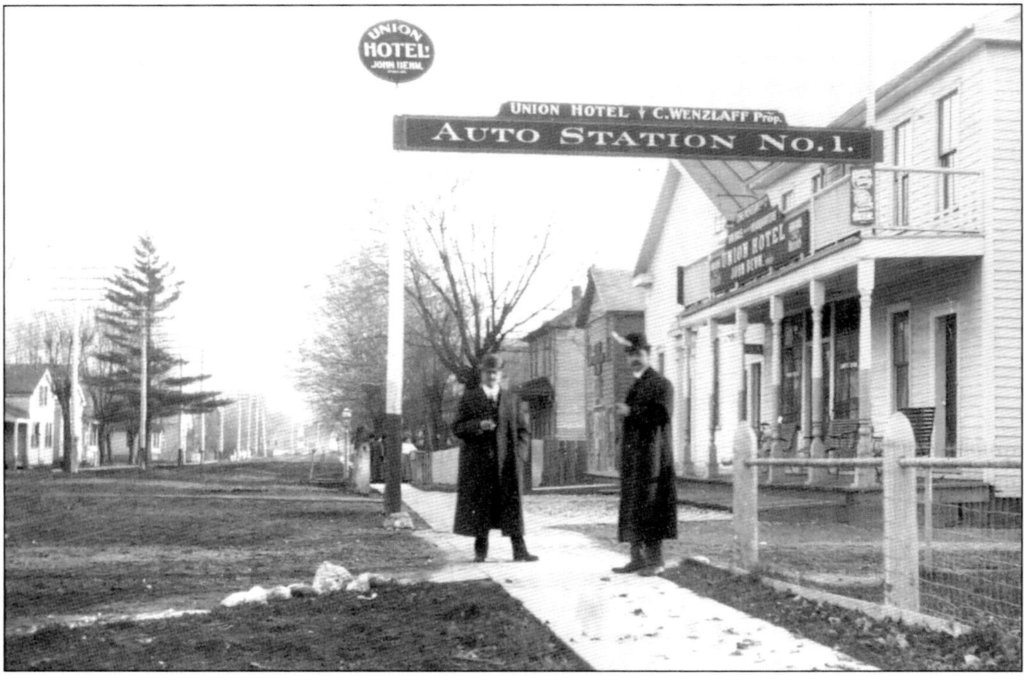

On Thanksgiving, the club took a walking trip to Wheeling. A handwritten note on this photo says that the club is inside the Union Hotel. (November 25, 1909.)

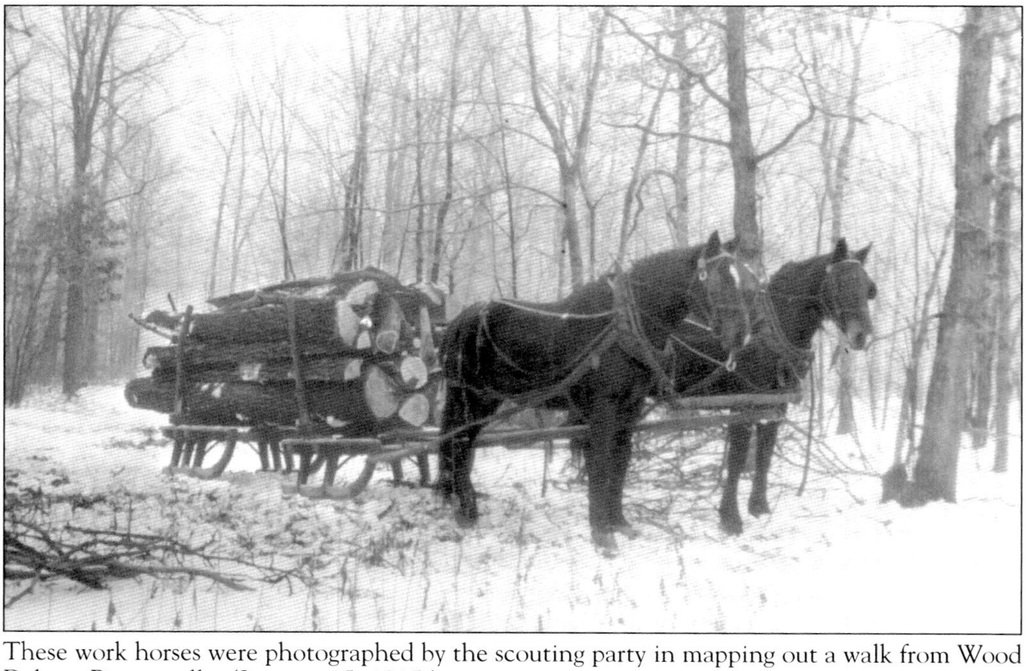

These work horses were photographed by the scouting party in mapping out a walk from Wood Dale to Bensenville. (January 15, 1915.)

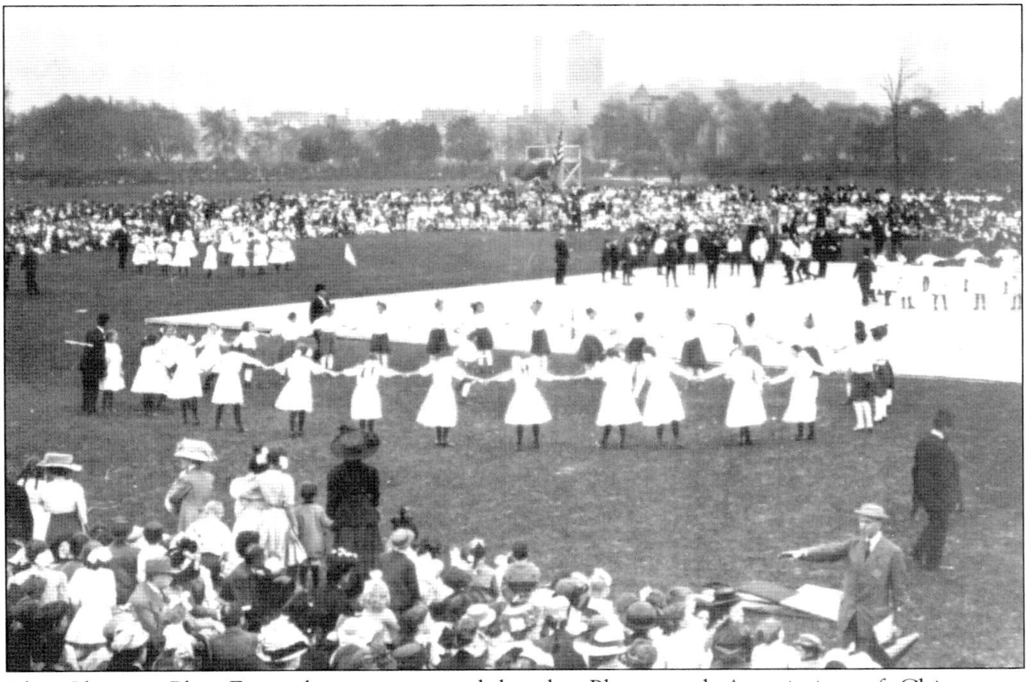

The Chicago Play Festival was sponsored by the Playground Association of Chicago to highlight the variety of outdoor recreation activities among Chicago's various ethnic groups. The club walked from Humboldt Park to Garfield Park, where this game was photographed. (October 9, 1909.)

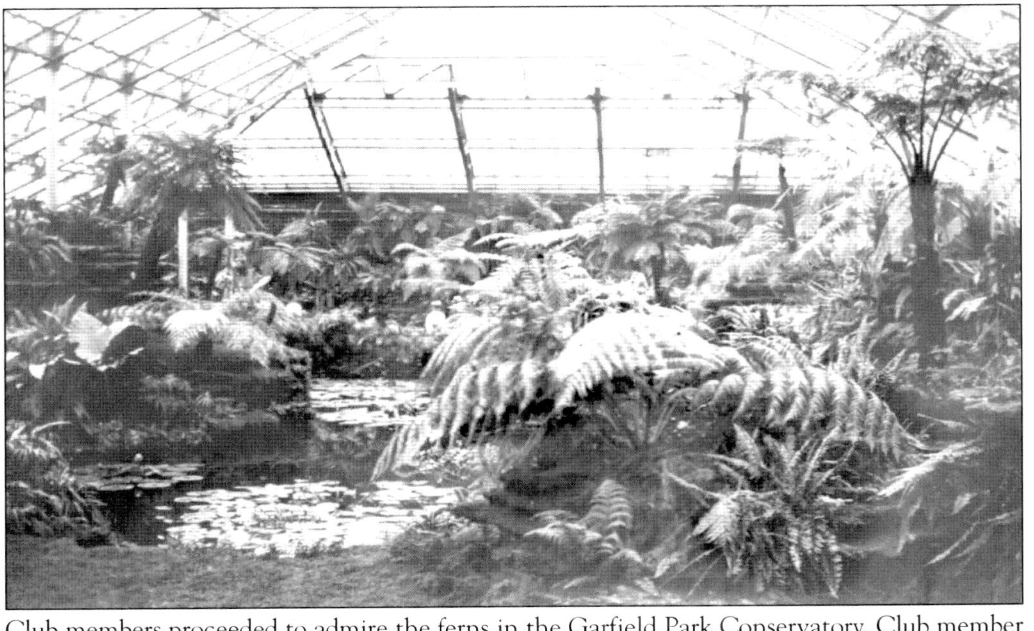

Club members proceeded to admire the ferns in the Garfield Park Conservatory. Club member and the so-called "Dean of Prairie Landscape Architecture," Jens Jensen, redesigned the conservatory and most of the West Parks. (October 9, 1909.)

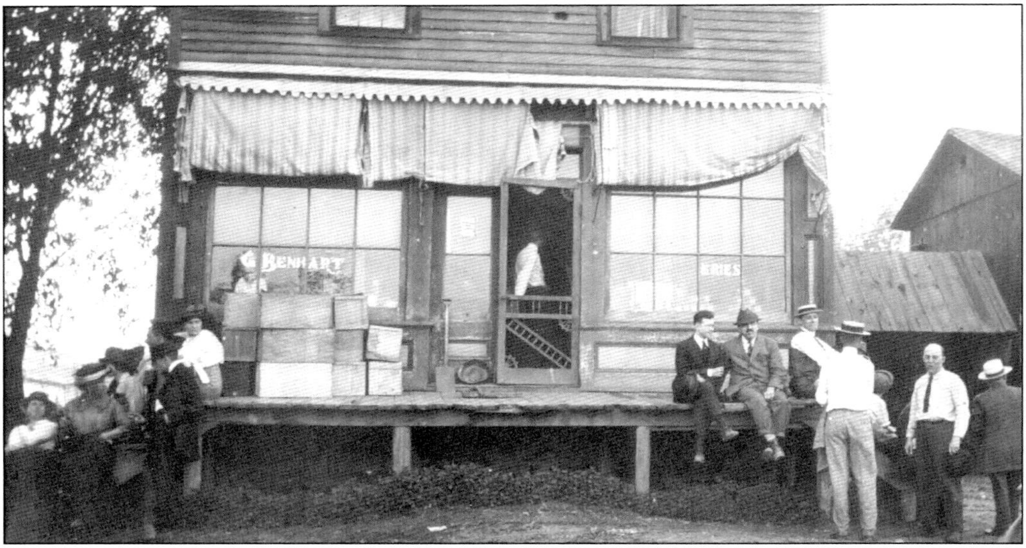

This country store near Meachem offered a place to rest. Note the ties on the gentlemen—all dressed for a walk. (June 6, 1914.)

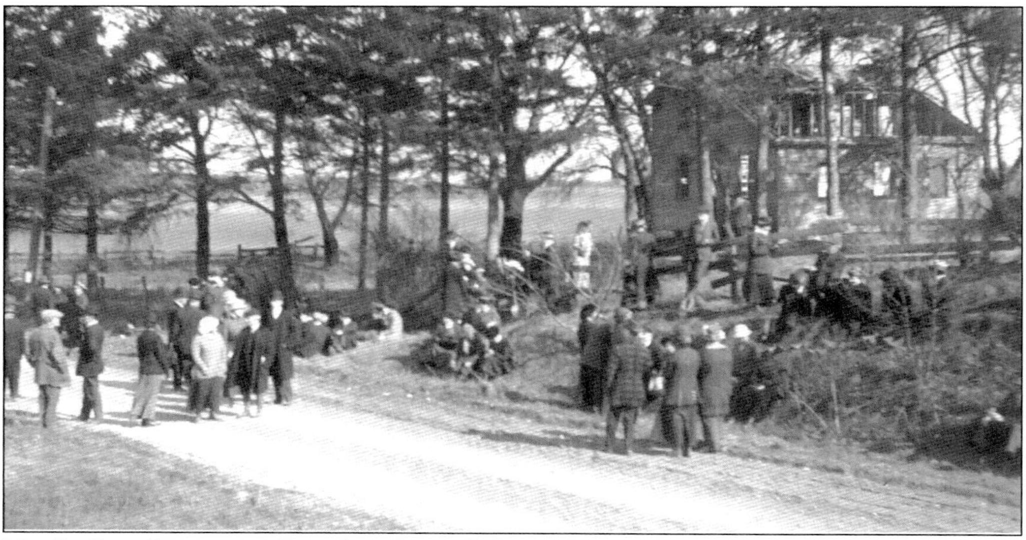

The Du Page River was followed on this walk from Lisle to Naperville. This shot was taken near Naperville. (March 27, 1915.)

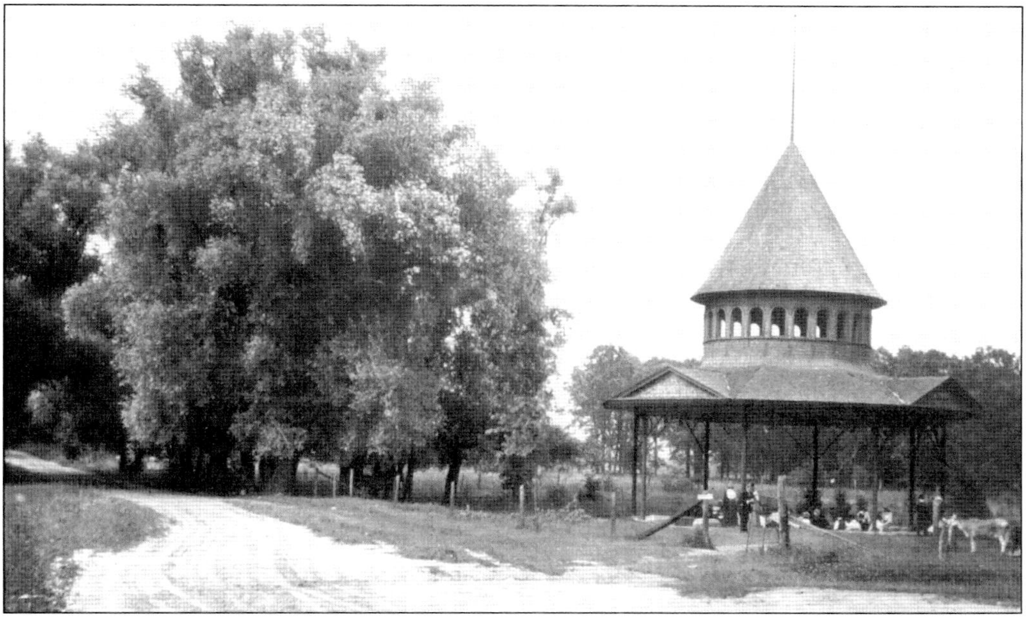

The views at Glen Ellyn Springs were shared by Prairie Club members and a cow. (June 20, 1914.)

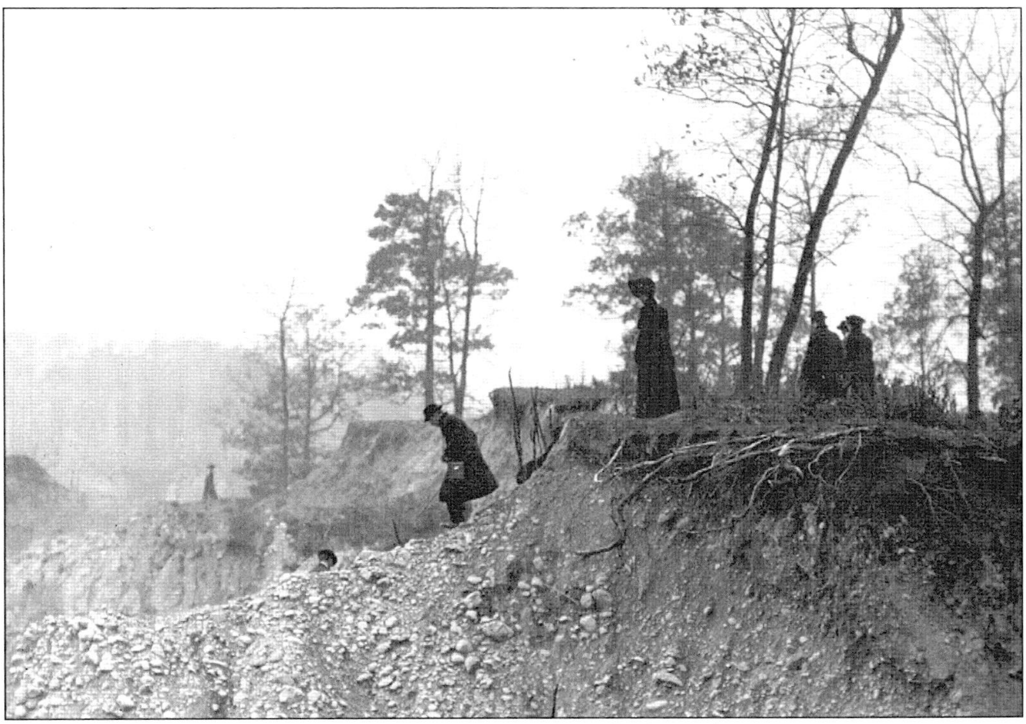

This gravel pit was seen near Glen Ellyn on an early walk. (1910.)

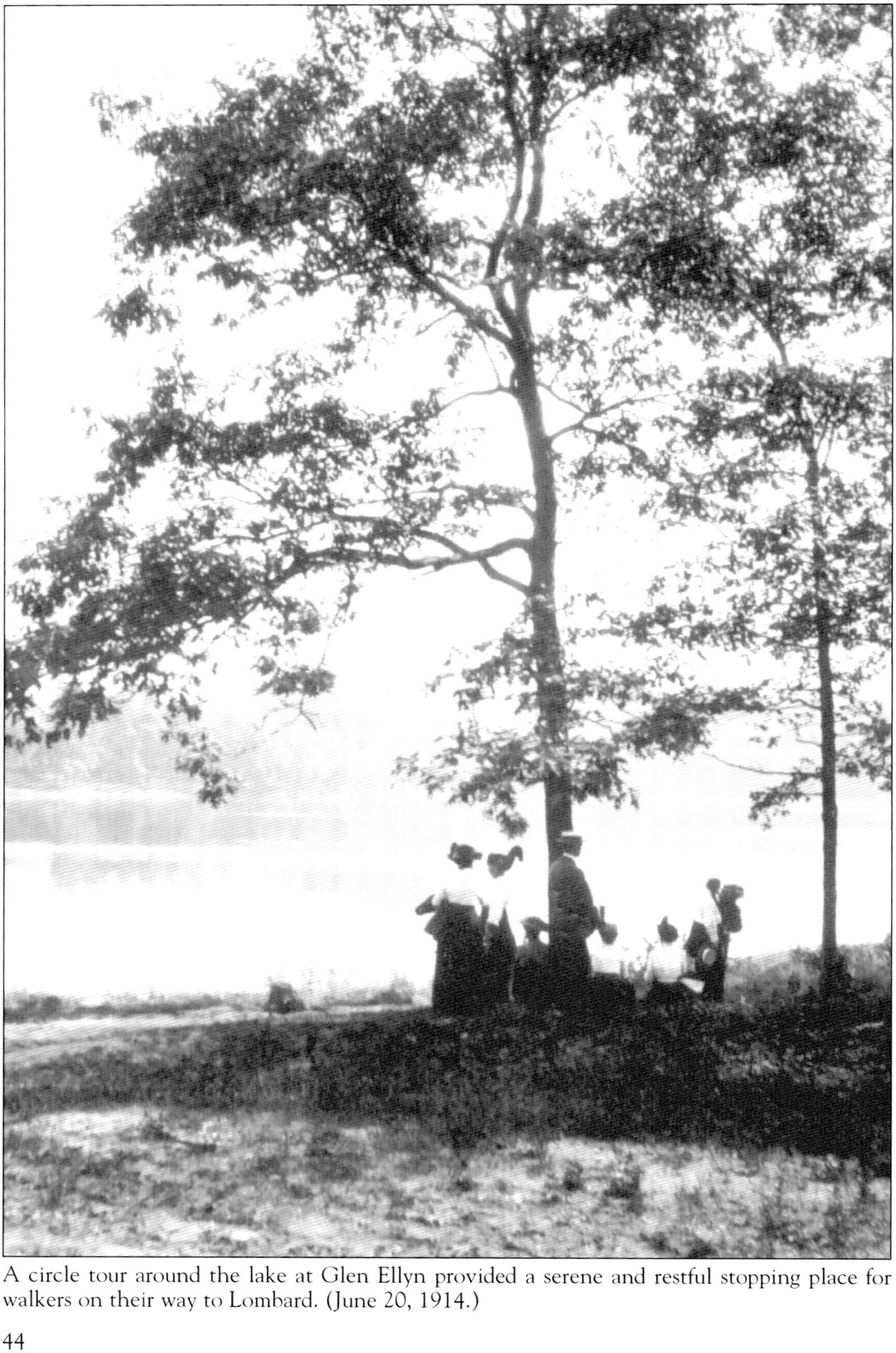

A circle tour around the lake at Glen Ellyn provided a serene and restful stopping place for walkers on their way to Lombard. (June 20, 1914.)

Four

NORTHERN EXPOSURE

In addition to moonlight strolls along Lake Michigan, Prairie Club members were often invited to walk amidst private estates on the North Shore, many of which were landscaped by Jens Jensen. The ravines around Lake Forest, Glencoe, and Ravinia provided plenty of challenging exercise while the lake offered cool breezes.

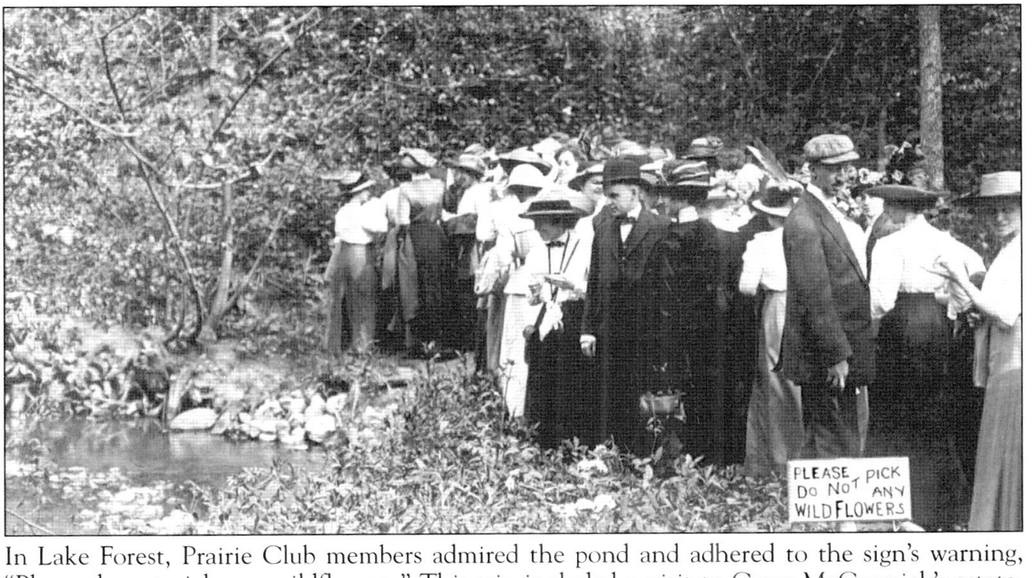

In Lake Forest, Prairie Club members admired the pond and adhered to the sign's warning, "Please do not pick any wildflowers." This trip included a visit to Cyrus McCormick's estate. (May 24, 1913.)

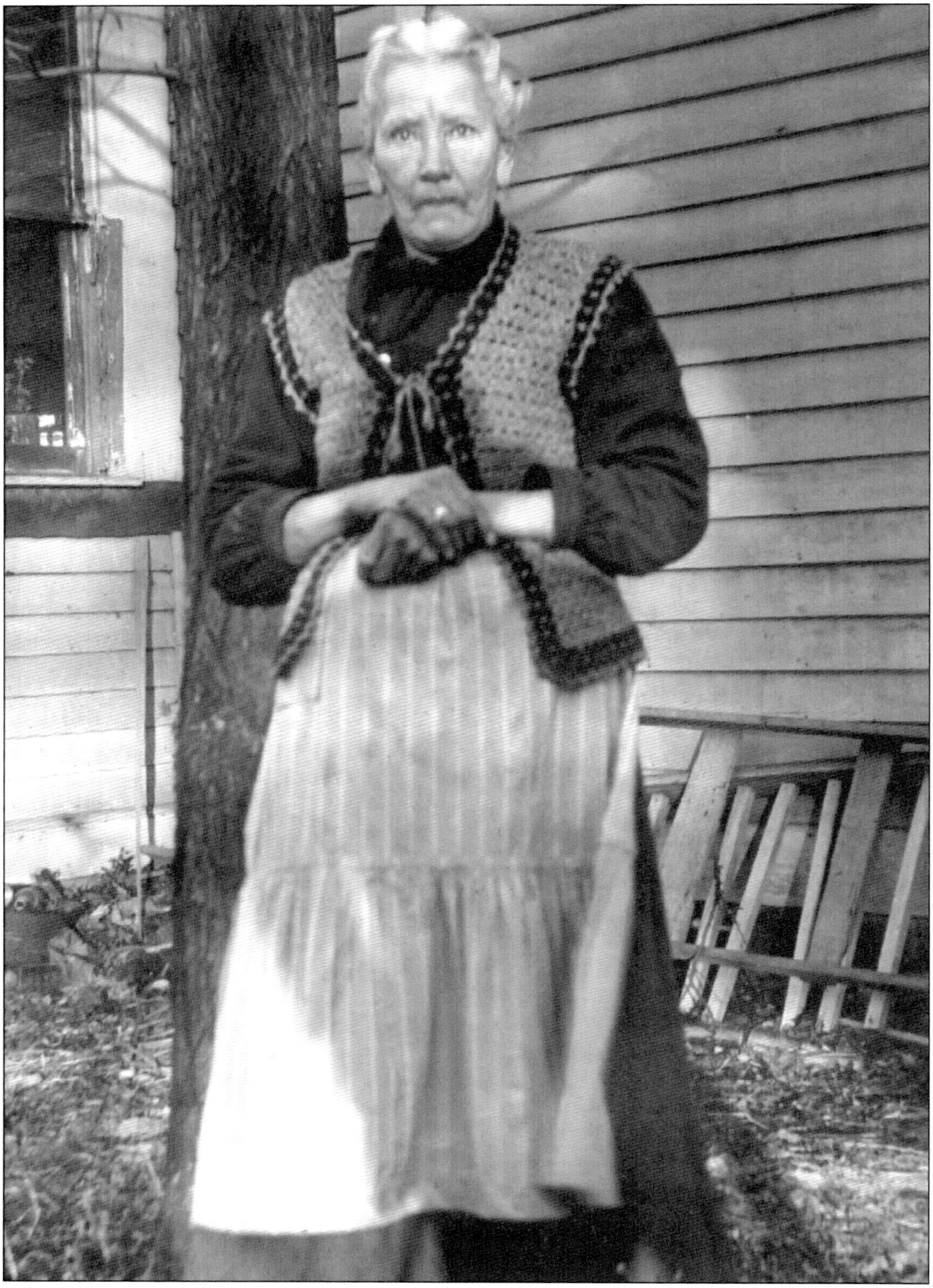

Along their walks, the Prairie Club was befriended by many colorful personalities. Here is Mrs. Mary Rager, daughter of Alexander Robinson, famous Pottawatomie Chief and Chicago notable. (November 21, 1915.)

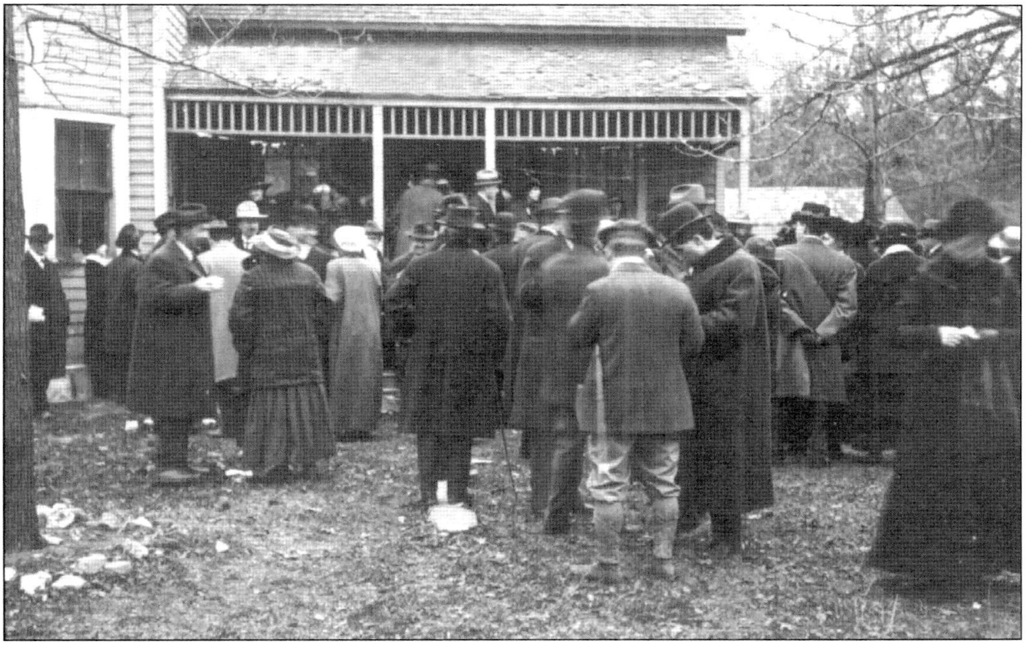

On the Park Ridge to River Grove hike, club members had refreshments at Mrs. Rager's home. Mrs. Rager's land near Park Ridge became part of the Cook County Forest Preserve. (December 4, 1915.)

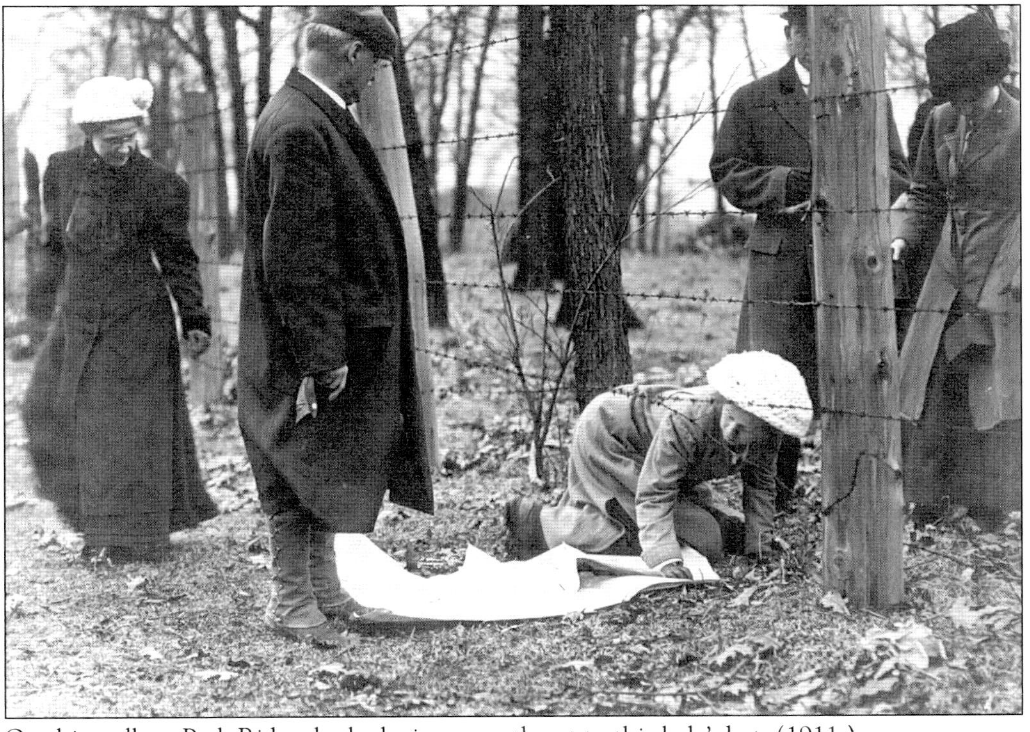

On this walk to Park Ridge, barbed wire was a threat to this lady's hat. (1911.)

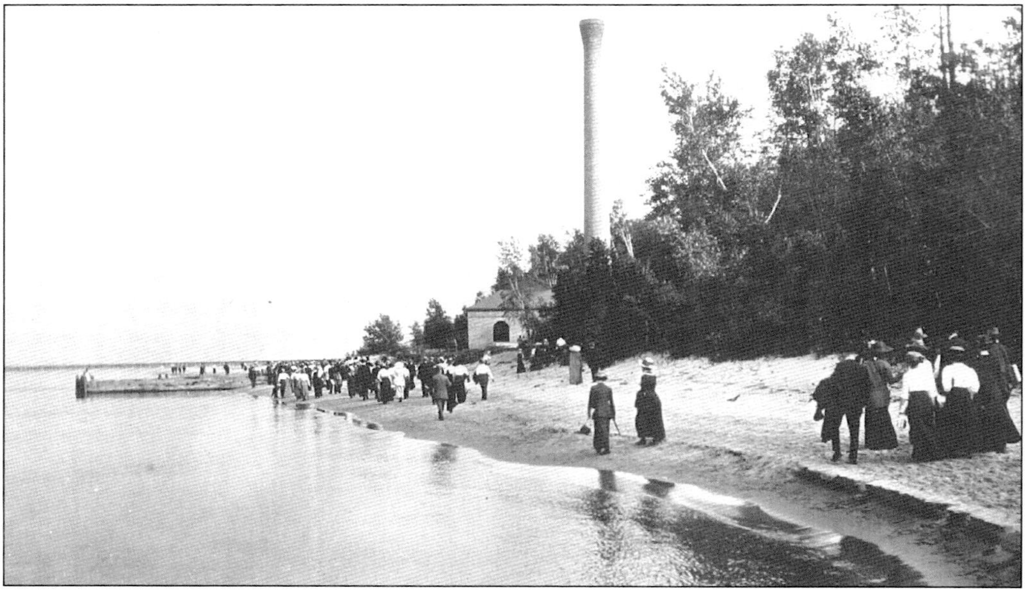

Hikers continued from Lake Forest to the Fort Sheridan water works. An optional 4-mile evening walk to Highland Park culminated in a bonfire on the beach. (May 24, 1913.)

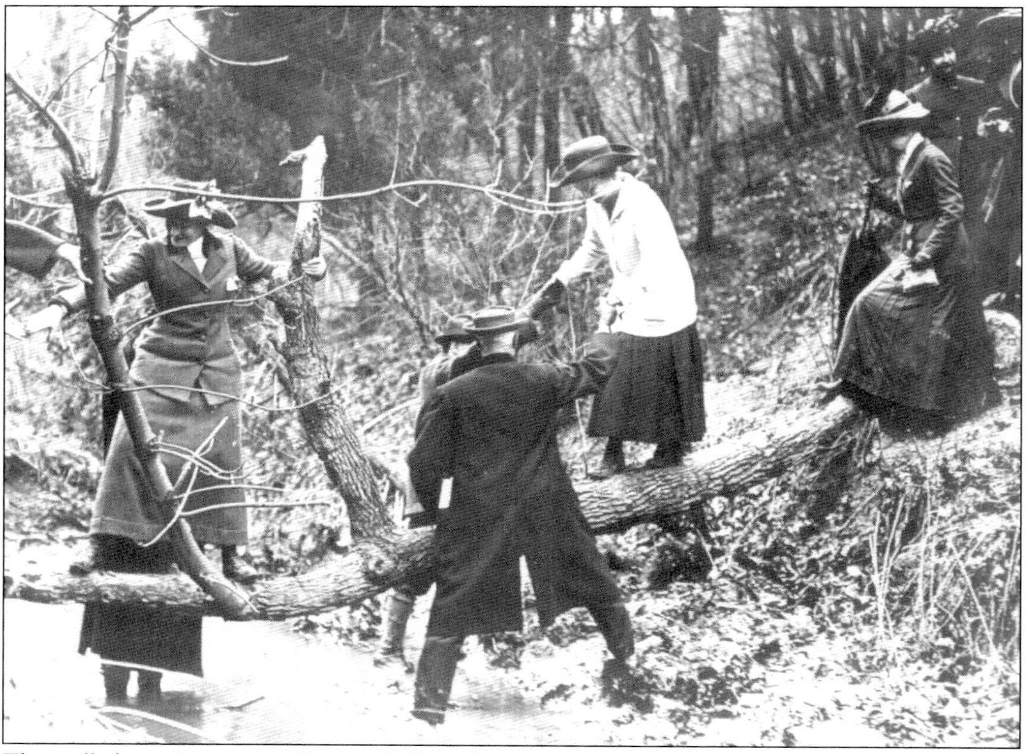

The walk from Ravinia to Glencoe followed one of the large ravines to the lake. An additional 2-mile walk to Hubbard Woods was optional in the evening. (April 12, 1913.)

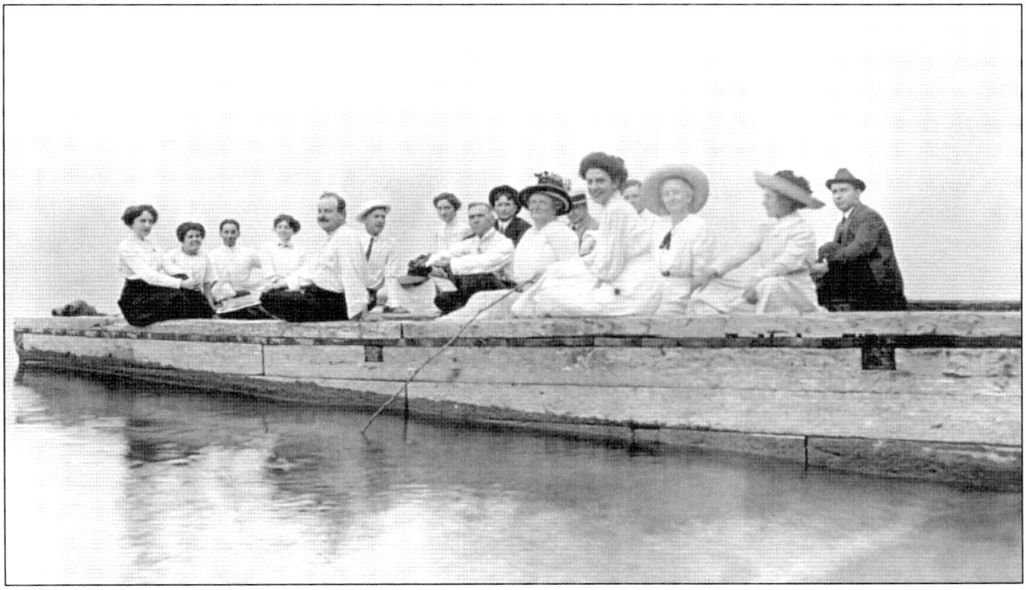

Prairie Club walkers enjoyed a view of the lake on their walk from Ravinia to Glencoe. (June 29, 1912.)

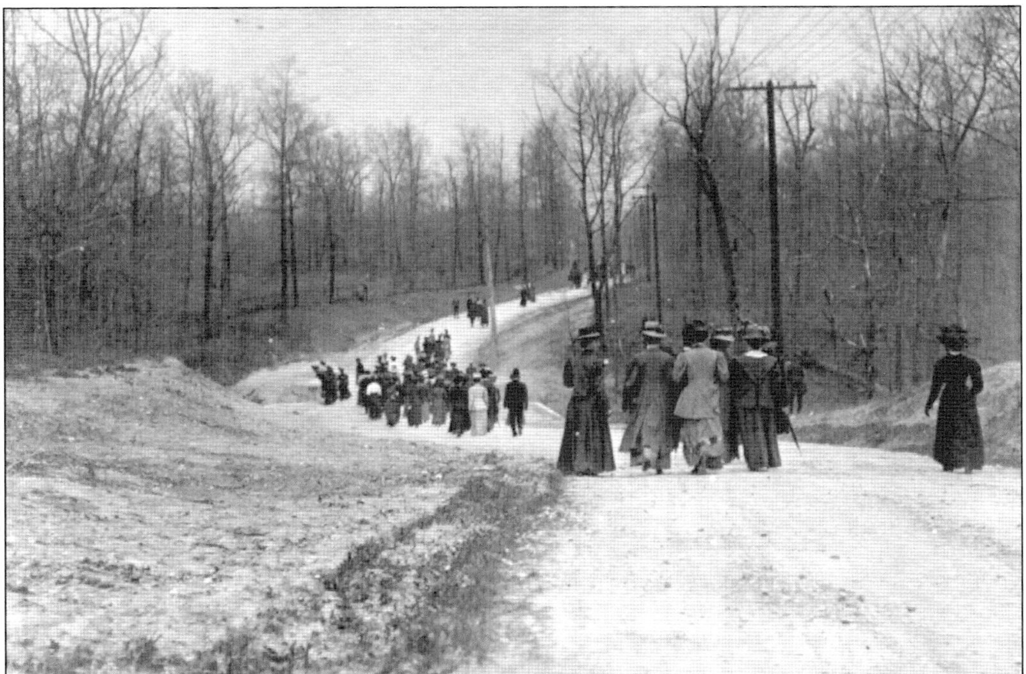

Sheridan Road in 1909 was not the well-paved thoroughfare it is today. Here, hikers take the popular trek from Ravinia to Glencoe. (May 8, 1909.)

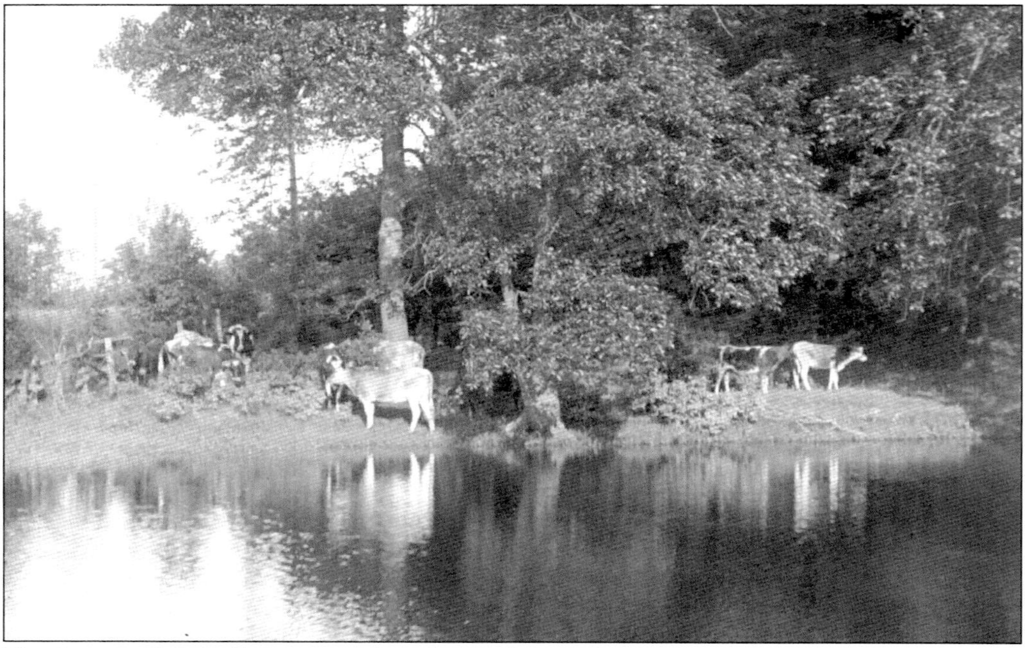

The Prairie Club Bulletin notes that the north branch of the Chicago River is "but a small stream," near the Glenview golf club. Prairie Club members walked from here to Morton Grove. (May 31, 1913.)

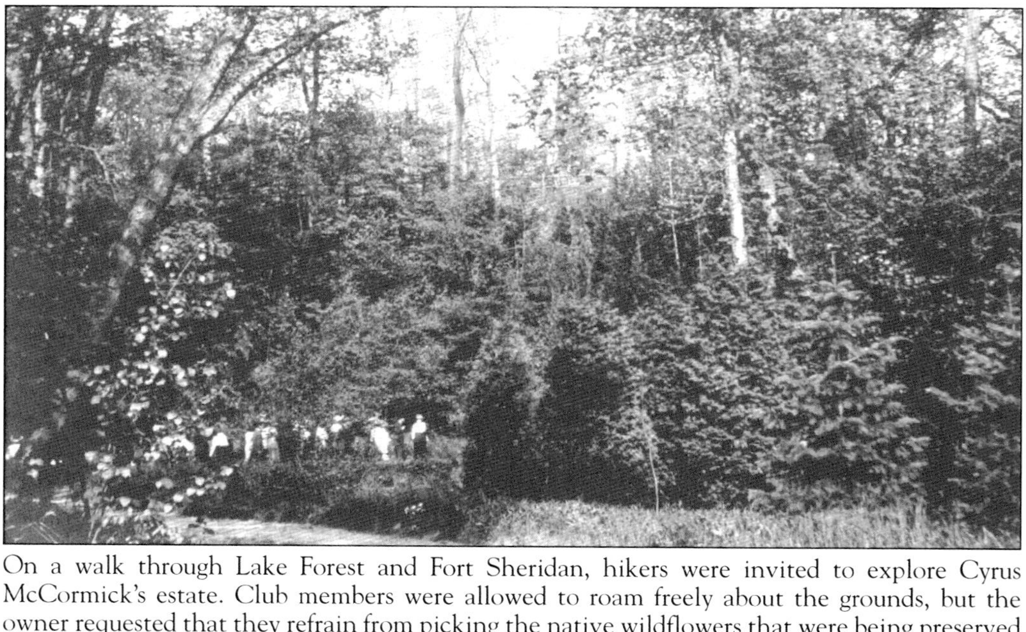

On a walk through Lake Forest and Fort Sheridan, hikers were invited to explore Cyrus McCormick's estate. Club members were allowed to roam freely about the grounds, but the owner requested that they refrain from picking the native wildflowers that were being preserved from extinction. (May 24, 1913.)

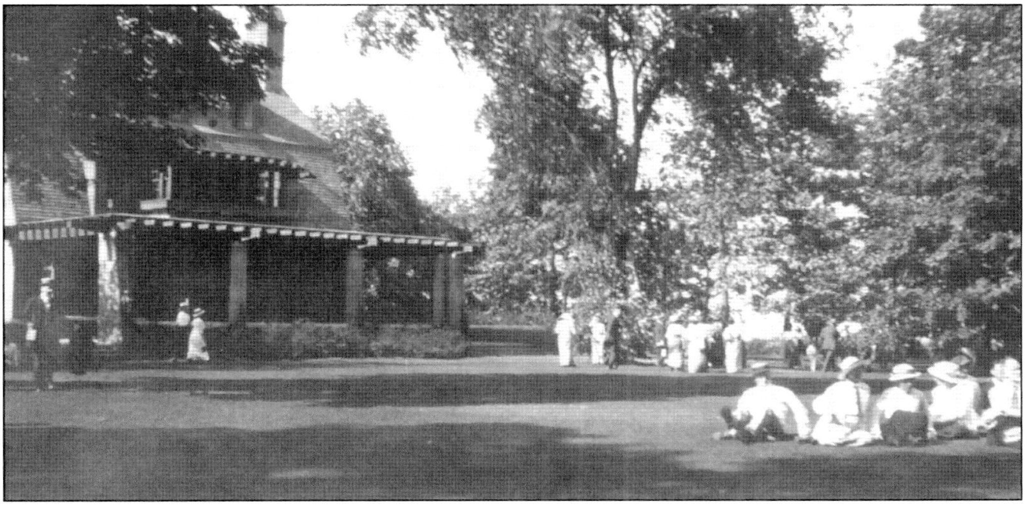

Club members were invited to visit the McCormick home in 1914 as well. The open lawn in front of the house provided a shady rest spot. (June 27, 1914.)

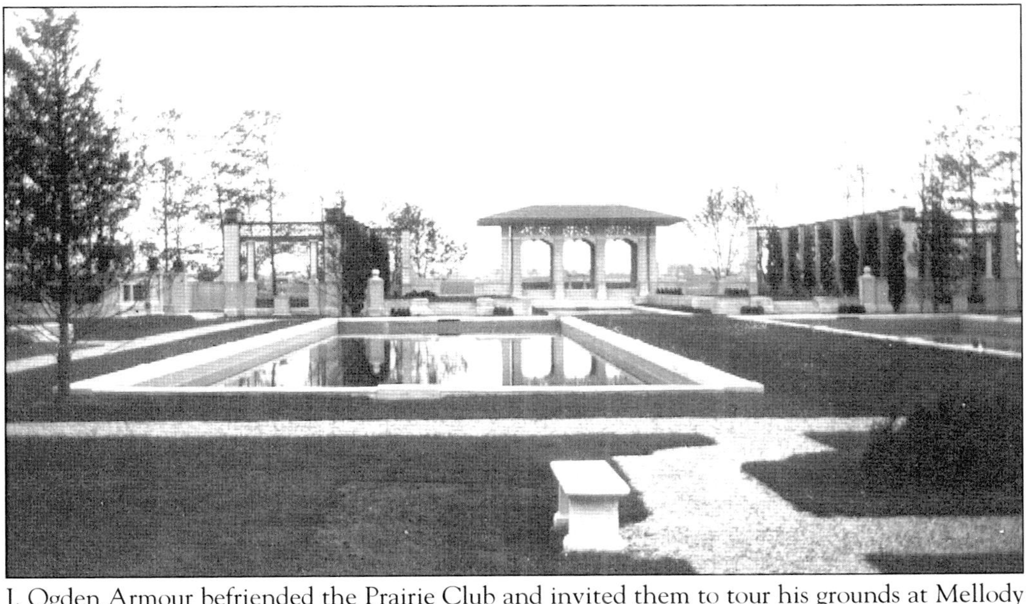

J. Ogden Armour befriended the Prairie Club and invited them to tour his grounds at Mellody Farm, shown here. Other estates were open on this walk including Samuel Insull's Hawthorn Farm, and Arthur Meeker's model dairy at Arcady Farm. (May 13, 1911.)

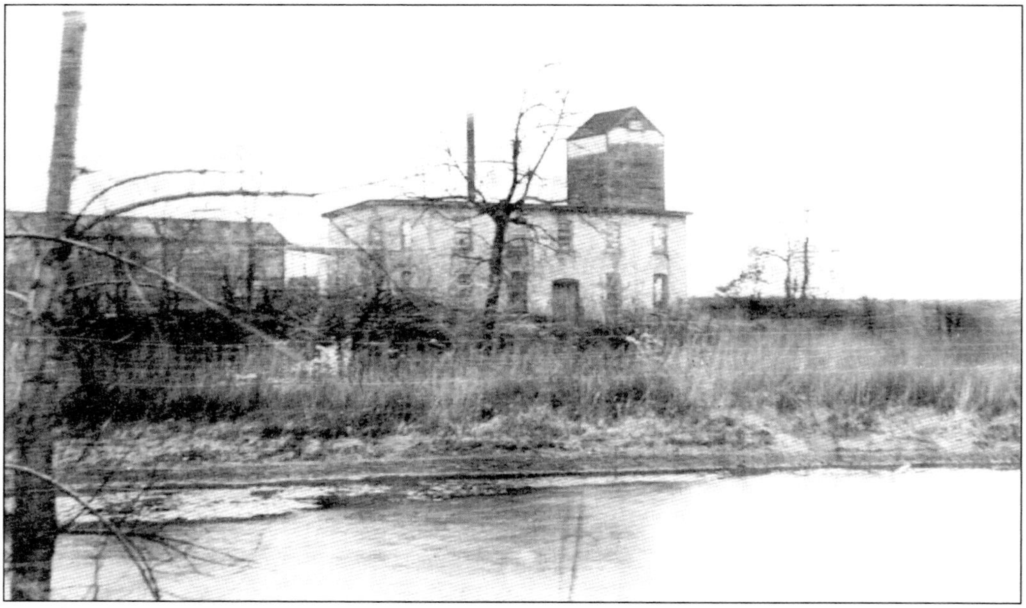

On Thanksgiving, the club walked from River Grove to Des Plaines. This old brewery was one of the sights. (November 6, 1908.)

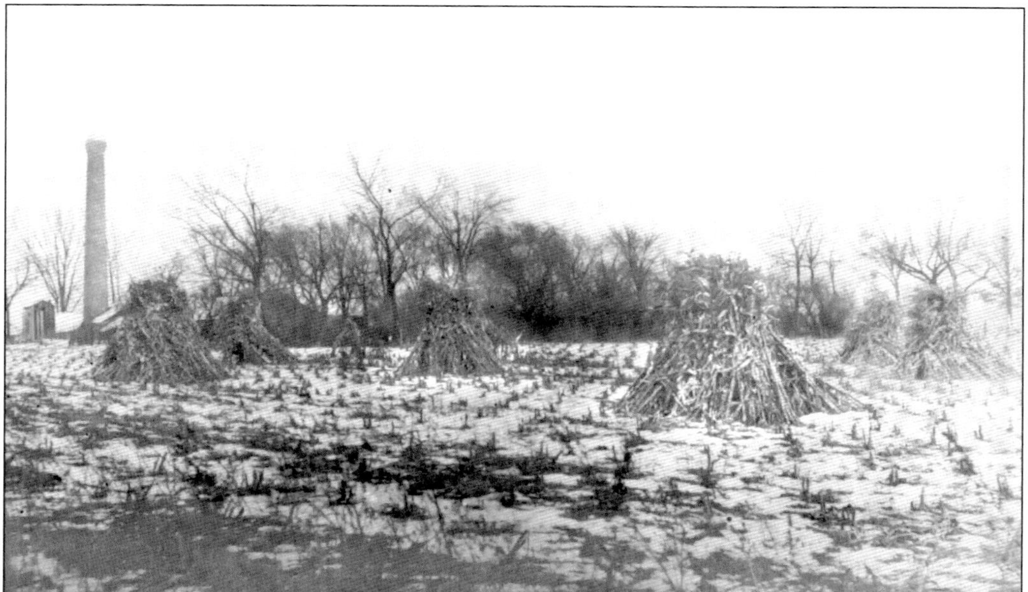

This early view of Foster Avenue shows the agrarian industry on the north side. (1908.)

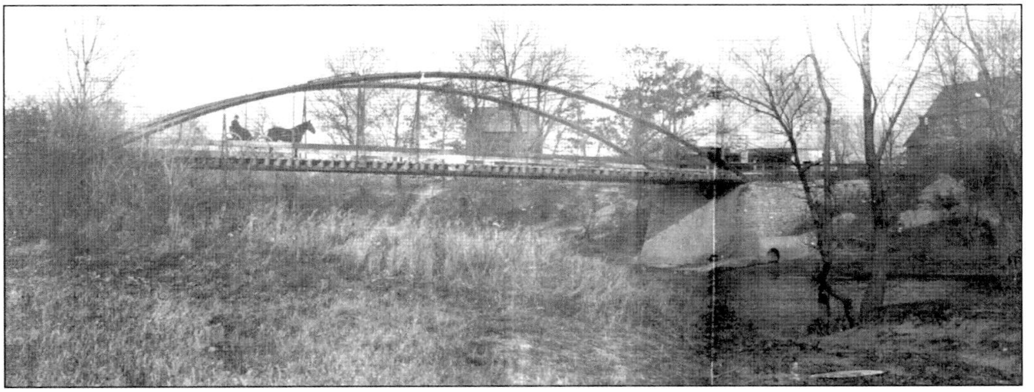

A horse and buggy cross the bridge on Irving Park Boulevard. (November 26, 1908.)

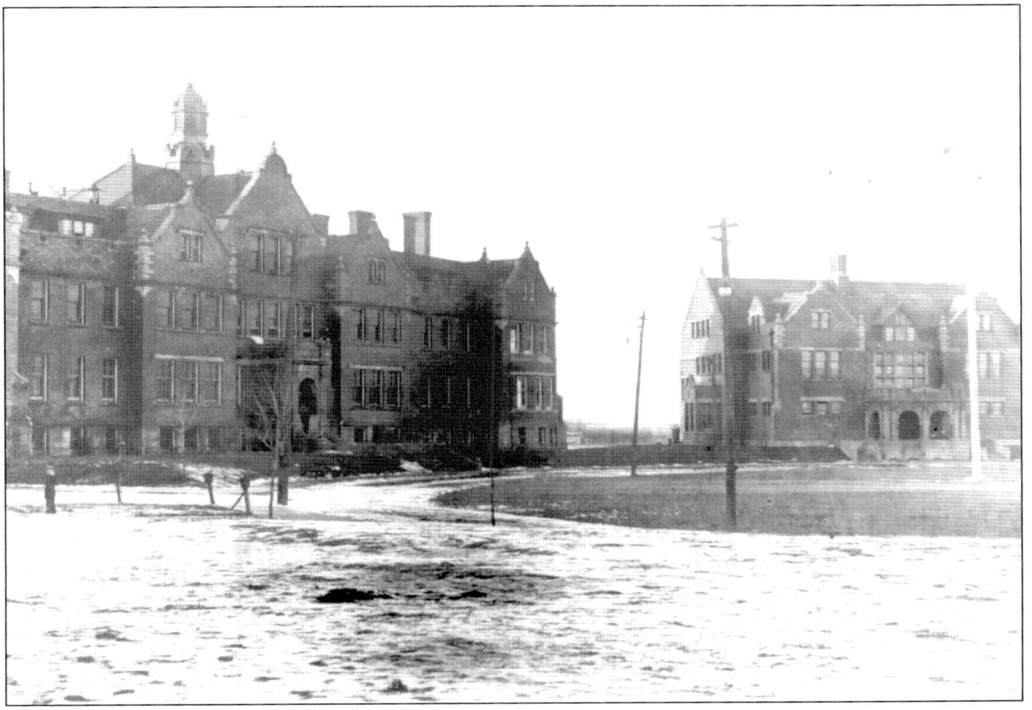

In addition to viewing Peterson's Nursery and Woods and the Chicago River near present day North Park Village Nature Center, a key attraction on this walk was a visit to the Parental School. (December 12, 1908.)

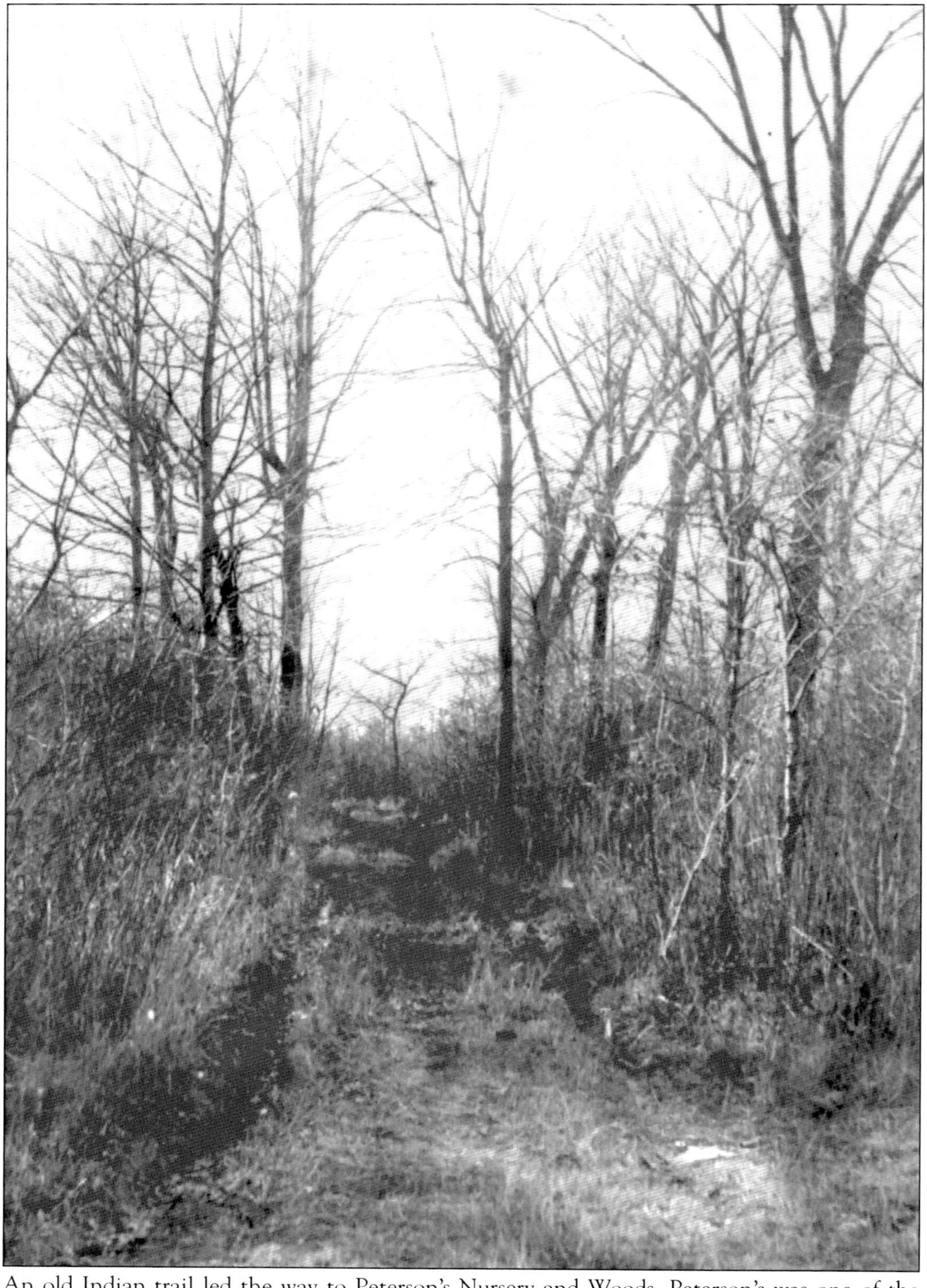

An old Indian trail led the way to Peterson's Nursery and Woods. Peterson's was one of the oldest greenhouses and nurseries in Chicago. It is now the site of the North Park Village Nature Center. (December 12, 1908.)

Five

Personalities Plus

As befit their rambling ways, Prairie Club members came from all walks of life. School teachers and tradesmen rubbed elbows with Chicago's elite. Learned academics joined hands with amateur naturalists, and women walked confidently next to men. The key prerequisite for joining the Prairie Club was a love of the outdoors. If that shoe fit, a Prairie Club member was ready to hike.

Some of the Prairie Club's early leaders were also prominent in Chicago and national environmental or artistic circles. The 1908 committee of the Playground Association of Chicago, from which the Prairie Club evolved, was chaired by Dwight H. Perkins. Perkins, a prominent Prairie School architect, was a pioneer in the movement to create the Cook County Forest Preserve district. Also on this first committee were high profile Chicagoans like Art Institute Director William M.R. French, writer Hamlin Garland, sculptor Lorado Taft, ecologist Henry C. Cowles, architect Walter Burley Griffin, landscape architect Jens Jensen, and settlement house leaders Graham R. Taylor and Amelia Hofer. Nine women were members of the original 40-person committee.

If not charter members of the Prairie Club, other Chicago luminaries were sympathetic to its cause. H.S. Pepoon, noted Chicago botanist, gave a lecture on a 1916 walk in Edgebrook. Charles L. Hutchinson, a leading businessman and Chicago Horticulture Society officer, entertained the group in his Lake Geneva summer home in that same year. In 1917, Hutchinson was a major contributor in organizing the spectacular Dunes pageant. Other eminent Chicagoans, like Harlow N. Higginbotham, led trips through his own estate, and Samuel Insull, J. Ogden Armour, and Cyrus McCormick opened up their grounds to Prairie Club hikers.

The club had its share of interesting individuals, but it also developed networks of special groups. The Prairie Players produced dramas and masques, while the square-dancing Prairie Swingers continue to meet after more than 50 years of dancing. Together, as individuals and groups, the Prairie Club personality shone through.

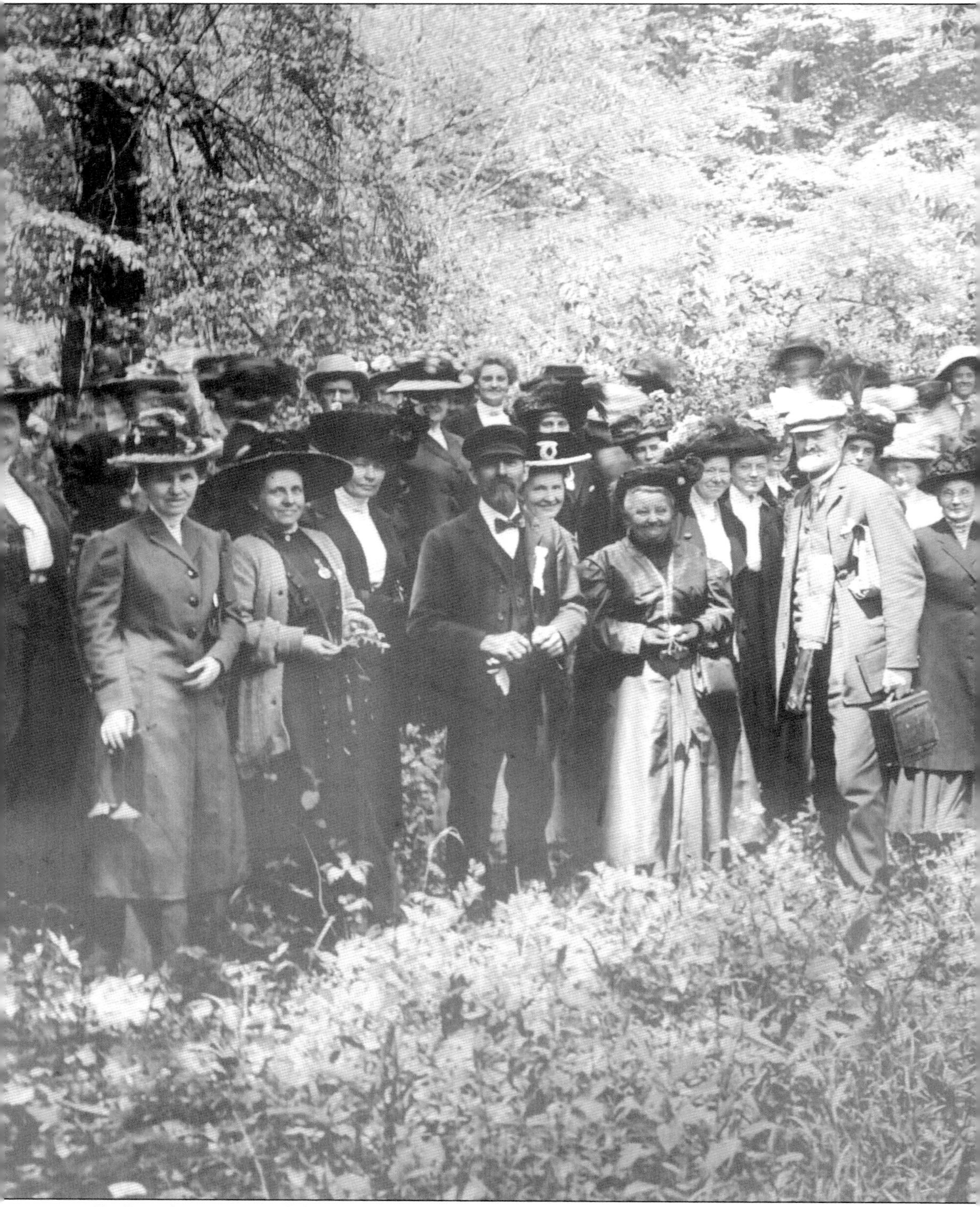

Each and every one of the Prairie Club members brings a unique contribution to the club. Here, according to the photo label, was "The Bunch in the Virgin Forest," at Three Oaks, Michigan.

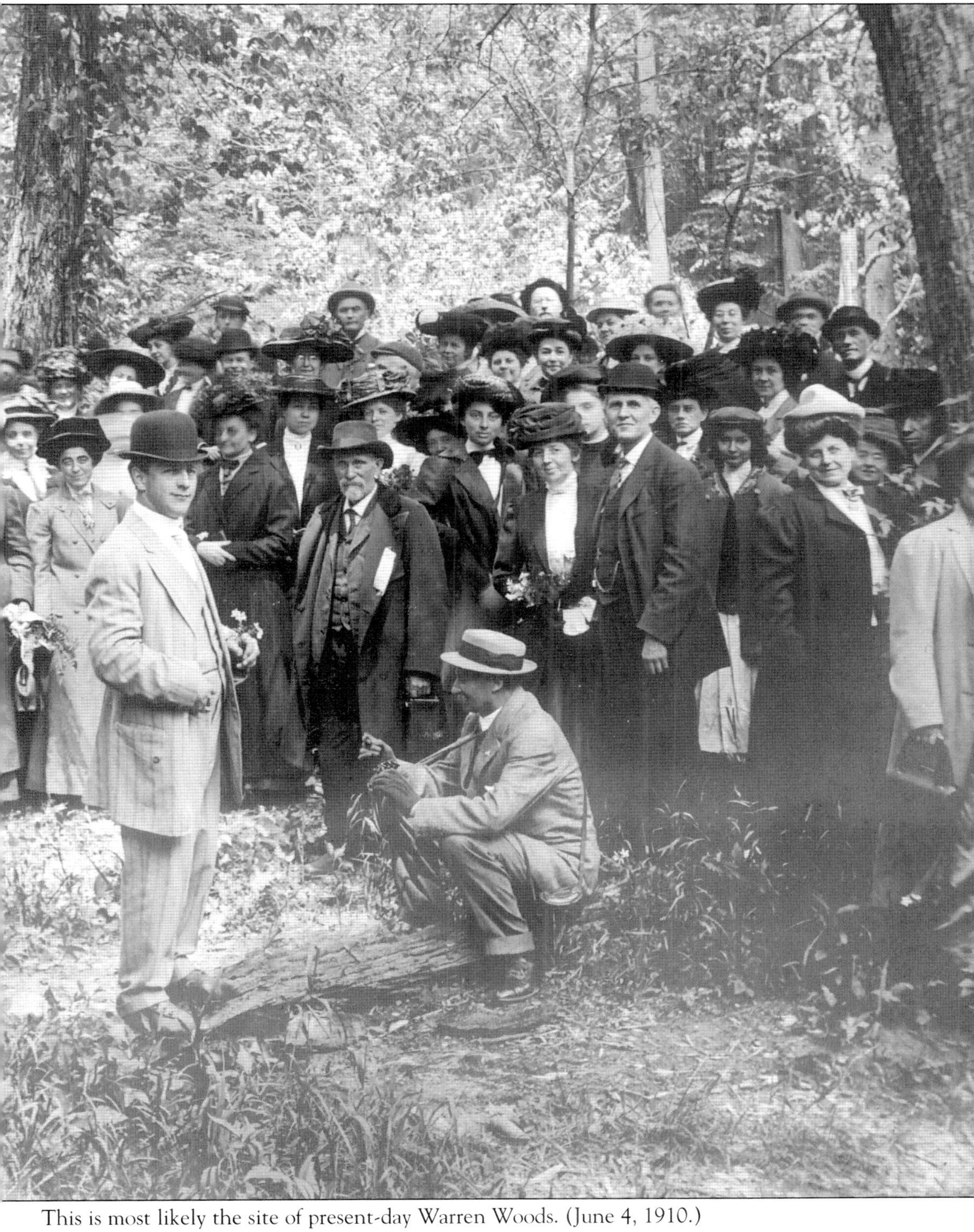

This is most likely the site of present-day Warren Woods. (June 4, 1910.)

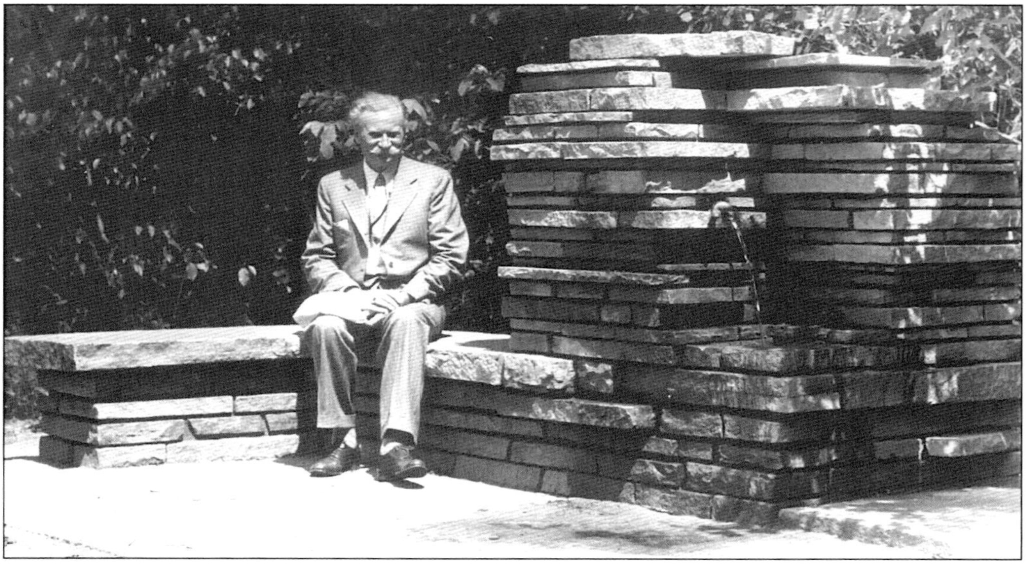

Jens Jensen (1860–1951) figures prominently among the Prairie Club's many personalities. A founder of the club and its president in 1914, Jensen is synonymous with the Prairie School of landscape architecture. Jensen designed this Prairie Club memorial fountain at the Indiana Dunes. (1932.)

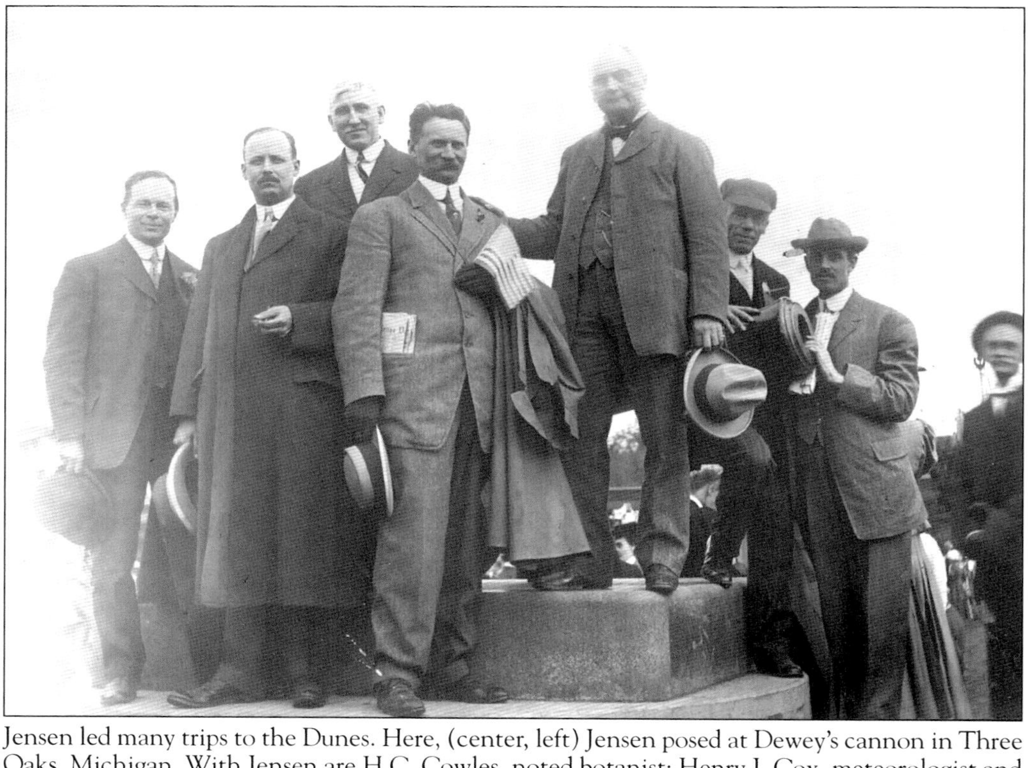

Jensen led many trips to the Dunes. Here, (center, left) Jensen posed at Dewey's cannon in Three Oaks, Michigan. With Jensen are H.C. Cowles, noted botanist; Henry J. Cox, meteorologist and geographer; and Edward K. Warren, industrialist and philanthropist. (June 4, 1910.)

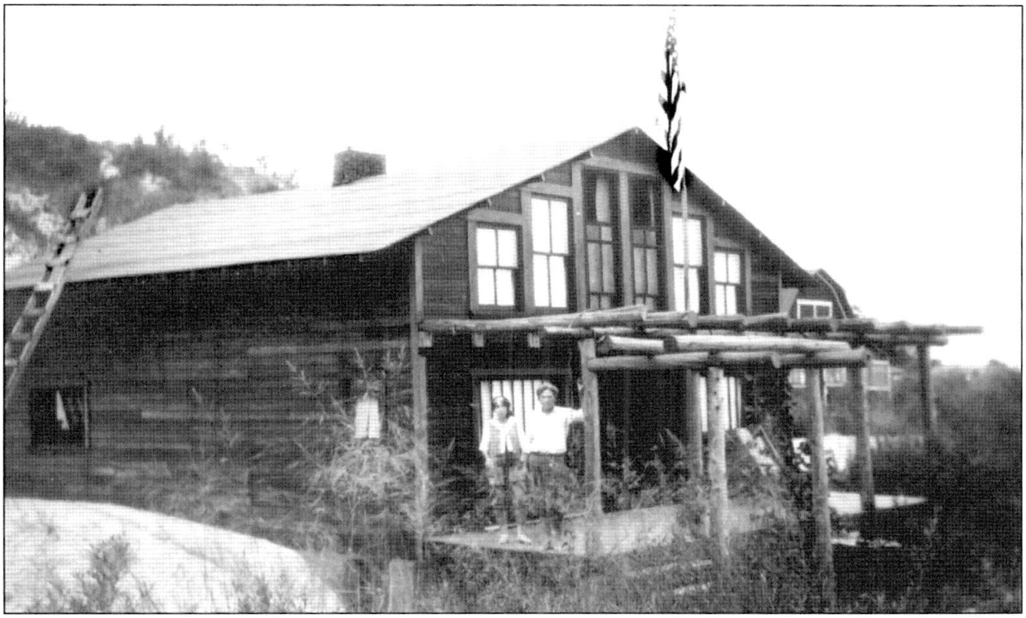

Eminent Dunes painter Frank V. Dudley and his wife lived at his cottage and studio in the Dunes, and often invited Prairie Club members here for a visit and conversation. Dudley served as a member of the Prairie Club's Board of Directors. He and his wife were later named as Honorary Life members. (September 5, 1925.)

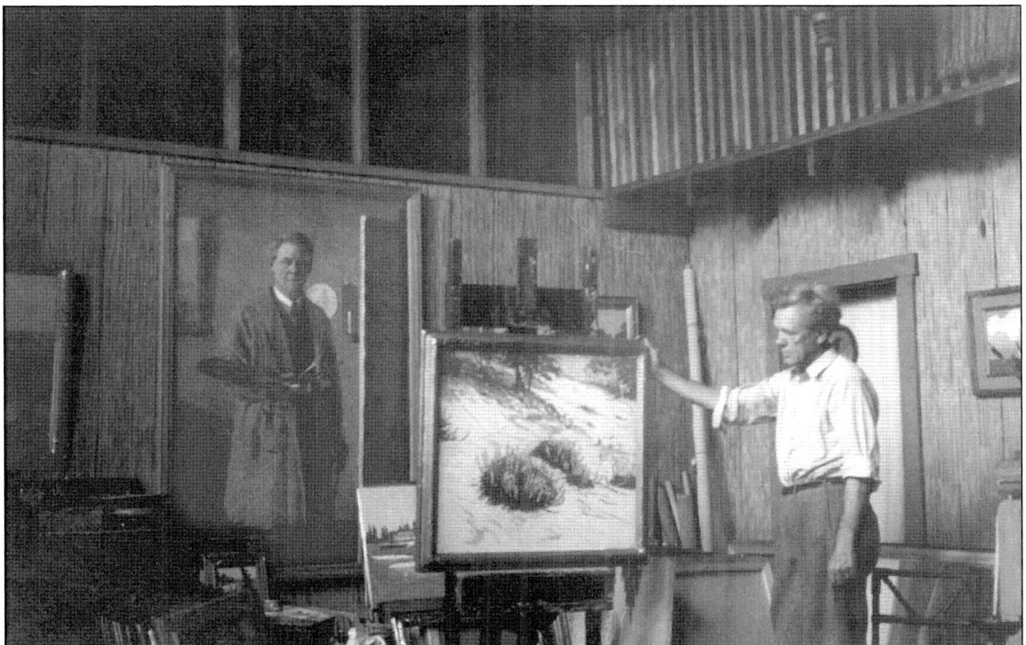

Dudley's paintings are very collectible today. Unlike most other structures in the state park, the Dudley cottage was allowed to remain in the Dunes for rent of one painting per year. Thus, the State of Indiana has by far the largest collection of Dudley paintings. (September 5, 1926.)

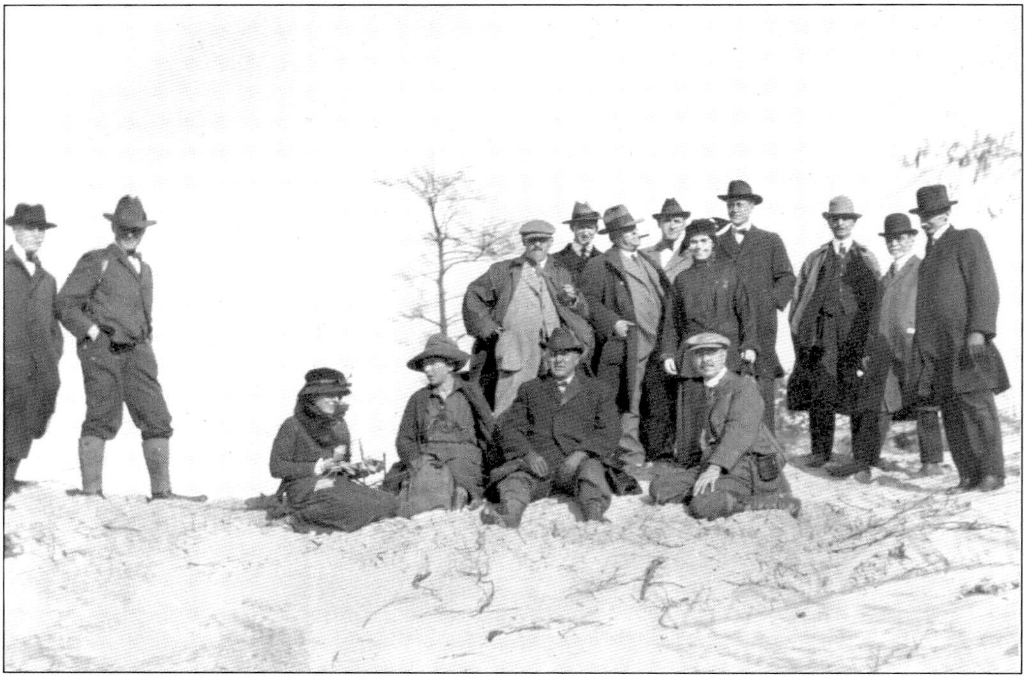

Stephen Tyng Mather (1867–1930) was an active Prairie Club member. A former Chicago businessman, he became the first director of the National Park Service. He was among the first to propose a 12,000-acre national site at the Dunes in 1916. He is shown here (fourth from right, back row, with bow tie) on a visit to the Dunes. (October 31, 1916.) (Photo courtesy of National Park Service).

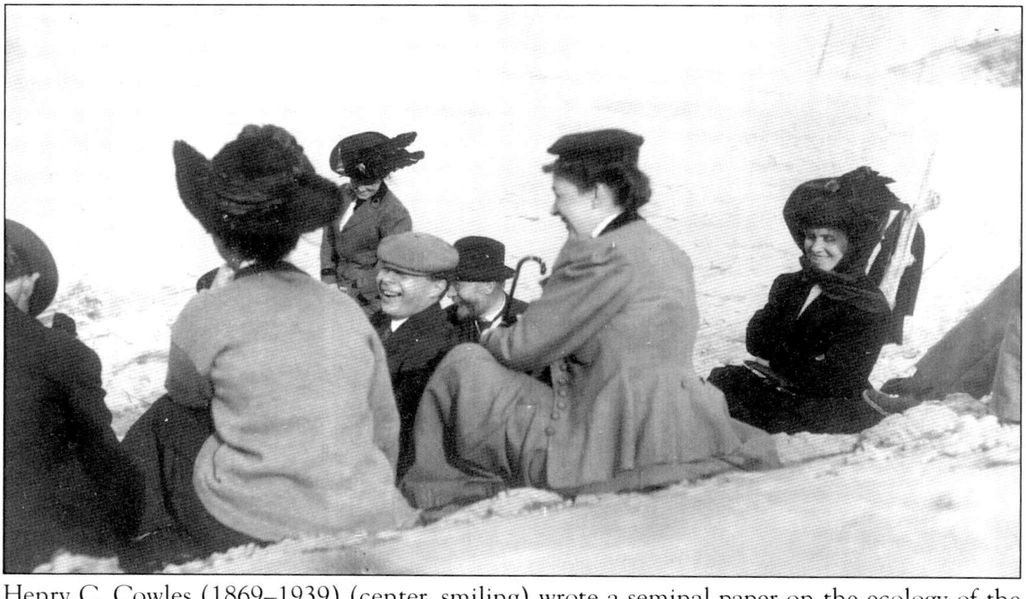

Henry C. Cowles (1869–1939) (center, smiling) wrote a seminal paper on the ecology of the Dunes and was very instrumental in the fight to save this precious resource. He was a botanist and professor at the University of Chicago. (November 13, 1909.)

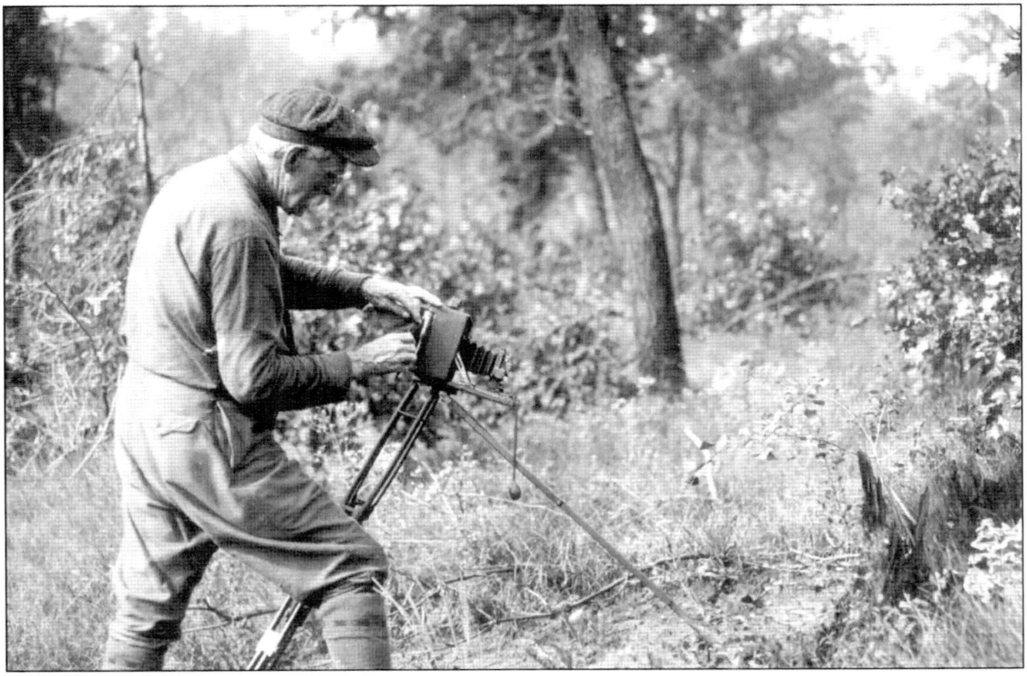

Captain Charles H. Robinson (1843–1940) was a colorful Prairie Club member who specialized in nature photography. He is said to be the last commissioned Civil War officer in this area, and was a congressman and mayor in Iowa. He joined the club in 1914. (No date.)

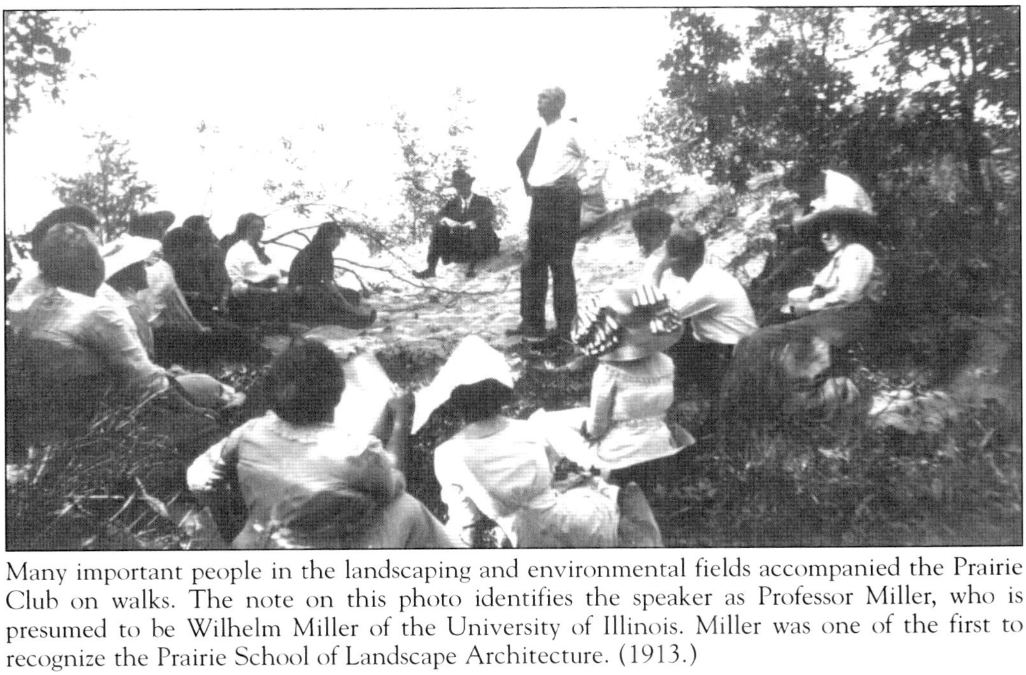

Many important people in the landscaping and environmental fields accompanied the Prairie Club on walks. The note on this photo identifies the speaker as Professor Miller, who is presumed to be Wilhelm Miller of the University of Illinois. Miller was one of the first to recognize the Prairie School of Landscape Architecture. (1913.)

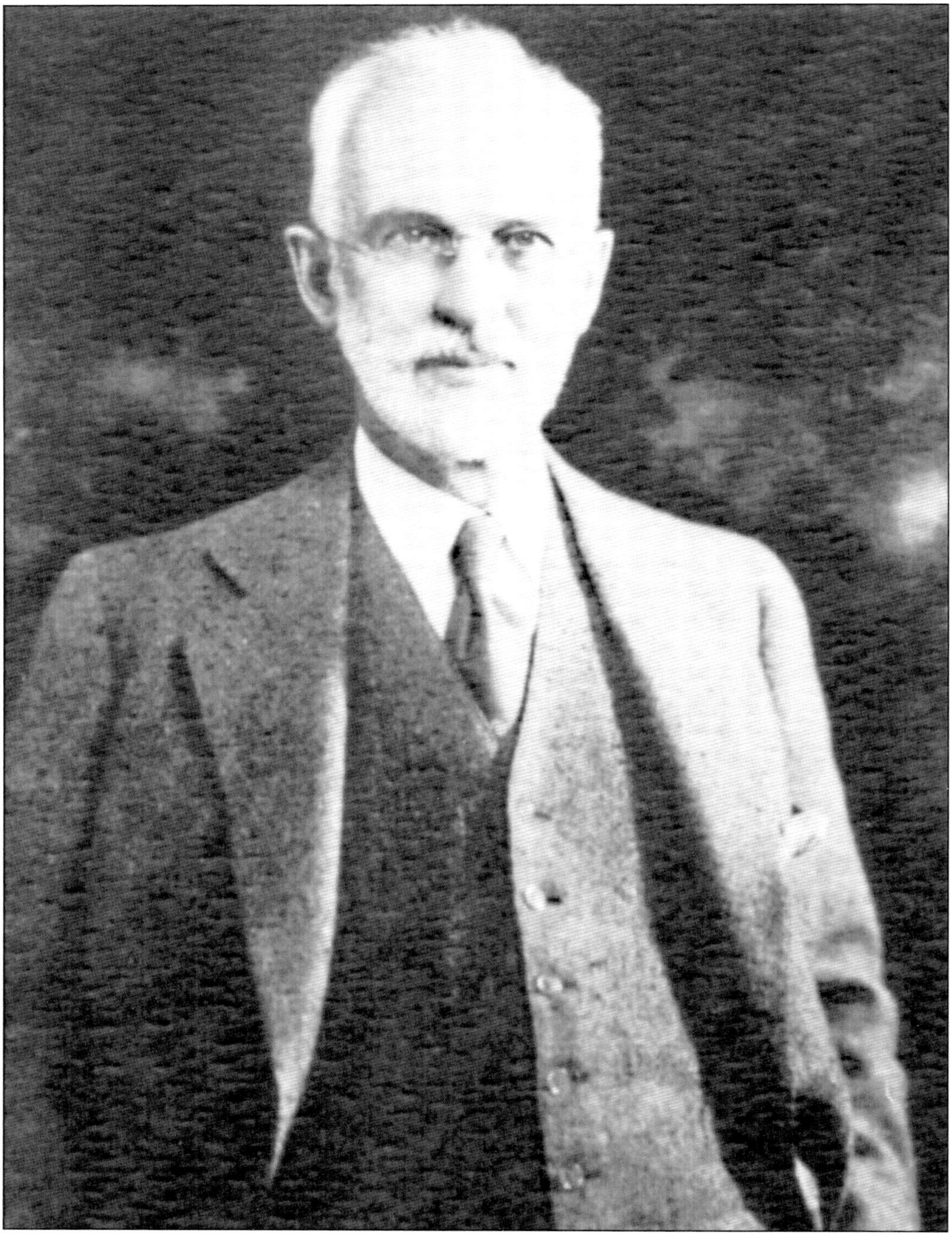

Dwight Heald Perkins (1867–1941), a Chicago architect, is generally recognized as spearheading the movement to create the Cook County Forest Preserves. The first president of the Chicago Regional Planning Commission, Perkins lobbied tirelessly for the acquisition and protection of the land, which would finally become the forest preserves we enjoy today. Perkins was an active and early Prairie Club member who often served as a walk leader. (Photo courtesy of Perkins & Will.)

Six

The Dunes

They climbed them. They walked through, swam around, and camped on them. Beginning with the Prairie Club's first walk to the Indiana Dunes in 1908, with 330 participants, it was love at first sight. When big industry and development threatened the very existence of the Dunes, the Prairie Club was in the front lines of the battle to save them.

The fragile Dunes ecosystem, with its great diversity in plant and animal habitats, was a source of delight for the Prairie Club hikers. With H.C. Cowles, Jens Jensen and other experts educating the public about this precious natural resource, fellow club members lobbied to preserve this magical place.

In 1913, Prairie Club members celebrated the dedication of their Dunes beach house with a pageant, "Duna—Spirit of the Dunes." This was the first of many masques, a popular dramatic art form of the times, produced to bring attention to the Dunes. In 1917, the Prairie Club led a large coalition of groups in staging the largest outdoor pageant ever held at that time, "Dunes under Four Flags." According to some estimates, attendance in the sandy hills and blowouts reached more than 40,000.

The first campaign to create a National Dunes Park, which included lobbying efforts from many groups, failed. Prairie Club conservationists and others appealed to the State of Indiana. Their efforts bore fruit when the Indiana Dunes State Park opened its gates in 1925. It wasn't until 1966, however, that Congress authorized an Indiana Dunes National Lakeshore.

Typically, club members boarded the South Shore train to begin all-day hikes in the Dunes. Climbing tall dunes like Mount Tom proved an irresistible challenge. Spotting rare plants and birds in the woodlands and bogs was another favorite pastime.

The club's first permanent camp was built in 1913, near Tremont in the Dunes, and for many years, club members enjoyed swimming, hiking, and nature at this rustic spot. In 1926, faithful to its mission of conservation, the Prairie Club sold its 46 acres (including 3,000 feet of beach frontage) at cost ($600 per acre) to form a key component of the newly formed Indiana Dunes State Park. Today, thousands of visitors frolic on what was once the private camp of the Prairie Club.

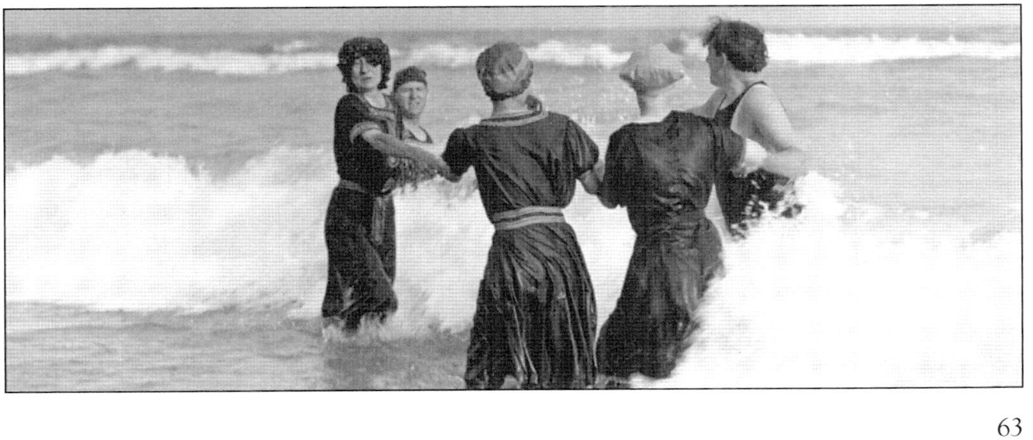

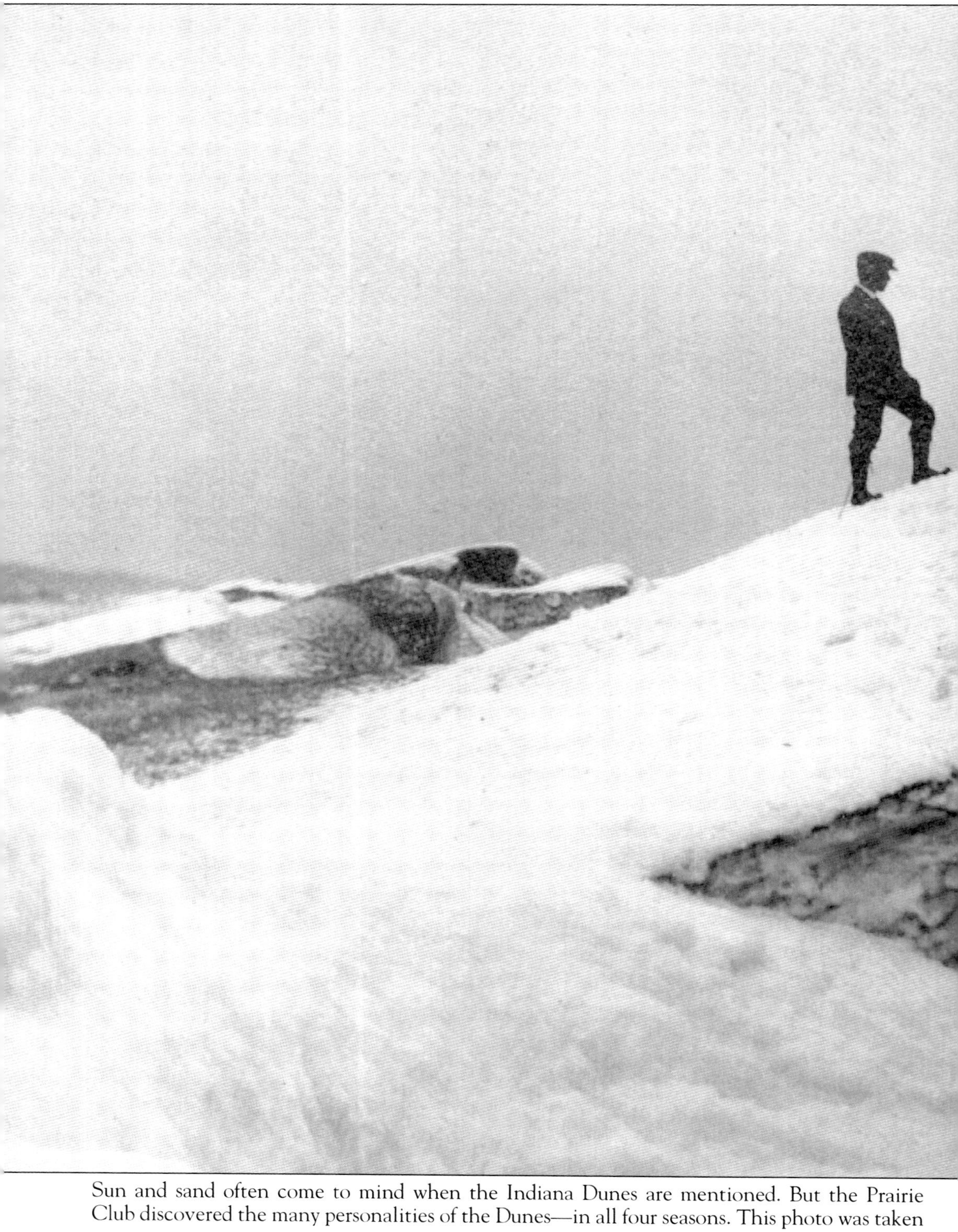

Sun and sand often come to mind when the Indiana Dunes are mentioned. But the Prairie Club discovered the many personalities of the Dunes—in all four seasons. This photo was taken

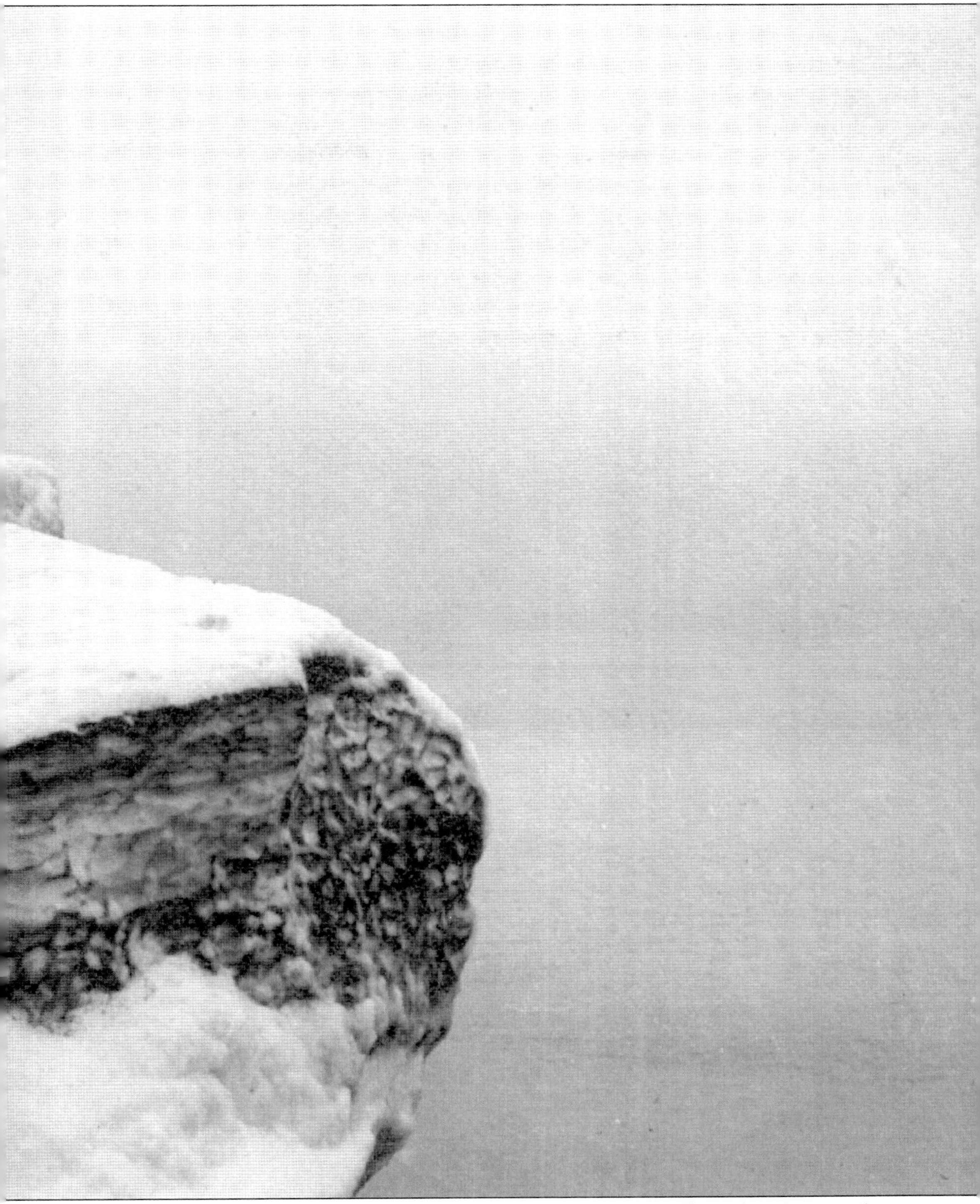

south of Gary and is signed "Dudley." It could be from artist Frank V. Dudley or his photographer brother, Clarence. (February 1913.)

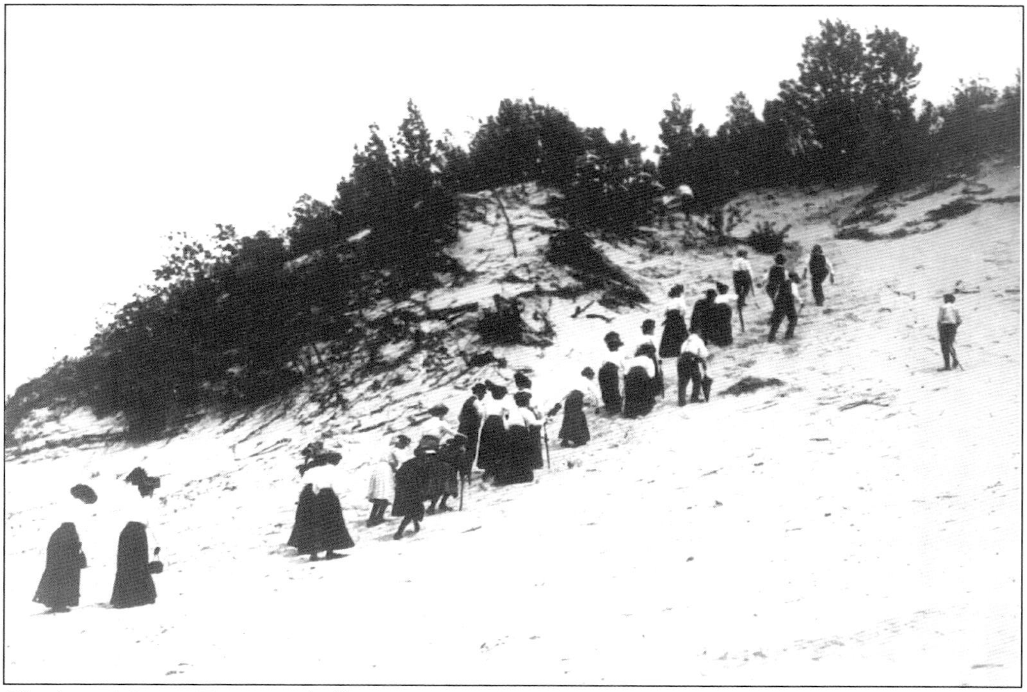

Climbing Mount Tom is a challenge even today, without the long skirts worn by early Prairie Club women. (May 31, 1908.)

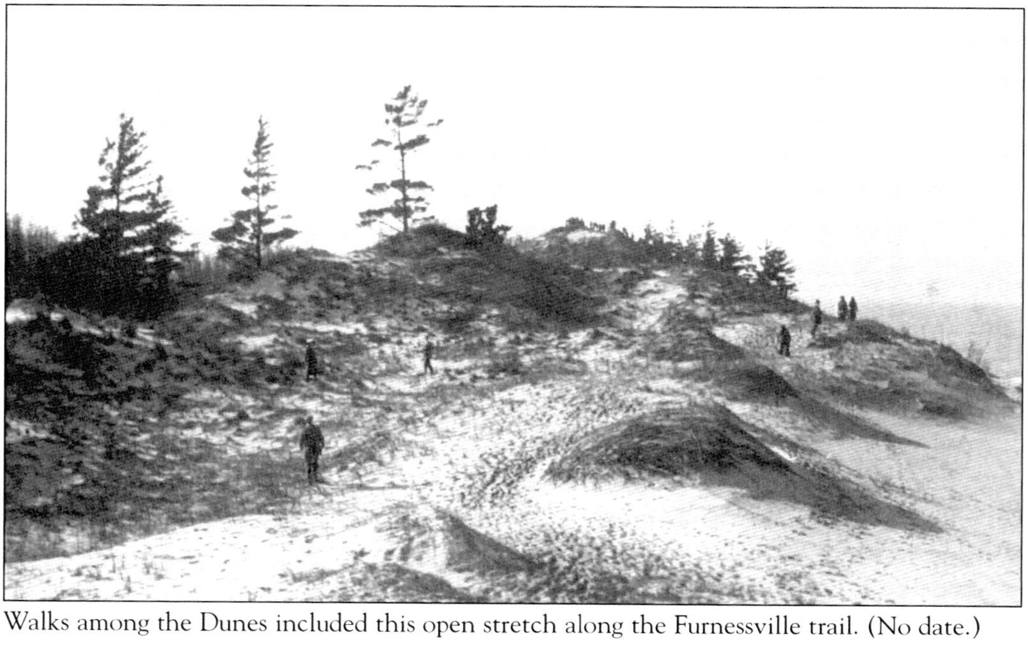

Walks among the Dunes included this open stretch along the Furnessville trail. (No date.)

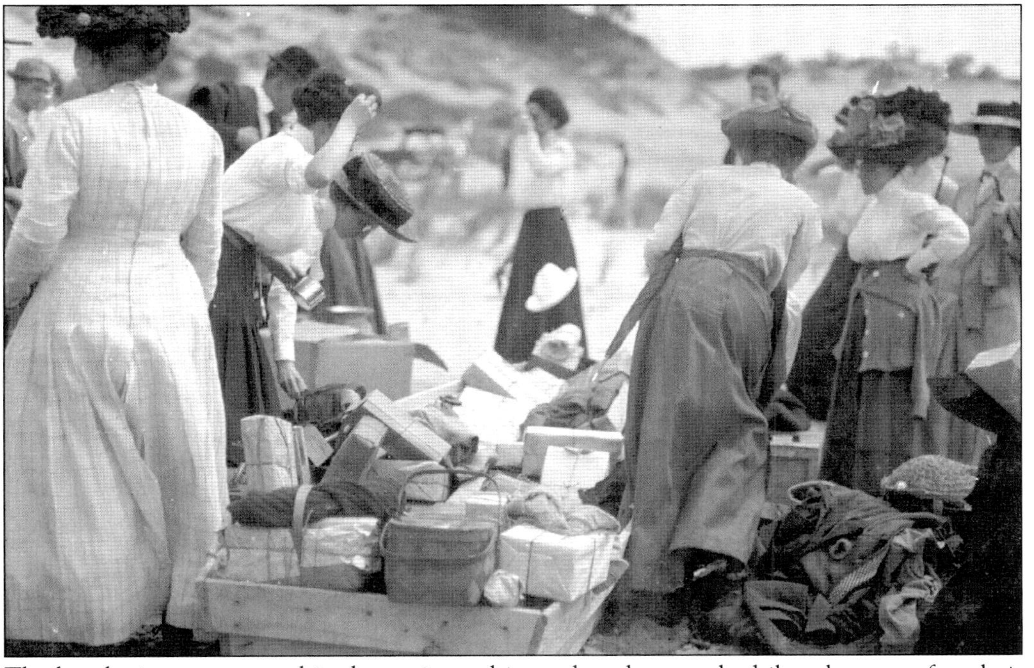

The handwritten note on this photo gives a hint at how hungry the hikers became after their walk from Furnessville: "the scramble when the wagon arrived." (July 4, 1910.)

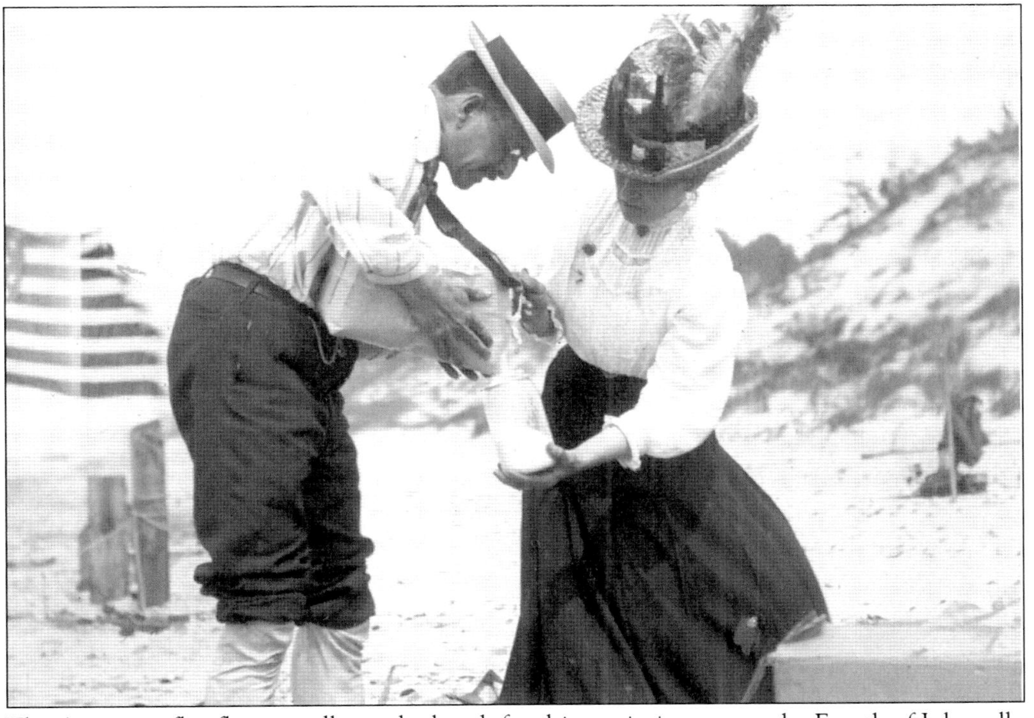

The American flag flew proudly on the beach for this patriotic crew on the Fourth of July walk. Here, two club members sweeten the lemonade. (July 4, 1910.)

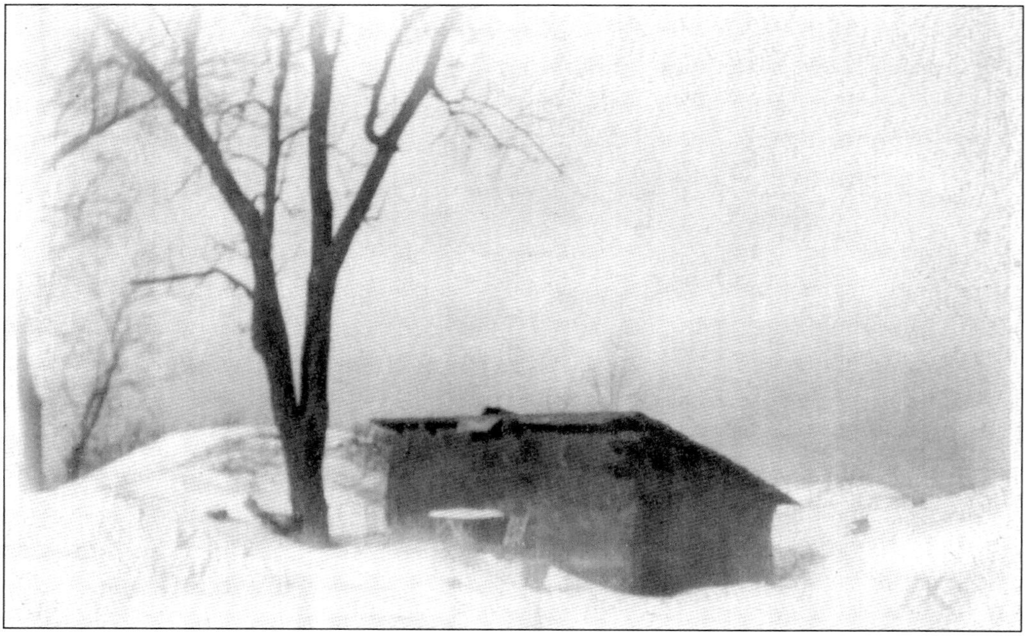

Notations on this photo suggest it was taken by C.H. Robinson, with his note, "A girl who was a graduate of the University. . . turned hermit and lived in this shack. . . ." Presumably he refers to Alice Gray, the legendary "Diana of the Dunes," who lived in the dunes between 1915 and 1923.

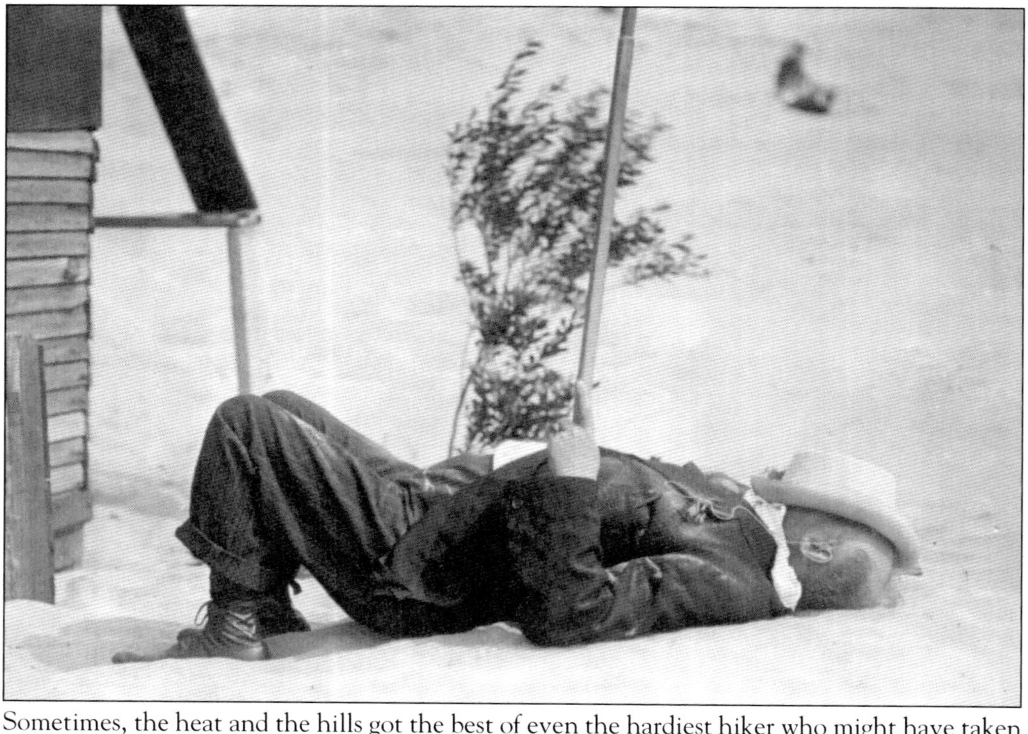

Sometimes, the heat and the hills got the best of even the hardiest hiker who might have taken a well-earned nap. (July 4, 1910.)

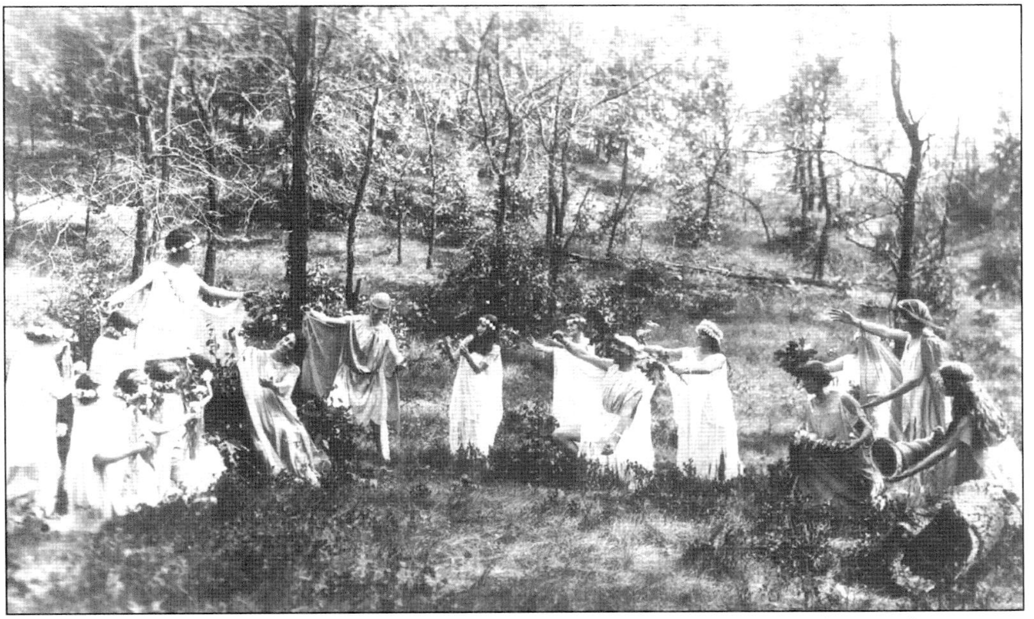

Outdoor masques were frequently performed by Prairie Club members to mark special events, or to bring attention to a cause, like the conservation of the Dunes. This play, *Duna, the Spirit of the Dunes*, was written by Mrs. Jacob J. Abt and marked the opening of the Prairie Club's Beach House in Tremont. In this scene, Duna is hailed. (October 19, 1913.)

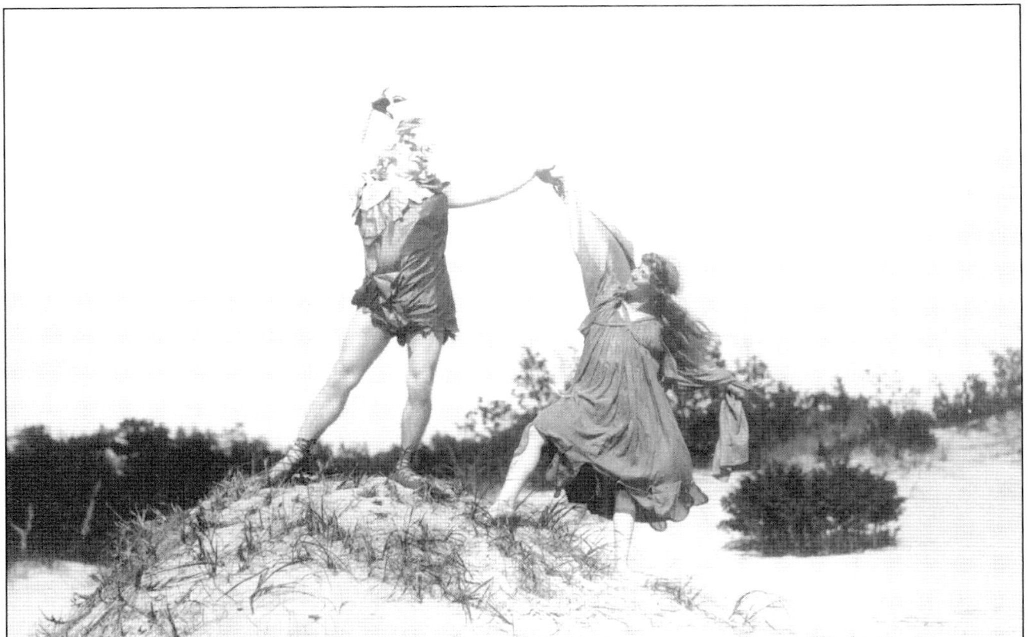

On Memorial Day in 1915, another masque, "The Awakening," celebrated the anniversary of the founding of the Prairie Club. This is the "Dance of the Nymph and Fawn." (May 31, 1915.)

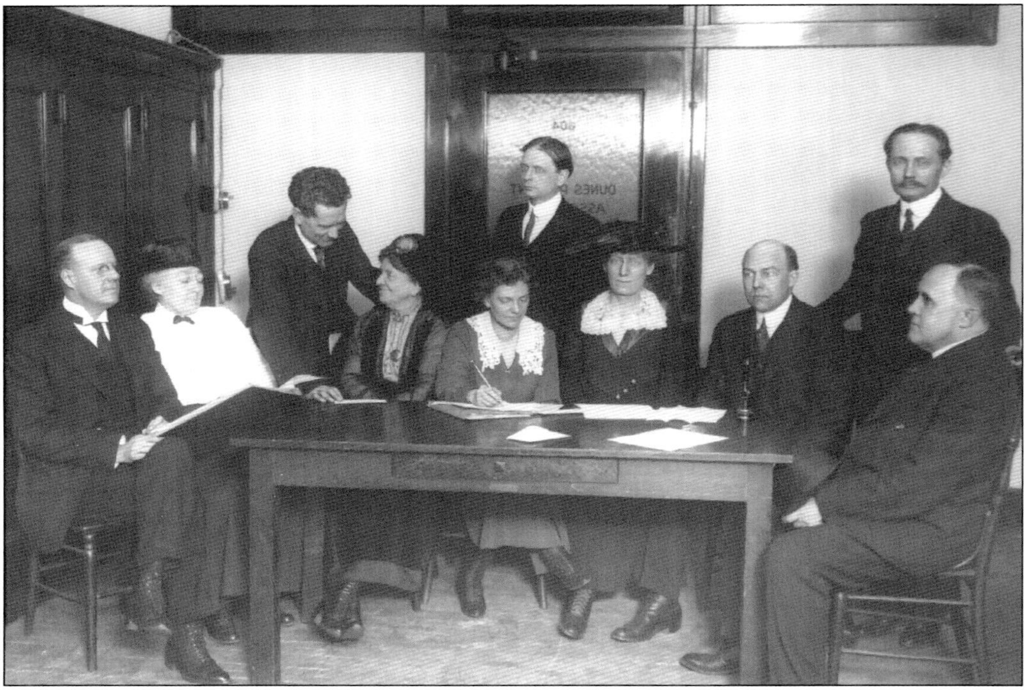

The most significant pageant, "The Dunes Under Four Flags," was held on two weekends in 1917, to bring widespread attention to the fight to save the Dunes. A prestigious and dedicated Pageant Board contributed much to the Pageant success. Pictured here, from left to right, are as follows: Eames MacVeagh, Anna H. Loeb, Thomas W. Allinson, Florence Holbrook, Ethel M. Durfee, Caroline M. McIlvaine, pageant author Thomas Wood Stevens (standing in back), James L. Houston Jr., Arthur Hercz, and Charles D. Platt.

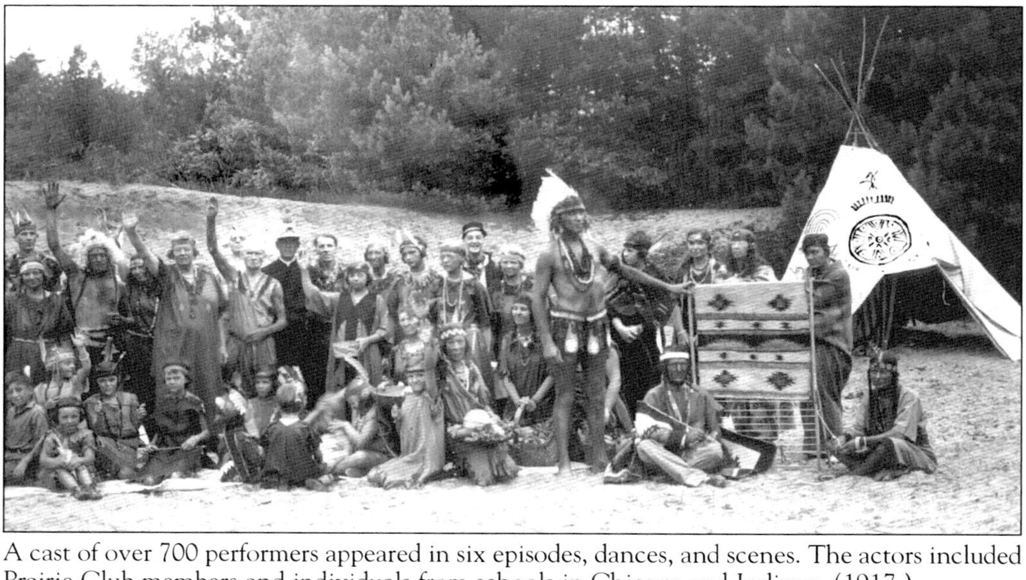

A cast of over 700 performers appeared in six episodes, dances, and scenes. The actors included Prairie Club members and individuals from schools in Chicago and Indiana. (1917.)

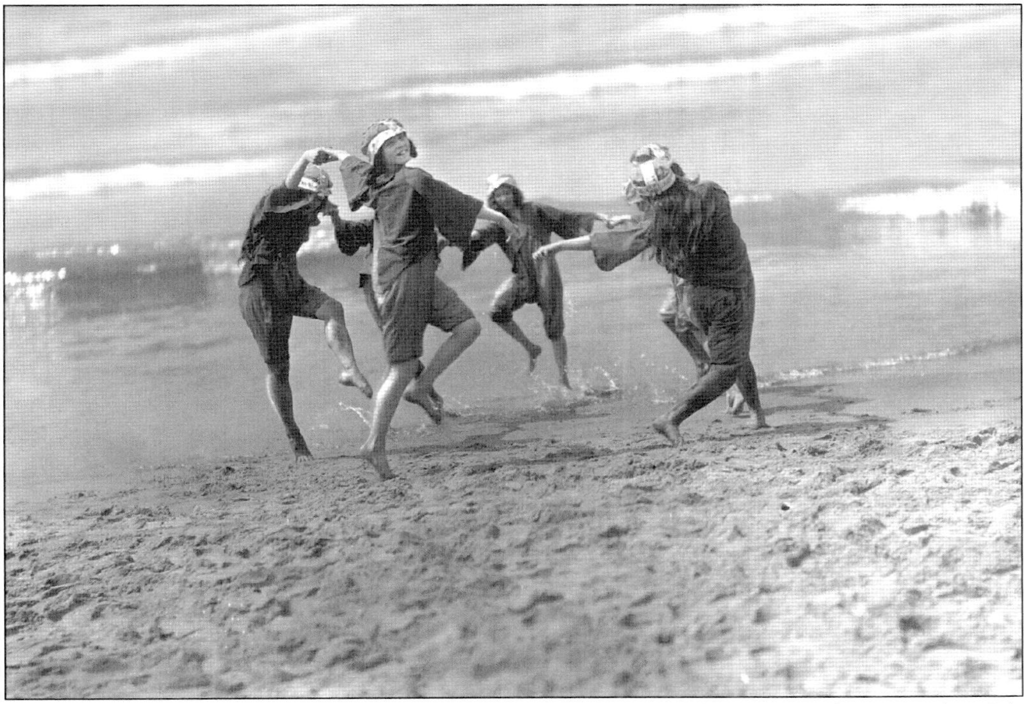

Fittingly, on the shores of Lake Michigan, young ladies interpret the "Dance of Waves." (1917.)

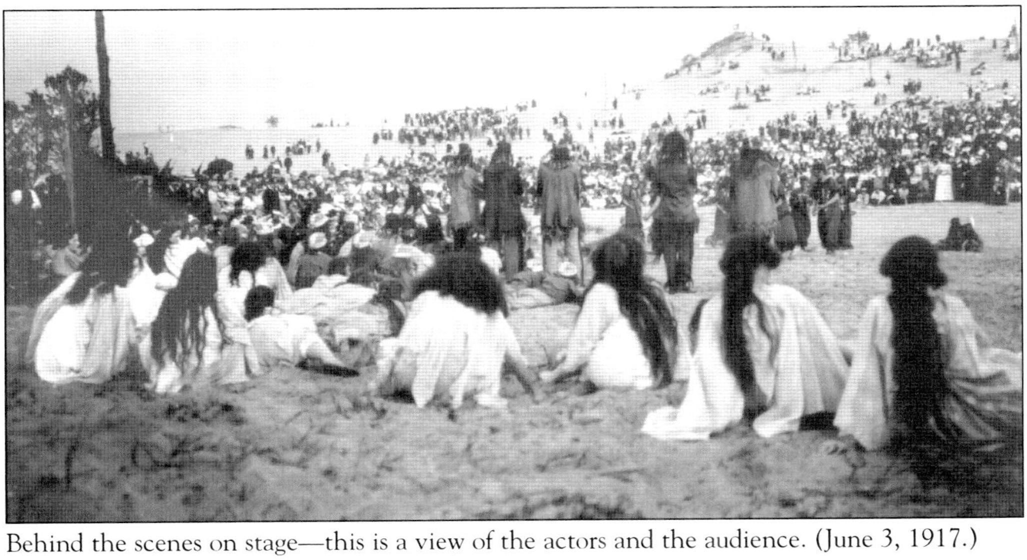

Behind the scenes on stage—this is a view of the actors and the audience. (June 3, 1917.)

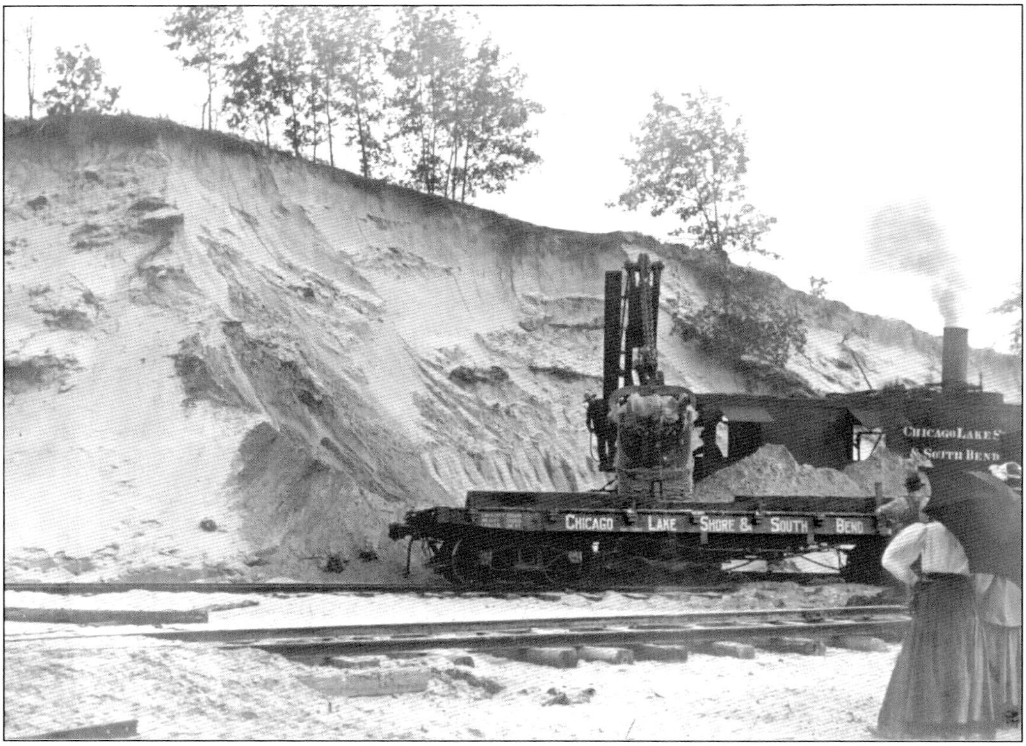

Threats to the Indiana Dunes were early and persistent. Steel mills and other development threatened the natural and delicate beauty. Here, a sand-mining operation depletes the dunes near Miller, Indiana. (May 30, 1908.)

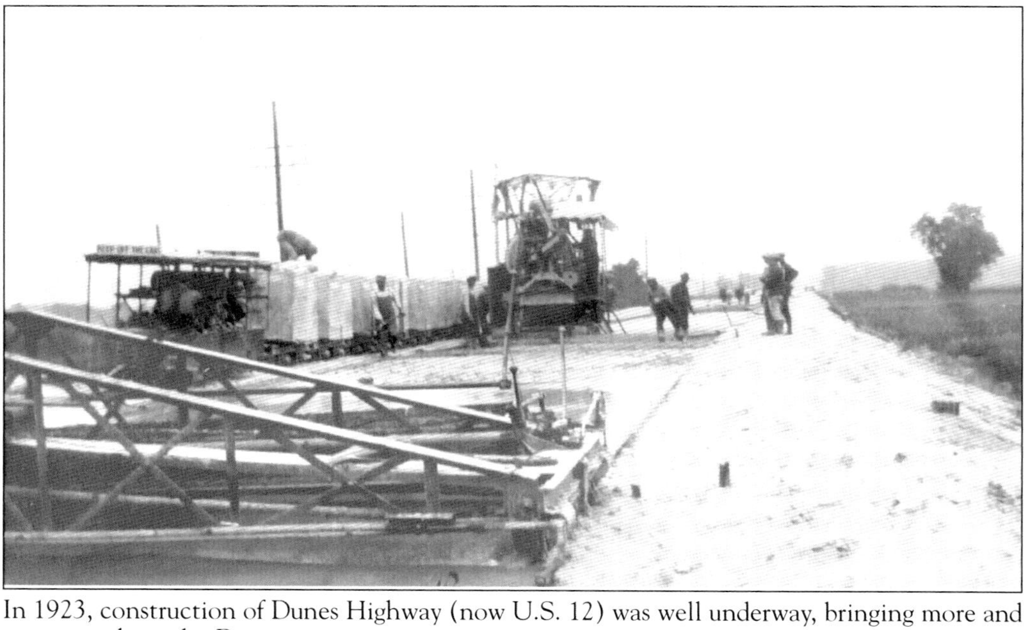

In 1923, construction of Dunes Highway (now U.S. 12) was well underway, bringing more and more people to the Dunes.

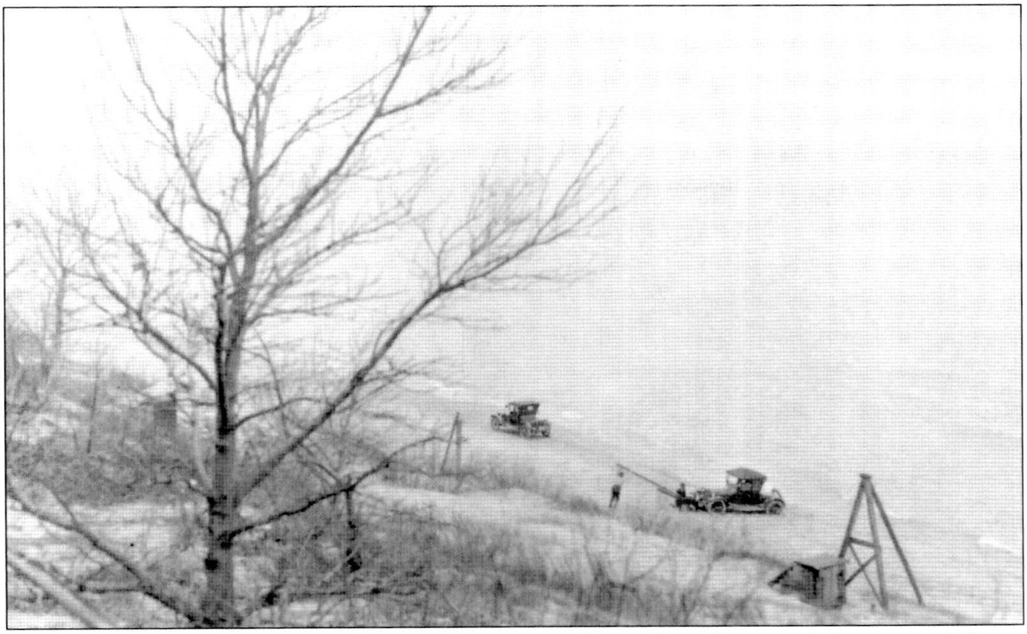

The handwritten note on this photo, "Tin Lizzies," shows the advance of the automobile on the beach in the 1920s.

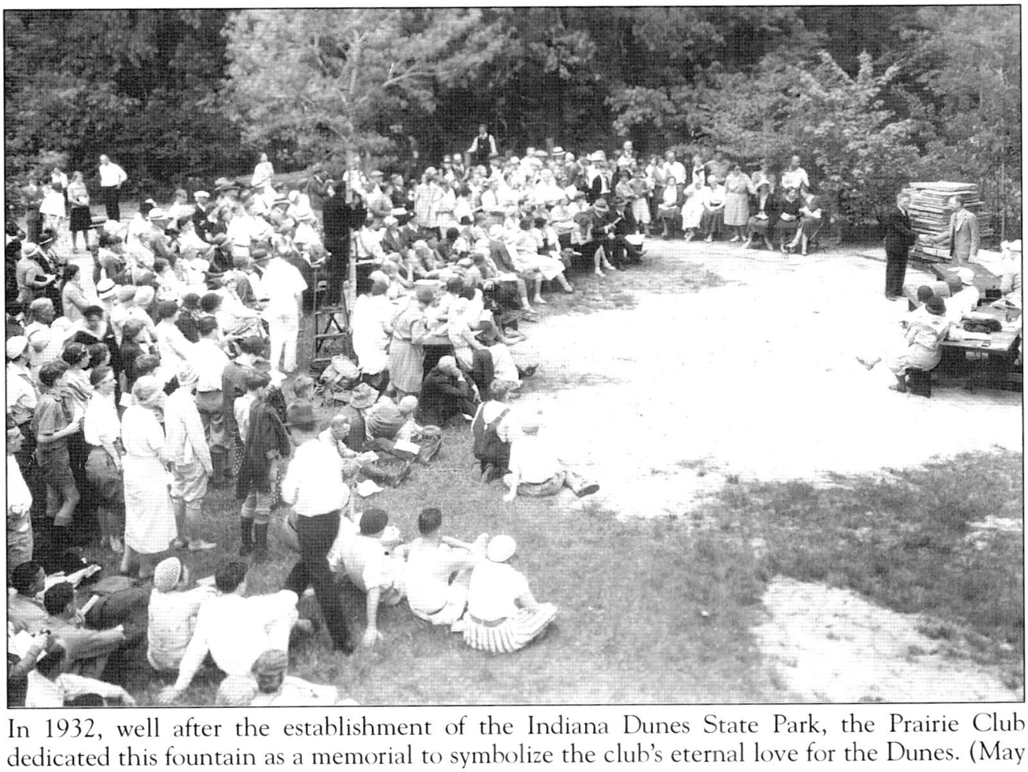

In 1932, well after the establishment of the Indiana Dunes State Park, the Prairie Club dedicated this fountain as a memorial to symbolize the club's eternal love for the Dunes. (May 30, 1932.)

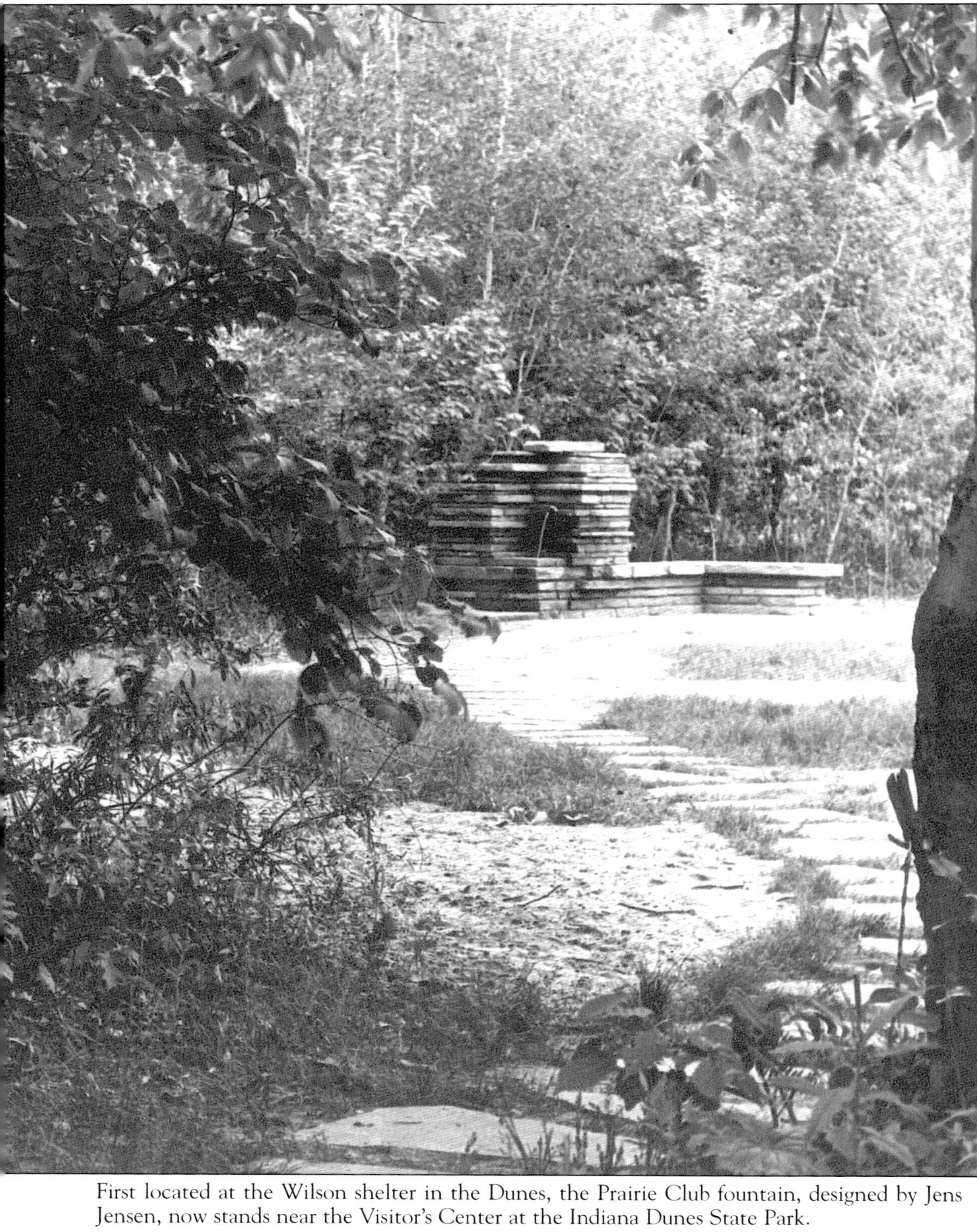

First located at the Wilson shelter in the Dunes, the Prairie Club fountain, designed by Jens Jensen, now stands near the Visitor's Center at the Indiana Dunes State Park.

Seven

The Camps

Even diehard tramps must stop and rest awhile. As the walks got longer, and as more weekend trips were planned, Prairie Club members began to see the potential of permanent campsites. The camps would allow members more time to explore nature, both on walks and in other outdoor activities. Never grandiose, the sites chosen for the camps let nature outshine man-made structure.

In June of 1911, the first camping trip was held at the Dunes in Tremont, Indiana. A later club bulletin explained, "The idea is to sleep out on the ground, using no tents, but simply a sleeping bag or pair of blankets. A deserted house and barn will provide shelter in case of rain."

By late summer 1912, the Tremont camp had proved to be a big success with 20 to 40 persons in camp each weekend. Finally in May of 1913, with Jens Jensen as chair of the Camp Committee, plans were approved to build a beach house at Tremont.

Shortly after World War I in 1919, another campsite was developed in the newly established Deer Grove Forest Preserve. To enjoy natural areas south of Chicago, permission was obtained from the Cook County Commissioners to establish a camp in Palos Park in 1922.

In 1930, the club purchased a partially developed, 60-acre tract of duneland, wooded terrain, and over 500 feet of shoreline to replace the Tremont camp, which had been sold to the Indiana Dunes State Park. This new camp was called Hazelhurst after the many witchhazel bushes on the property.

Many years of hiking and outdoor activities were enjoyed at these camps. Today, only two Prairie Club camps remain. Hazelhurst, on Lake Michigan in Harbert, Michigan, is in its 71st year. Spring Grove, the newest camp in northern Illinois, was founded in 1977. Both camps continue to provide Prairie Club members a natural haven to enjoy the outdoors.

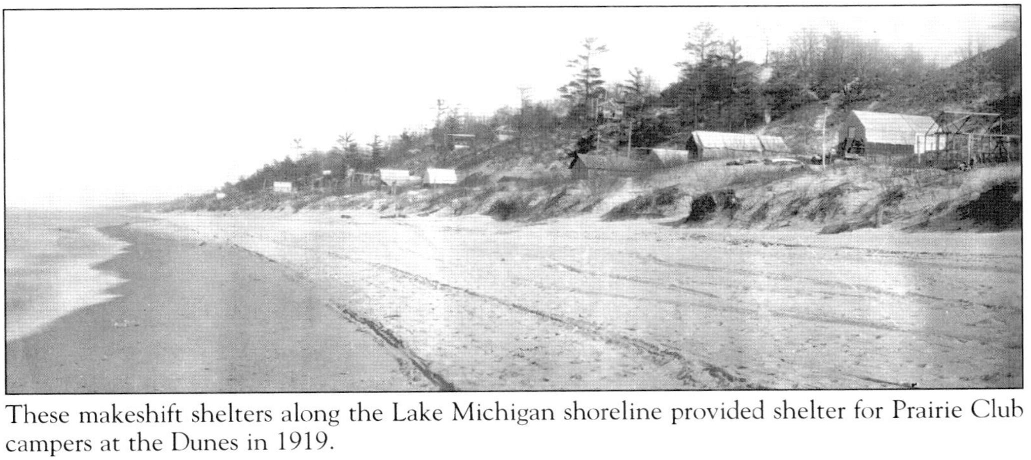

These makeshift shelters along the Lake Michigan shoreline provided shelter for Prairie Club campers at the Dunes in 1919.

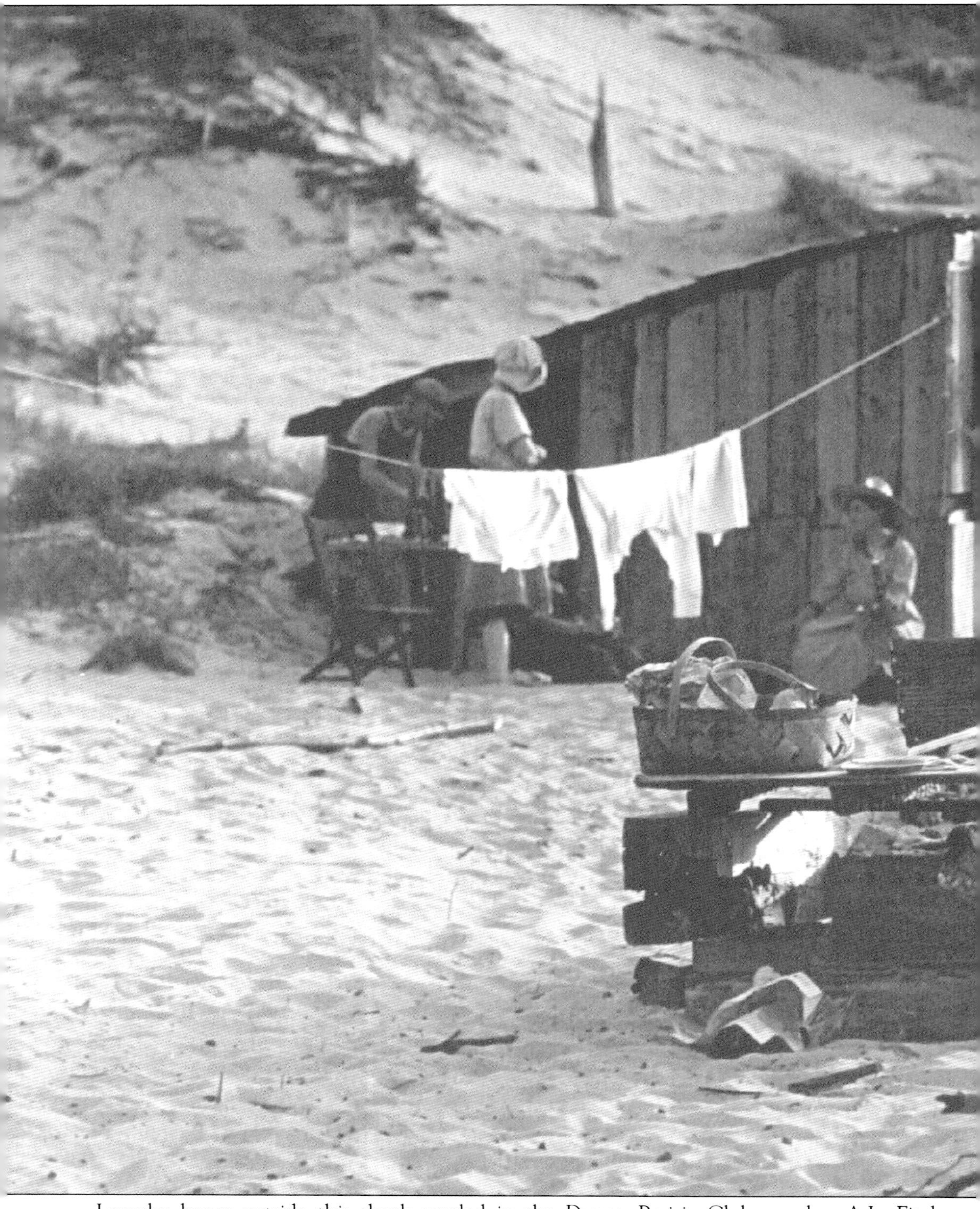

Laundry hangs outside this shack nestled in the Dunes. Prairie Club member A.L. Fitch took this picture and titled it, "The first Prairie Club Beach House (Unofficial) at Tremont."

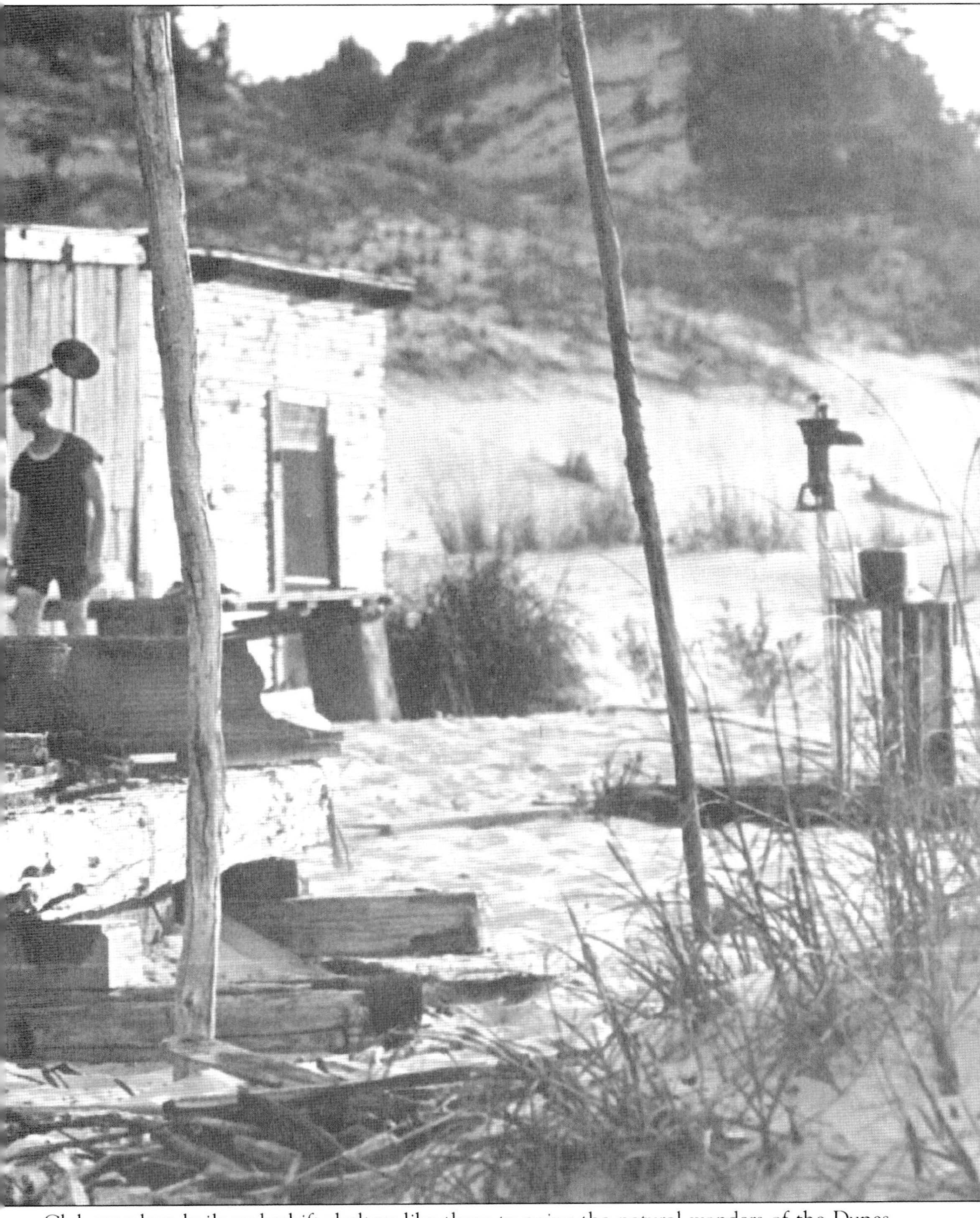

Club members built makeshift shelters like these to enjoy the natural wonders of the Dunes. (September 1, 1912.)

TREMONT CAMP

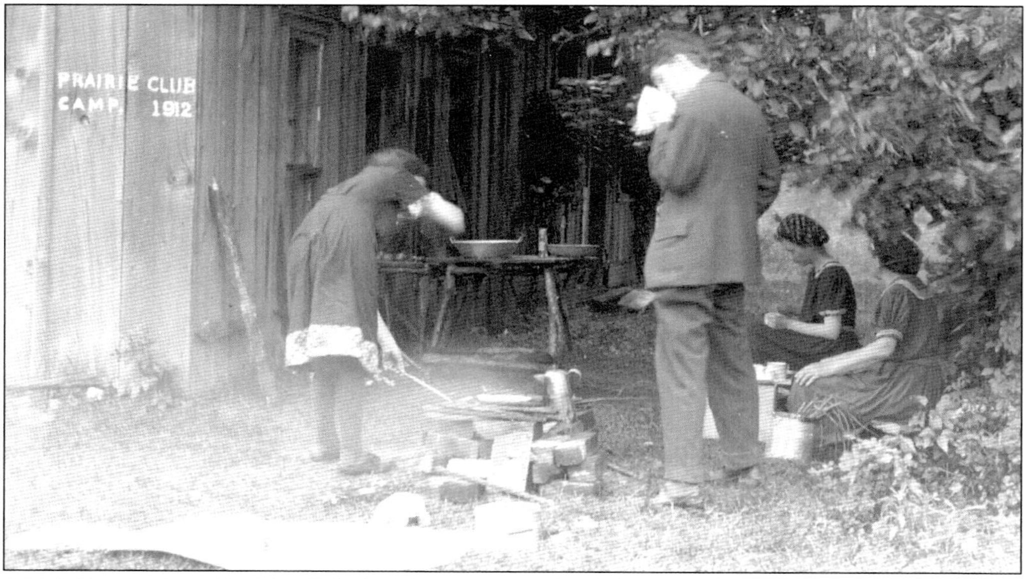

Officially, the first Prairie Club building was the Link House. The old, abandoned building was rented for a modest fee from a local farmer, Mr. Link. "Prairie Club Camp 1912" is clearly painted on the side of the Link Building. (June 23, 1912.)

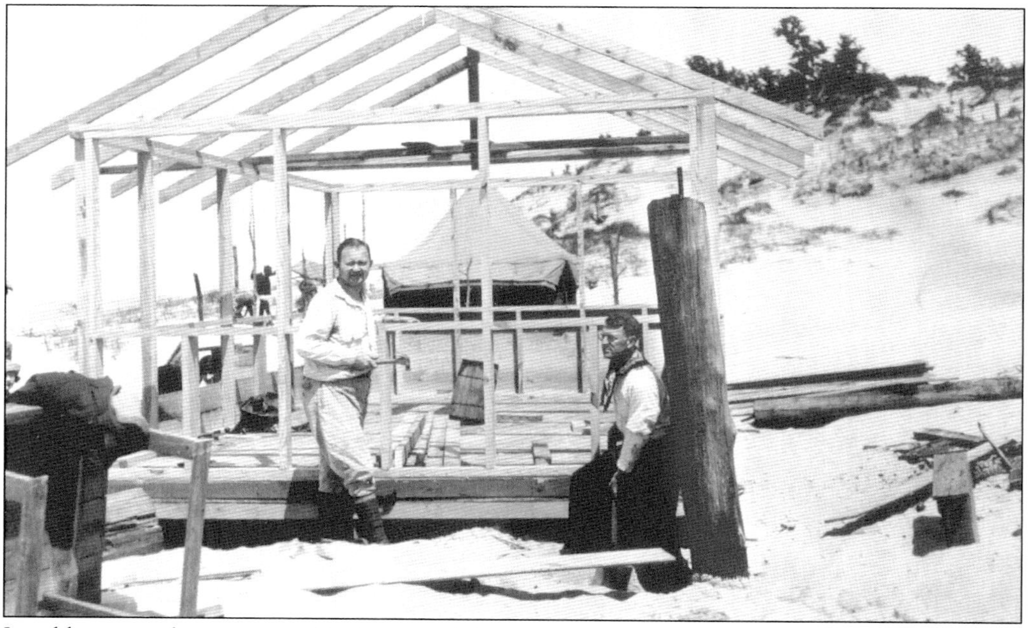

In addition to the communal buildings, club members could rent camping sites. Cabins at the Tremont beach site were very informal affairs, hand built by Prairie Club members. By the late 1920s, there were over 100 cottages spread along 3,000 feet of lakefront.

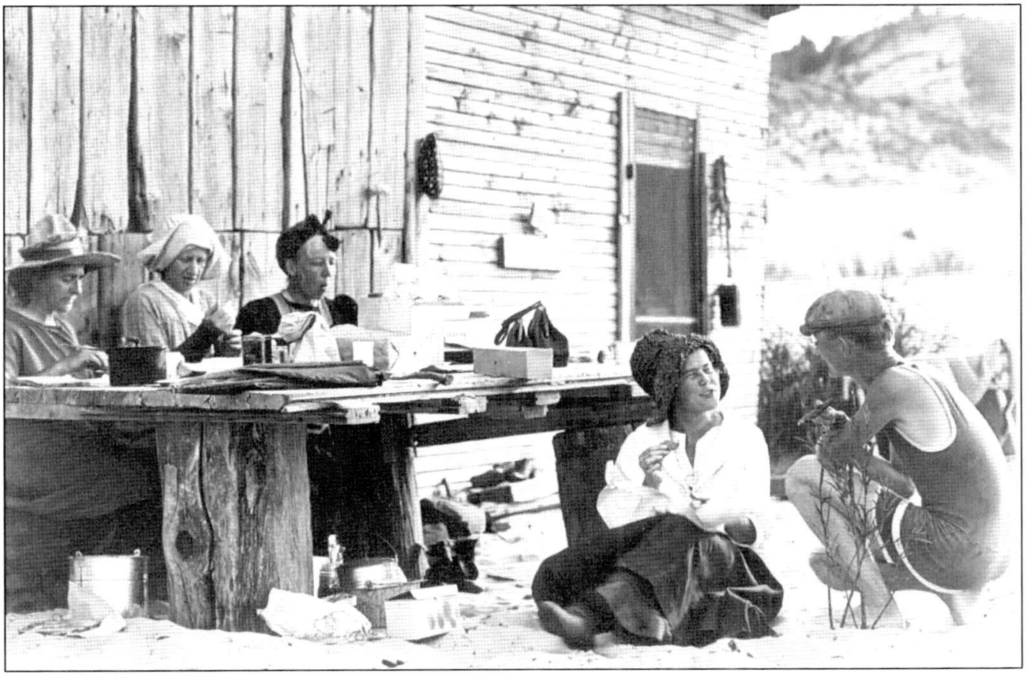

It must have still been warm on this day at the Dunes. A gentleman attired in a bathing suit converses with women at a cabin in Tremont. (September 2, 1912.)

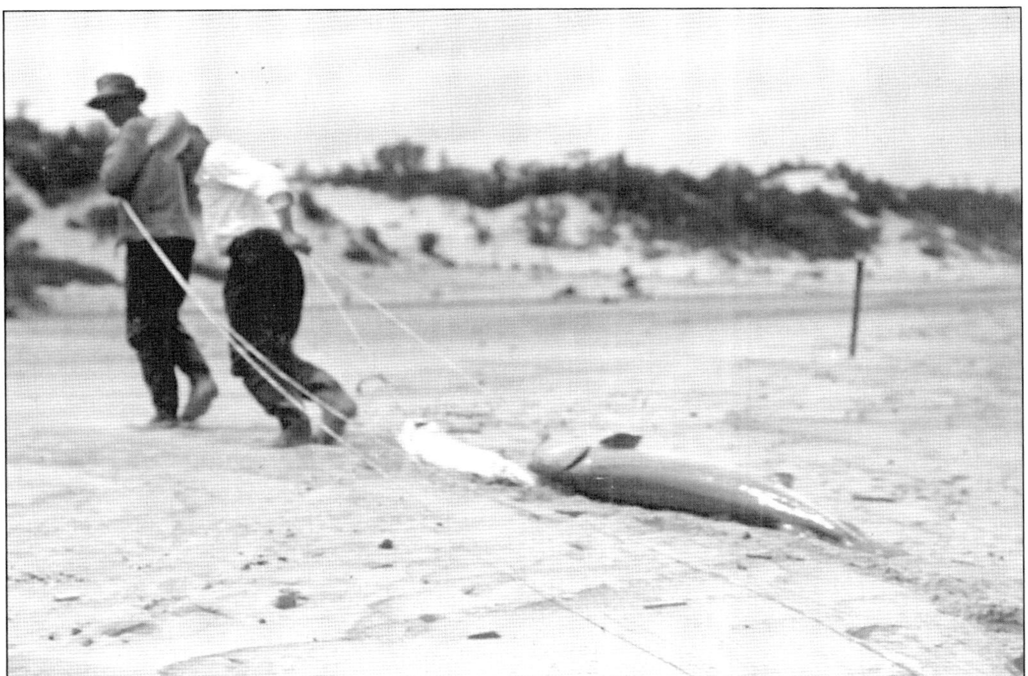

Dinner was often brought in from the lake, as shown by these men hauling the day's catch. (August 4, 1912.)

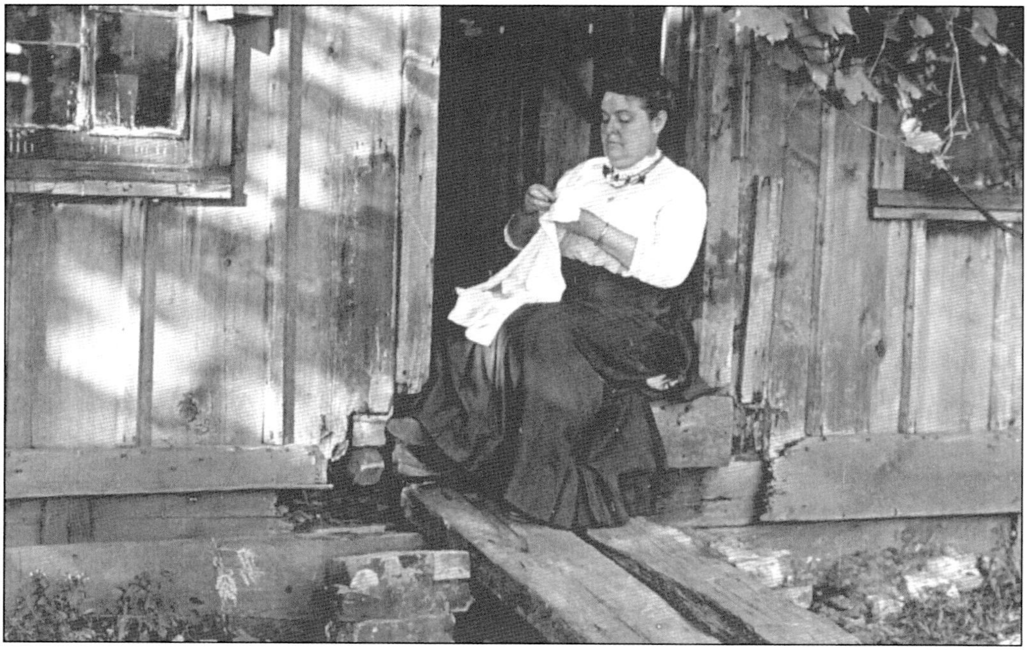

The shade of this cabin door yard provided a relaxing nook for sewing. (August 30, 1913.)

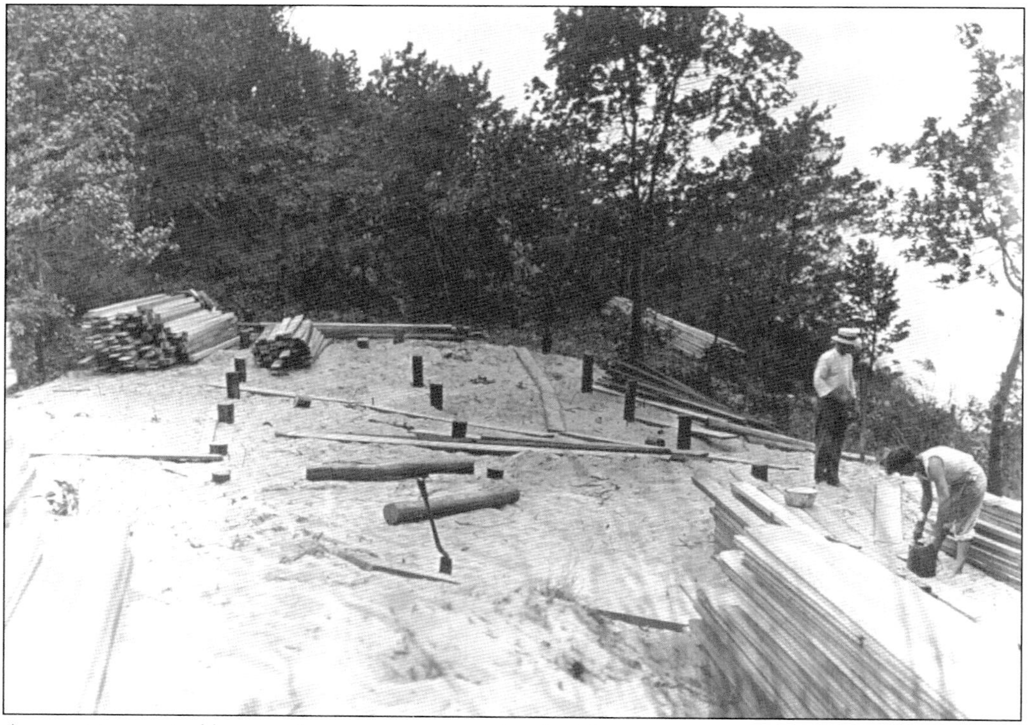

An exciting period began when members voted to build a new structure on the beach. Members helped build the communal Beach House, which was designed by Prairie Club member and architect Walter H. Kattelle. (September 11, 1913.)

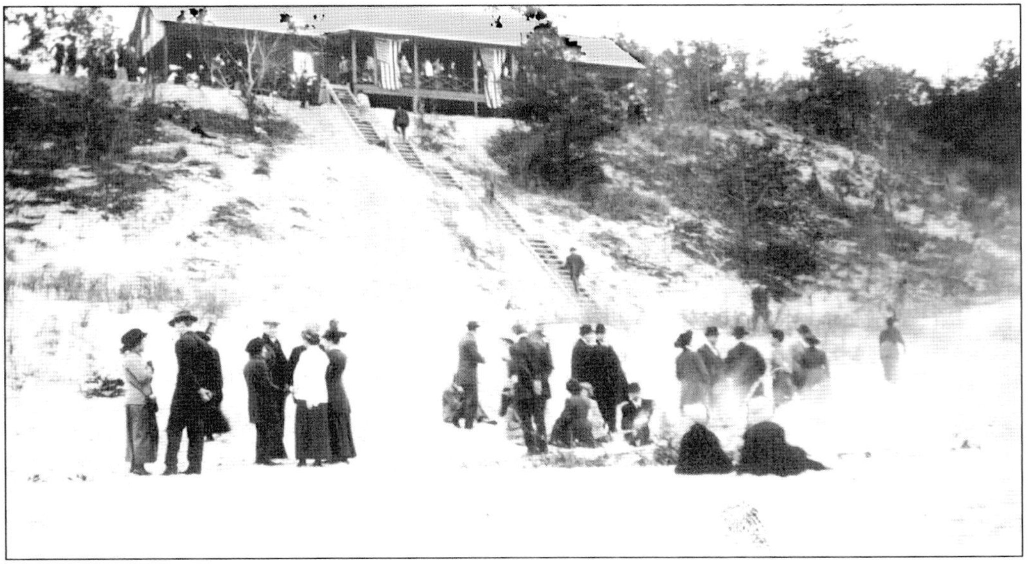

The Prairie Club celebrated the formal opening of their Beach House at Tremont in 1913. Dedication day ceremonies included singing, a masque, and, of course, hiking. (October 21, 1913.)

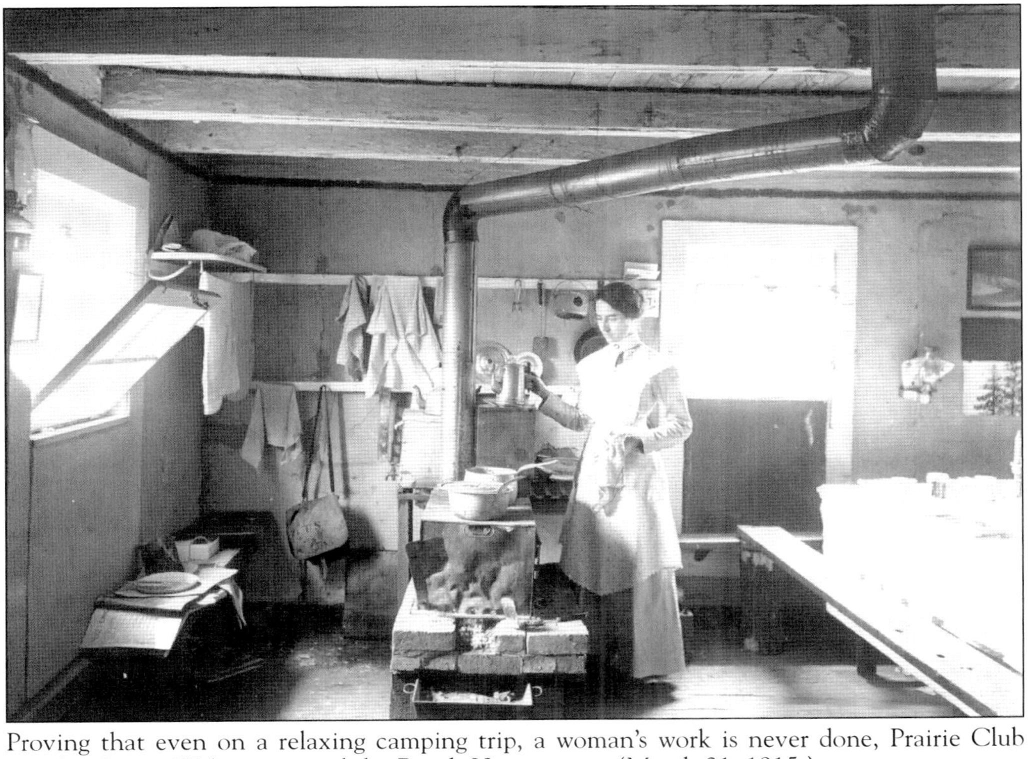

Proving that even on a relaxing camping trip, a woman's work is never done, Prairie Club member Bessie Weber managed the Beach House stove. (March 21, 1915.)

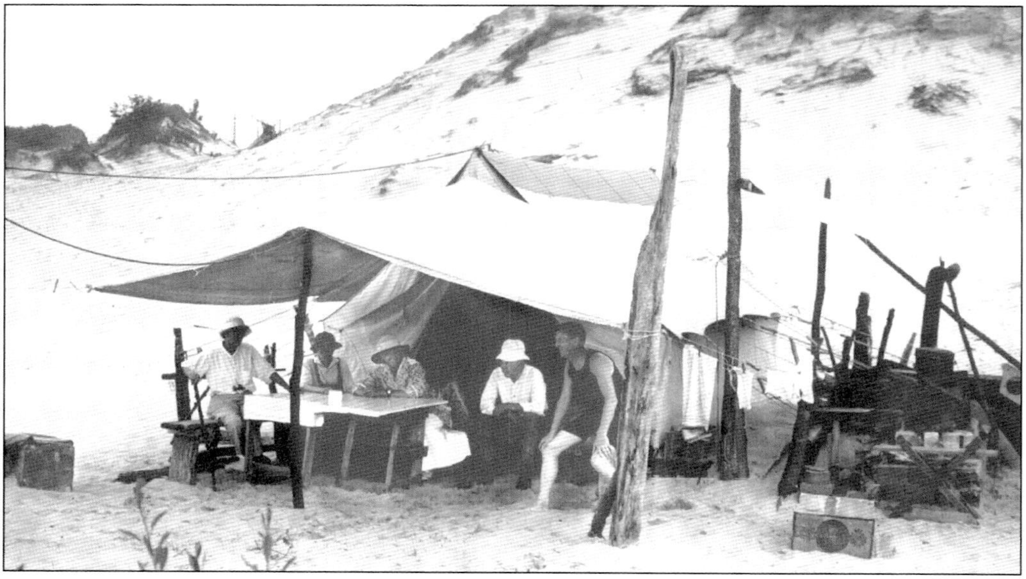

This photo has a handwritten note, "Golden Smith's camp in the Dunes." (August 22, 1915.)

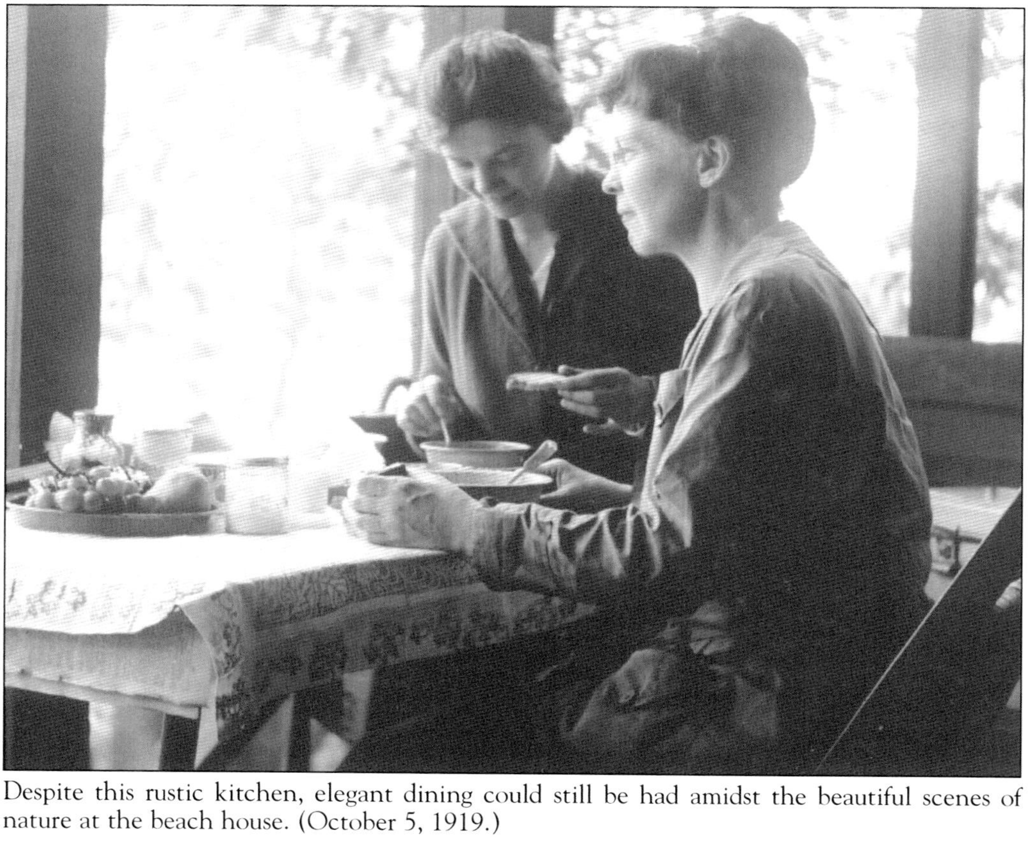

Despite this rustic kitchen, elegant dining could still be had amidst the beautiful scenes of nature at the beach house. (October 5, 1919.)

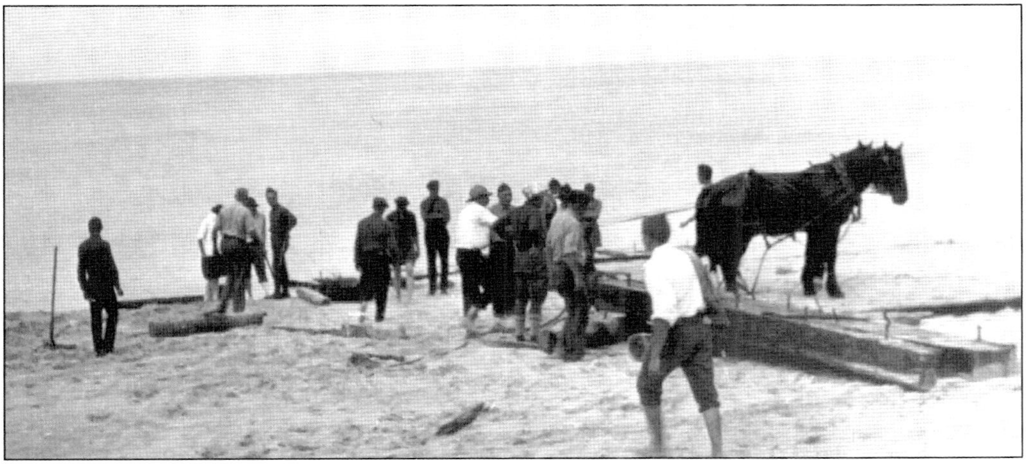

Even in the 1930s, horses were used to pull driftwood out of the lake, and also haul timber for the campsites.

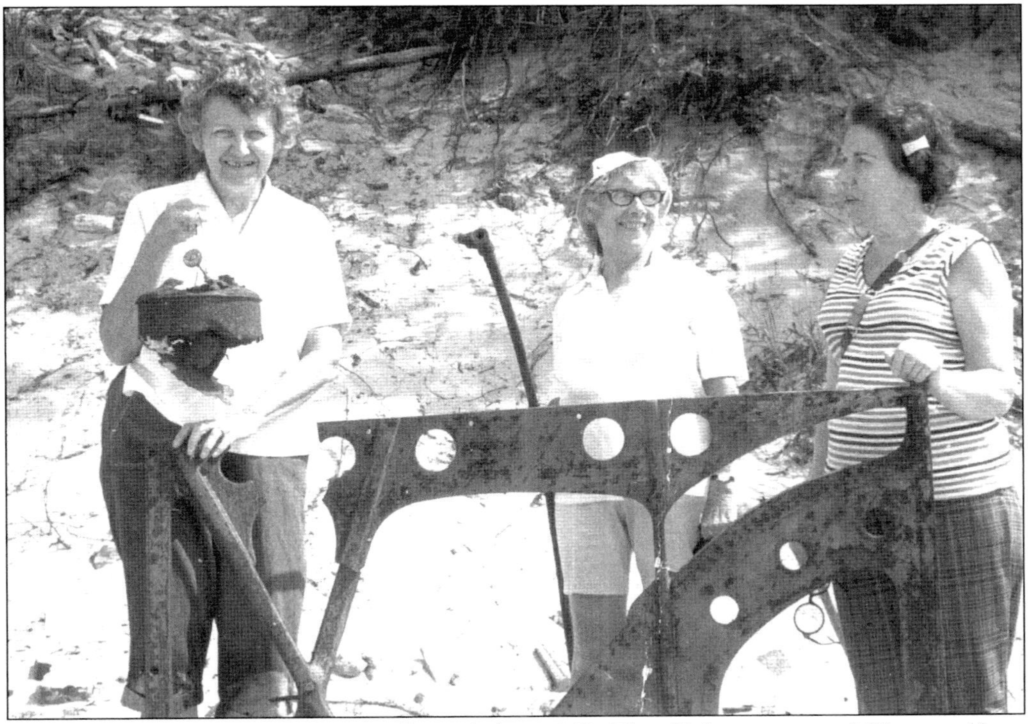

The Tremont Beach House era finally ended in 1967. The Club was granted 35 years (from 1932 to 1967) to enjoy the beach house, although all individual cabins had to be moved or torn down. Here, Jo Wilson, Marge Saindon, and Gertrude Brashevetz show the last remnants of the beach house in 1974.

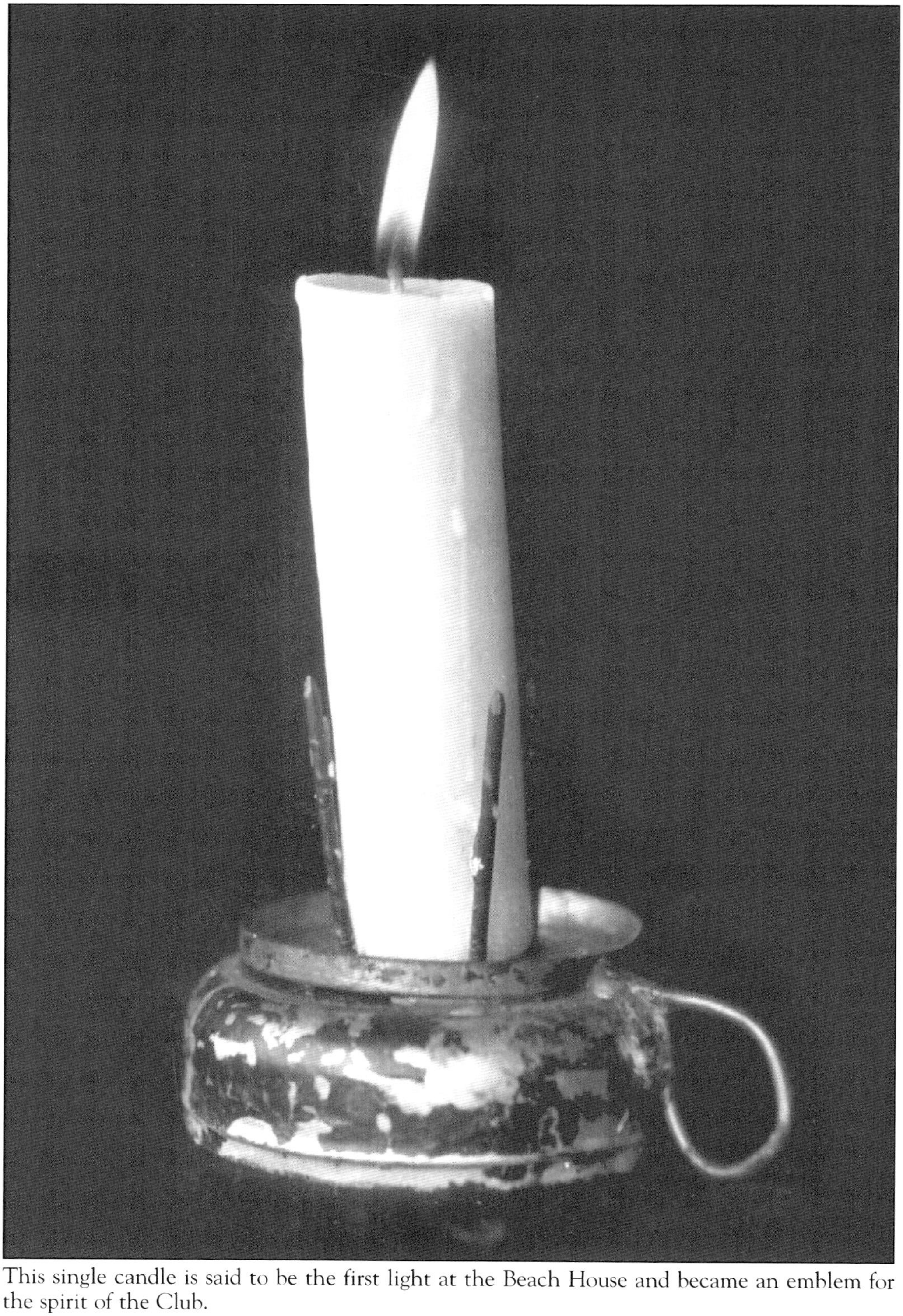

This single candle is said to be the first light at the Beach House and became an emblem for the spirit of the Club.

DEER GROVE CAMP

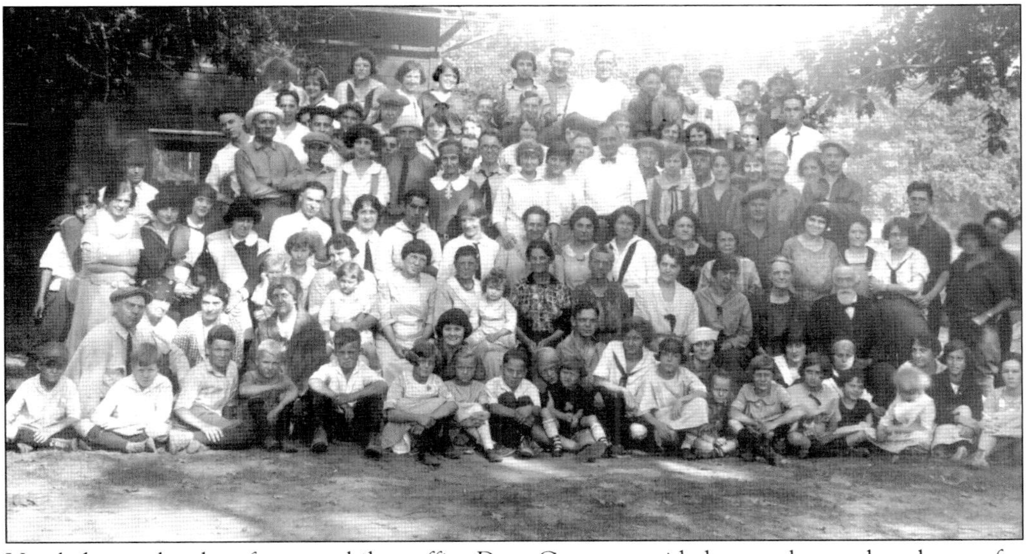

Until the onslaught of automobile traffic, Deer Grove provided a nearby outdoor haven for groups of families in the Prairie Club. (No date.)

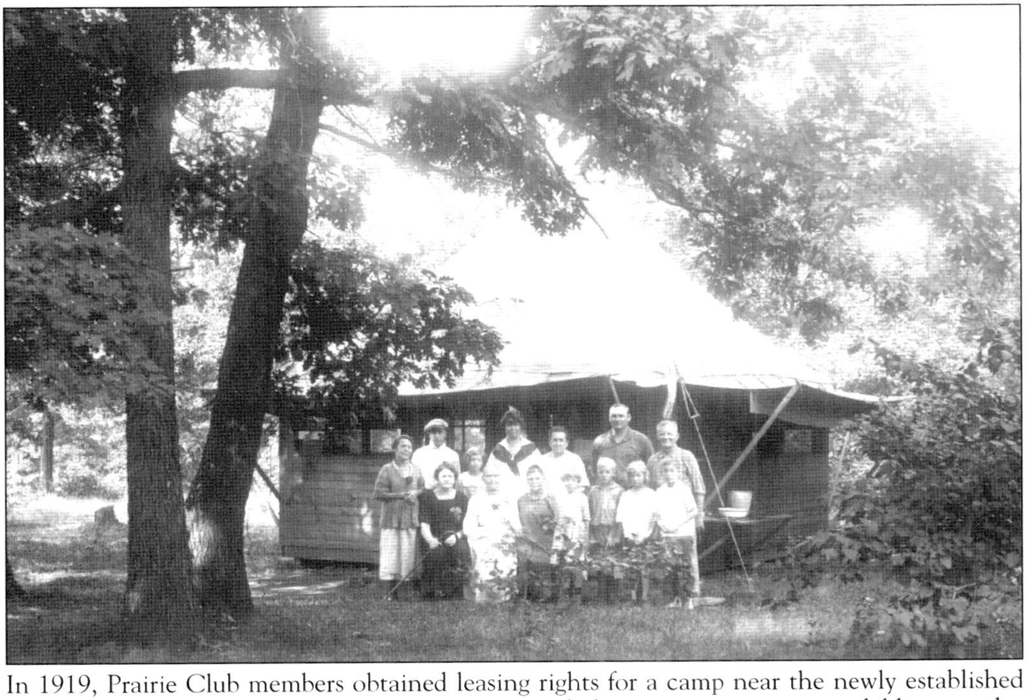

In 1919, Prairie Club members obtained leasing rights for a camp near the newly established Deer Grove forest preserve. Post-war equipment including army tents were available at surplus prices. (c. 1919.)

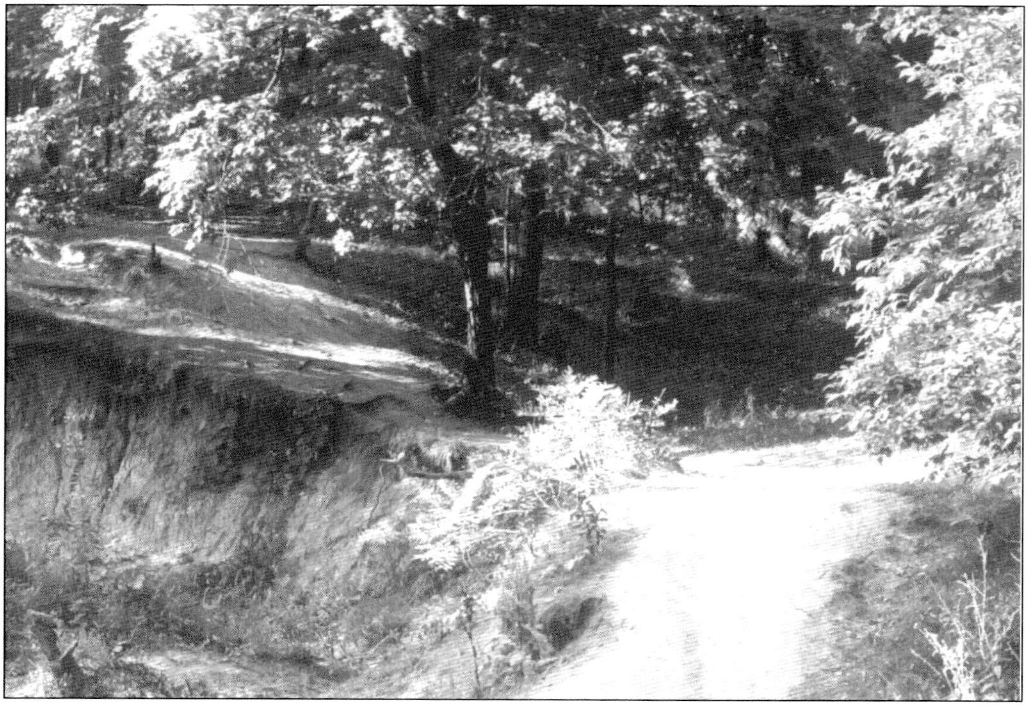

Deer Grove featured sloping hills and forested trails surrounding a spring-fed lake. (No date.)

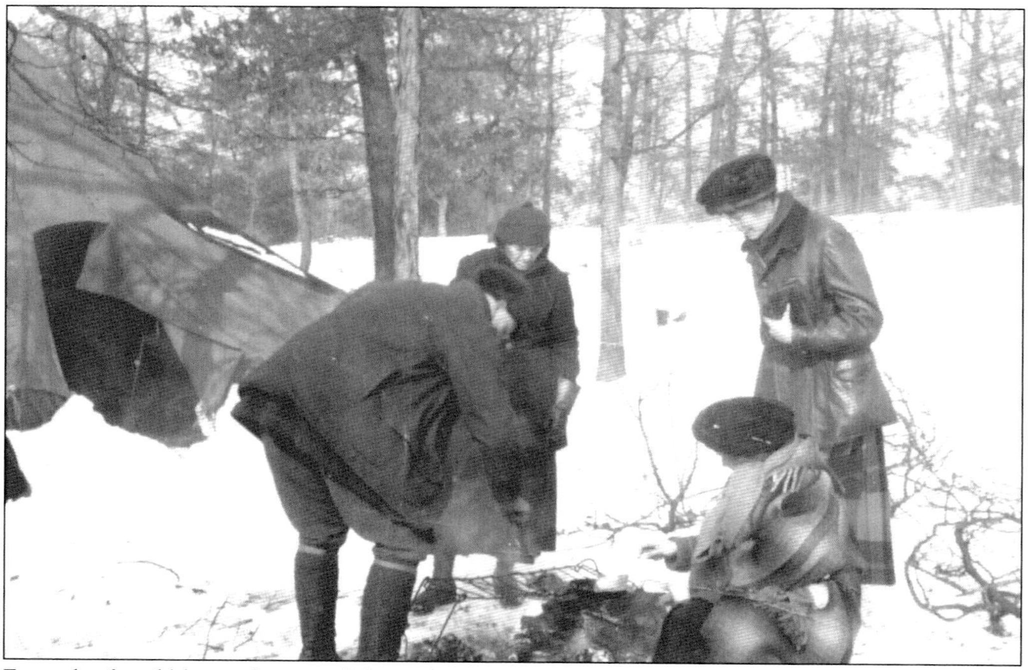

Even the frigid blasts of winter did not deter Club members from enjoying the outdoors at Deer Grove. (No date.)

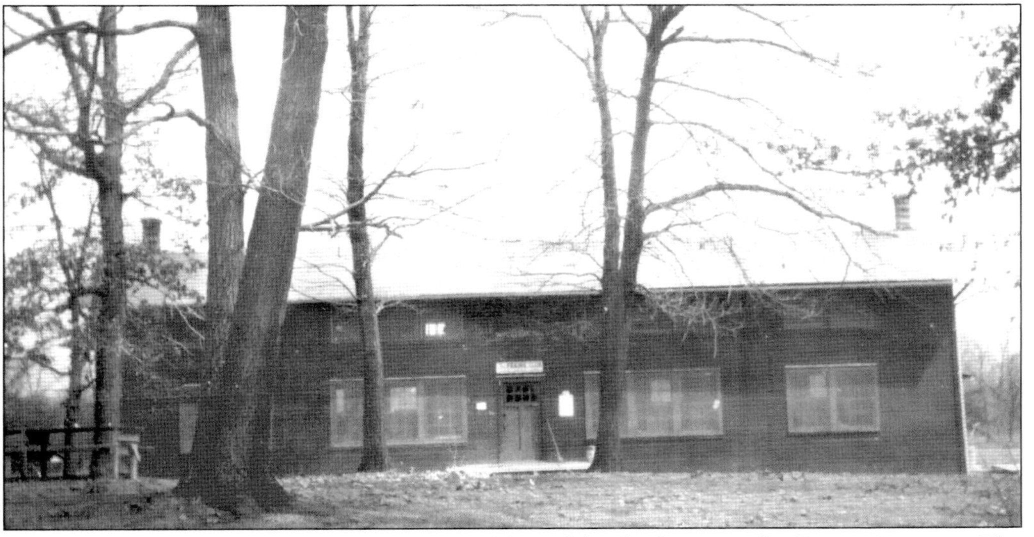

A modest club house was built on a strip of leased land adjoining the Forest Preserve. The Club lost the use of this clubhouse in the 1930s due to the expansion of the Forest Preserve. (April 1, 1923.)

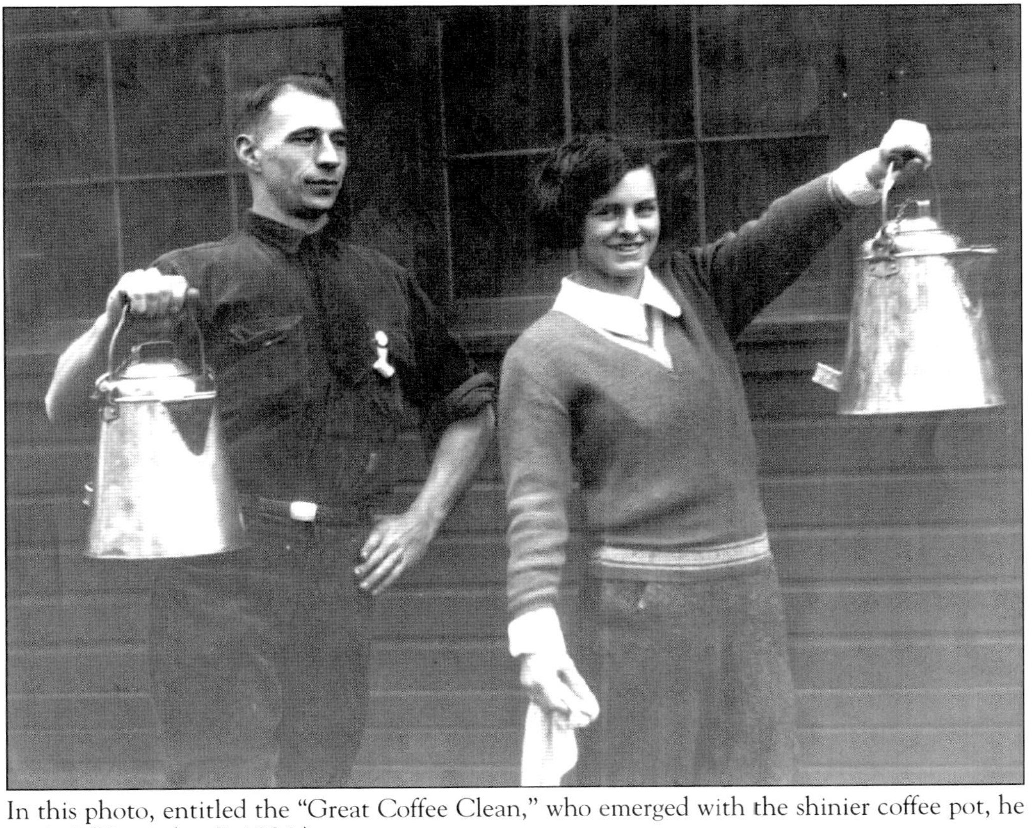

In this photo, entitled the "Great Coffee Clean," who emerged with the shinier coffee pot, he or she? (December 7, 1924.)

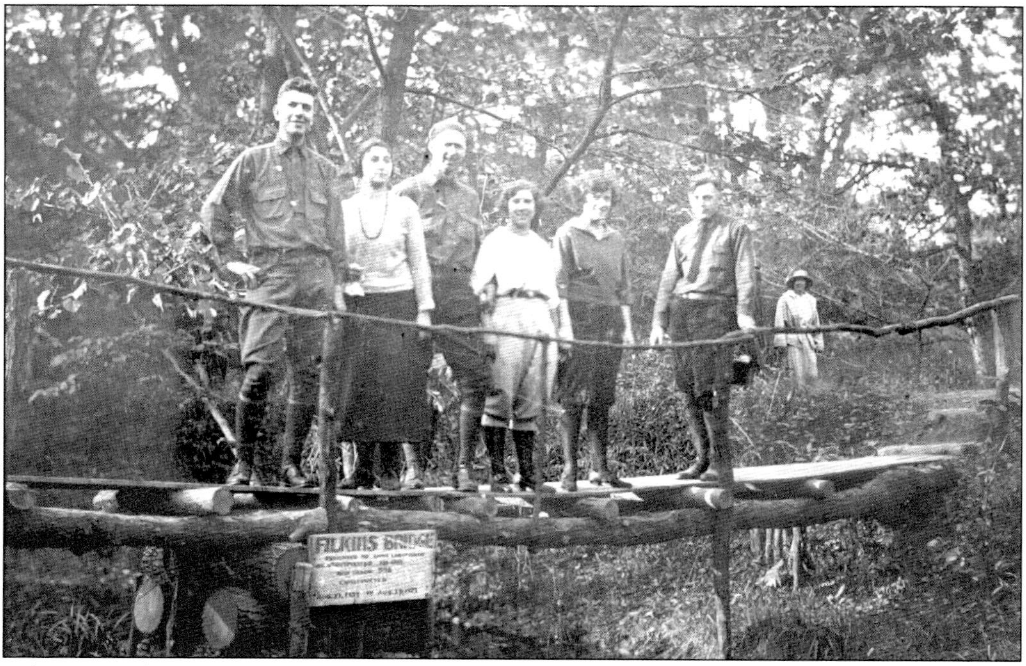

Hikers paused on this rustic bridge to view the sights on a walk around Deer Grove. (No date.)

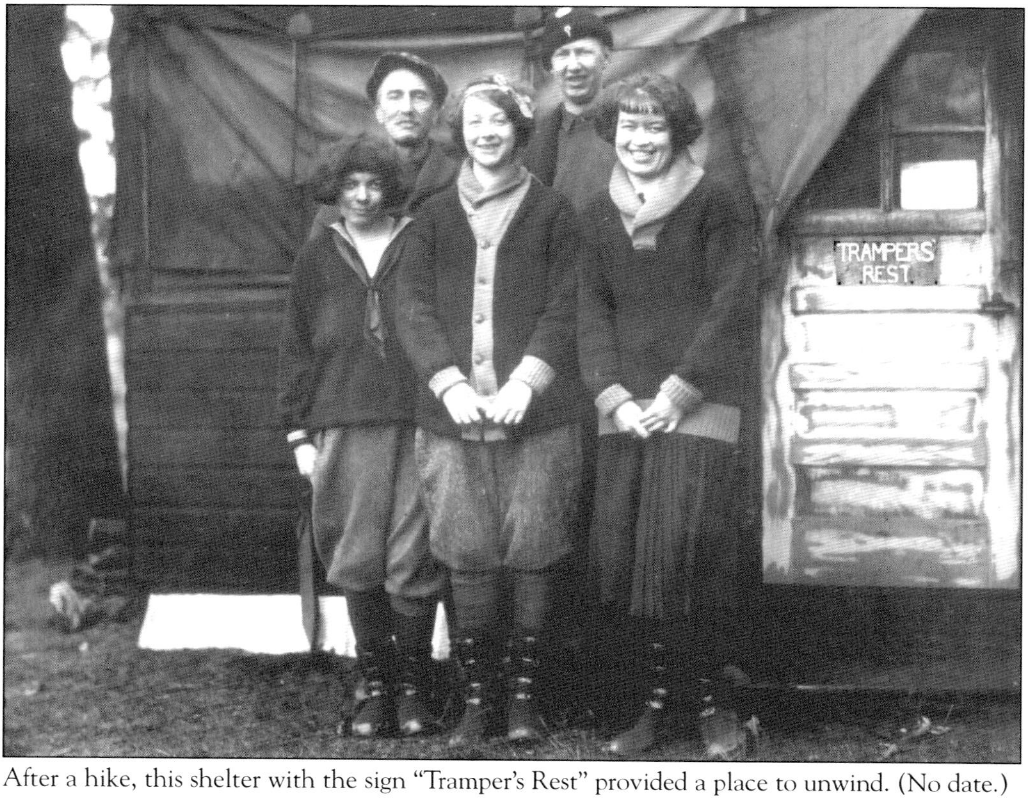

After a hike, this shelter with the sign "Tramper's Rest" provided a place to unwind. (No date.)

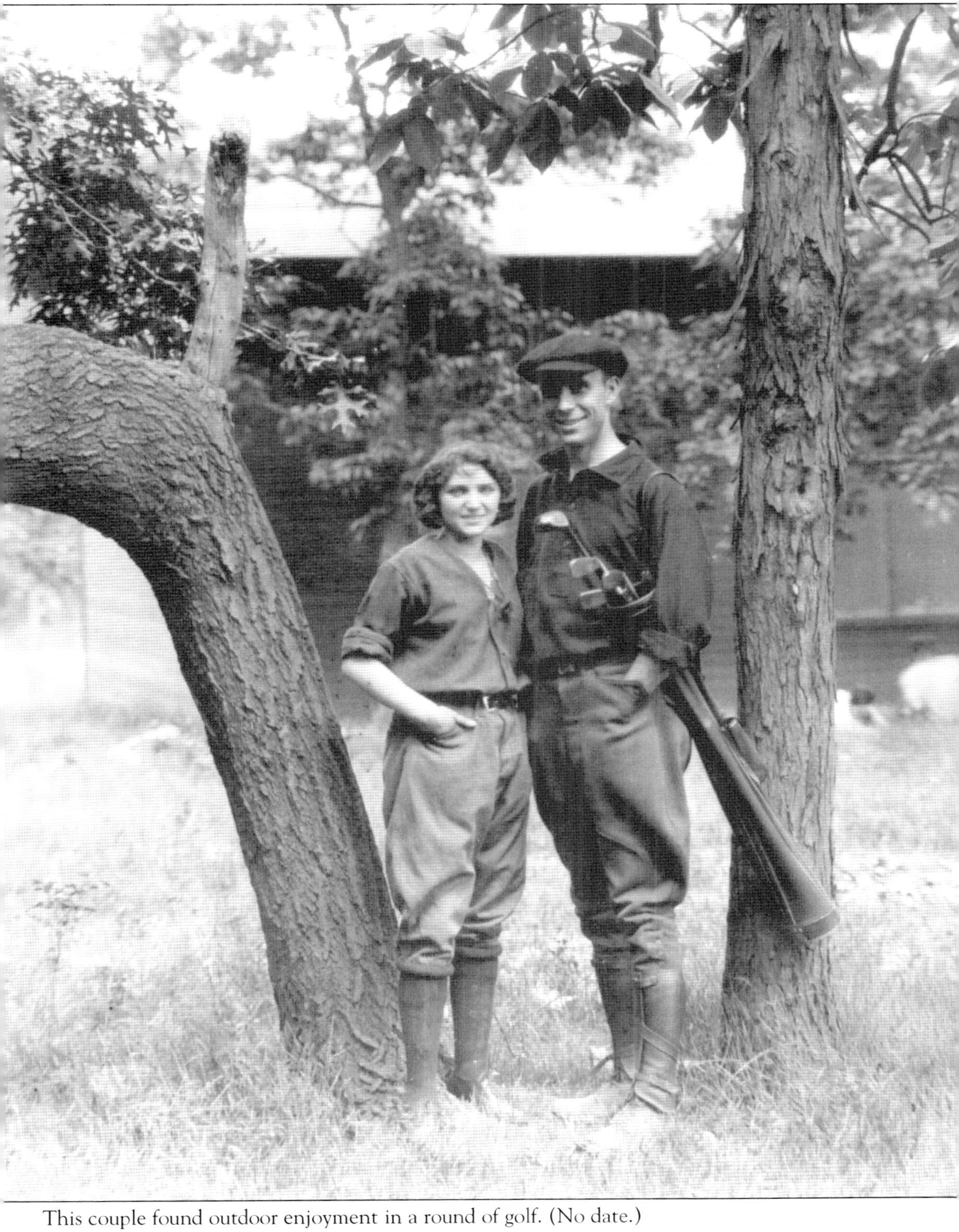

This couple found outdoor enjoyment in a round of golf. (No date.)

PALOS CAMP

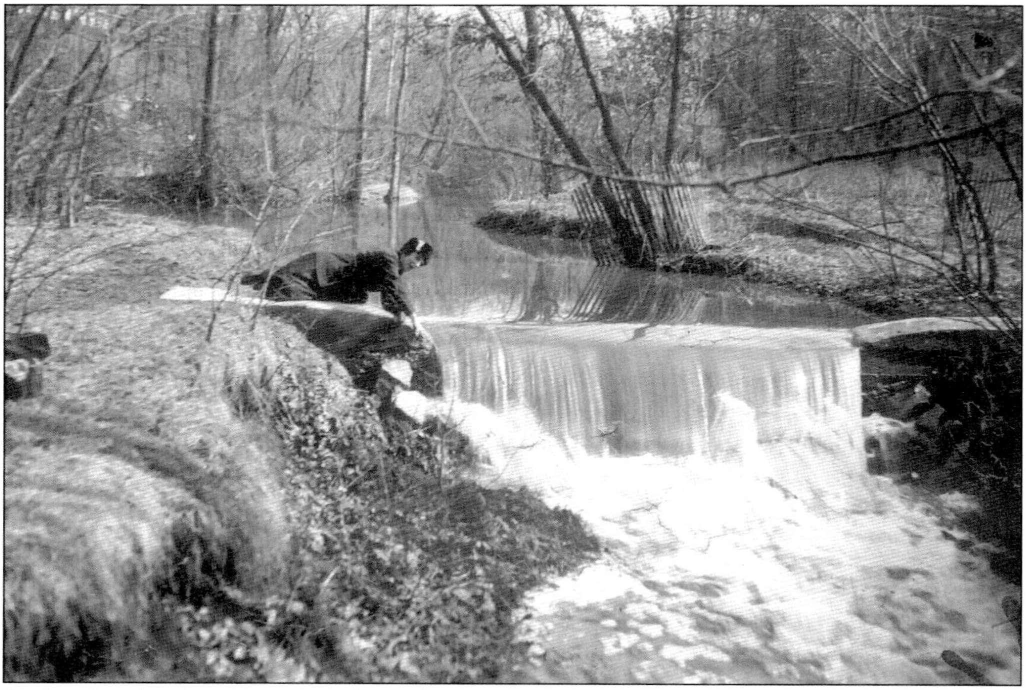

Said to be the first picture at the Palos Camp, this waterfall was one of the many natural features at Palos. The Camp was located near 91st Avenue and 126th Street. (1922.)

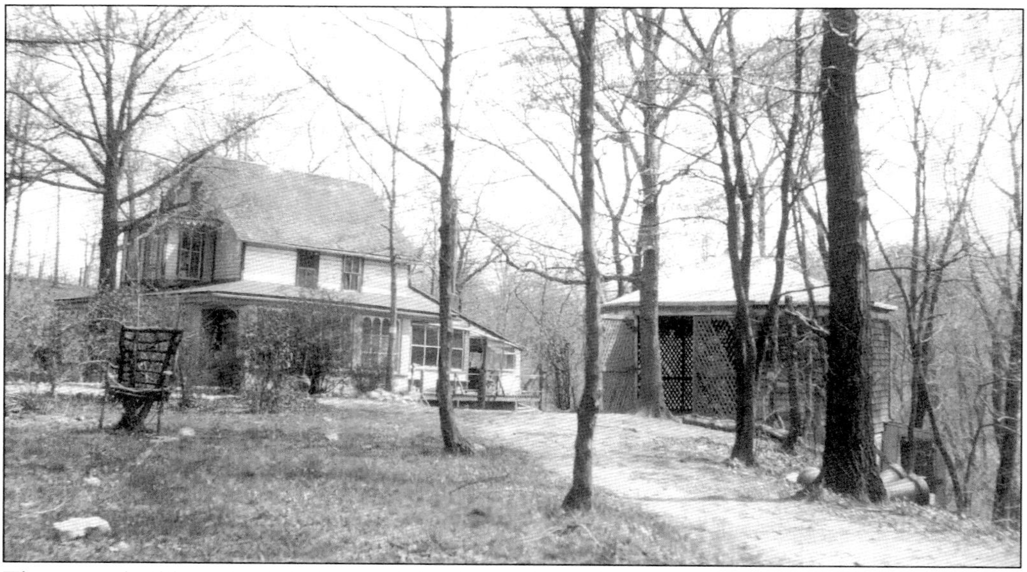

The camp buildings included an old farmhouse from Spencer Farm. Mr. Spencer was said to bottle water from the springs nearby. (1923.)

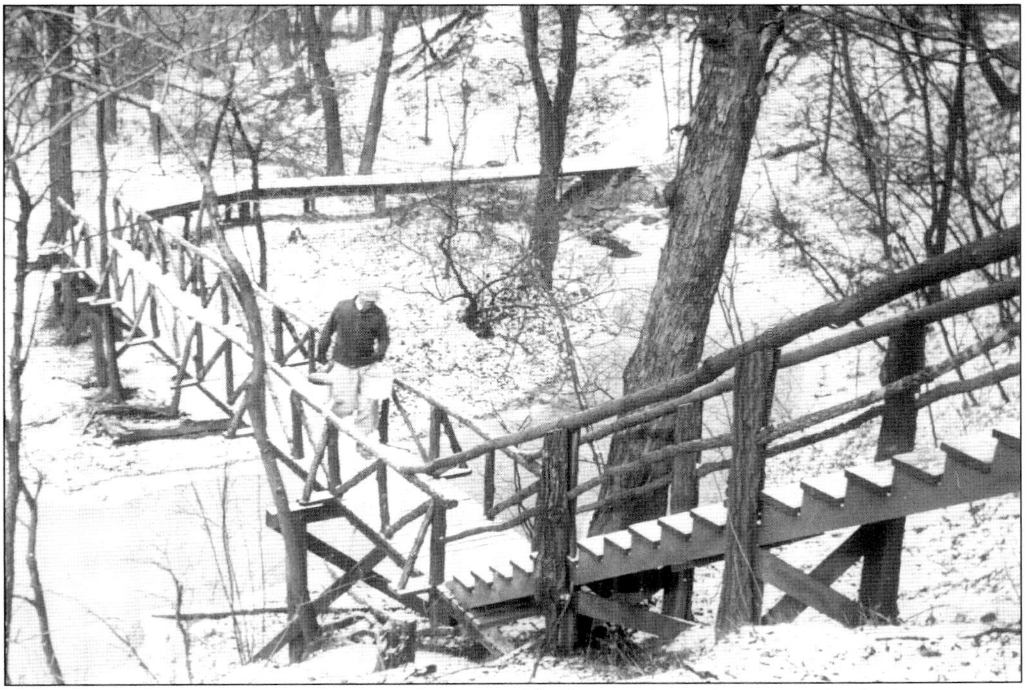

Many a step was needed to scale the ravines and hills near the Palos camp. (1934.)

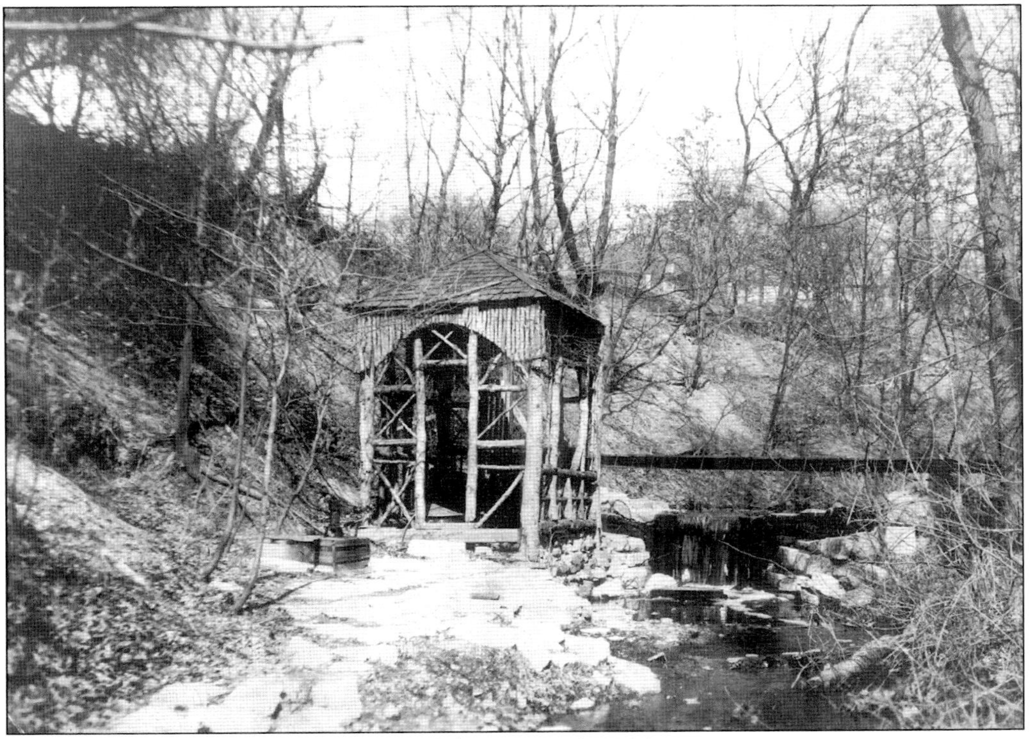

A picturesque gazebo marked the site of the springs. (1923.)

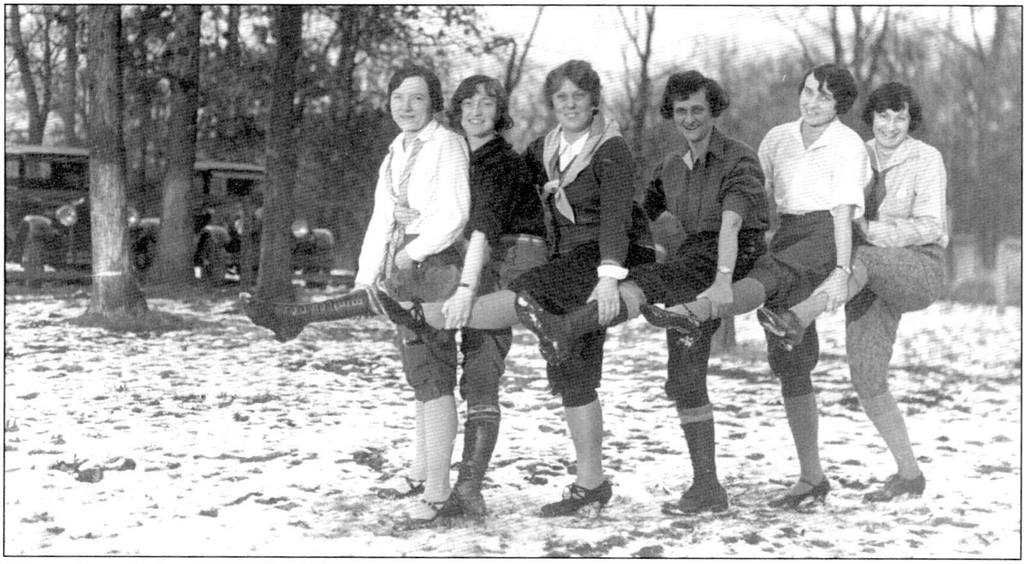

Were these ladies ready for hiking or dancing? (No date.)

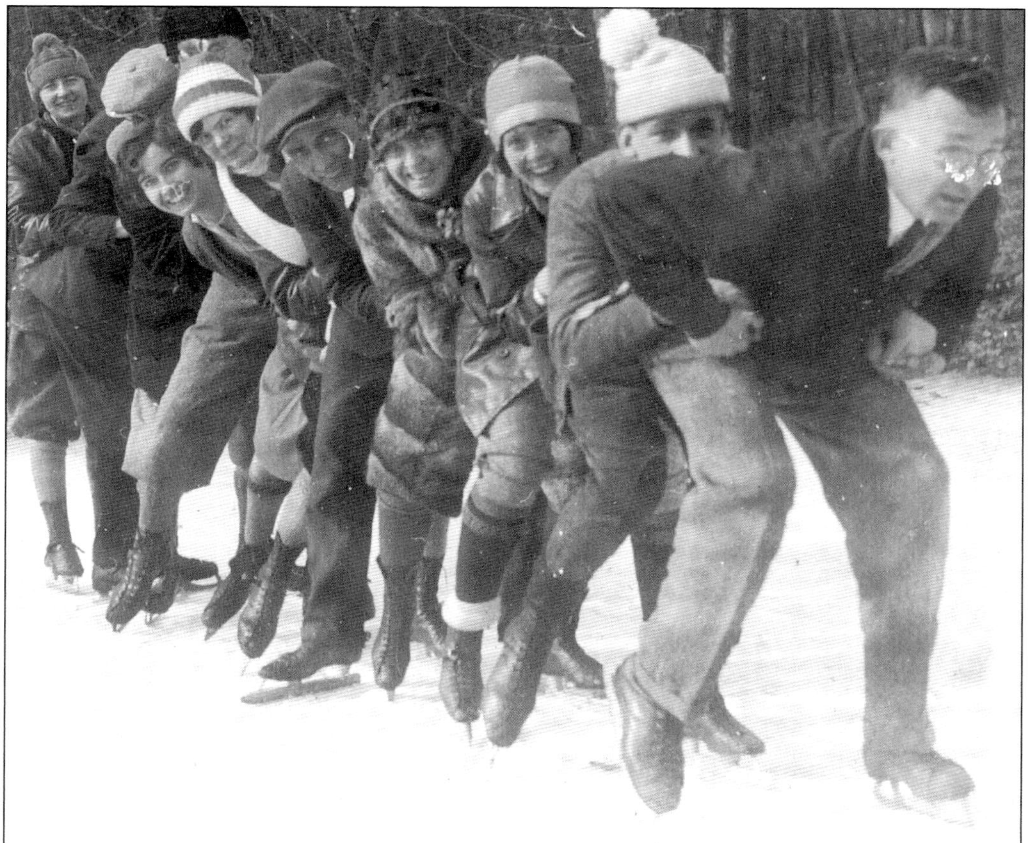

Among the many activities at Palos, skating was popular on the ponds and streams.

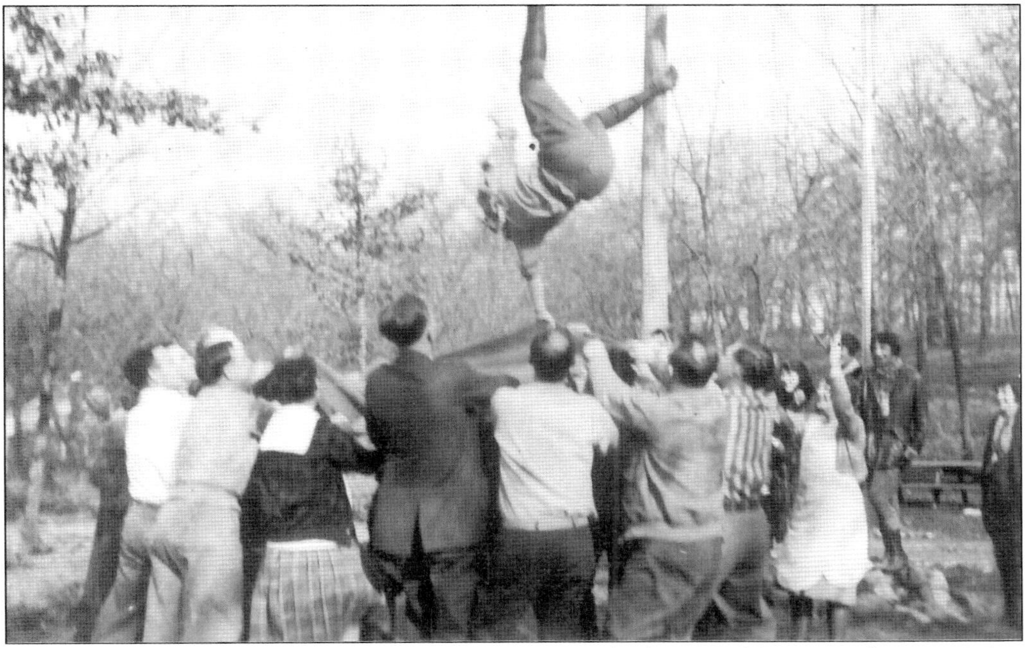

Some Club members were head-over-heels in love with the joy of being outdoors at Palos. (April 1, 1928.)

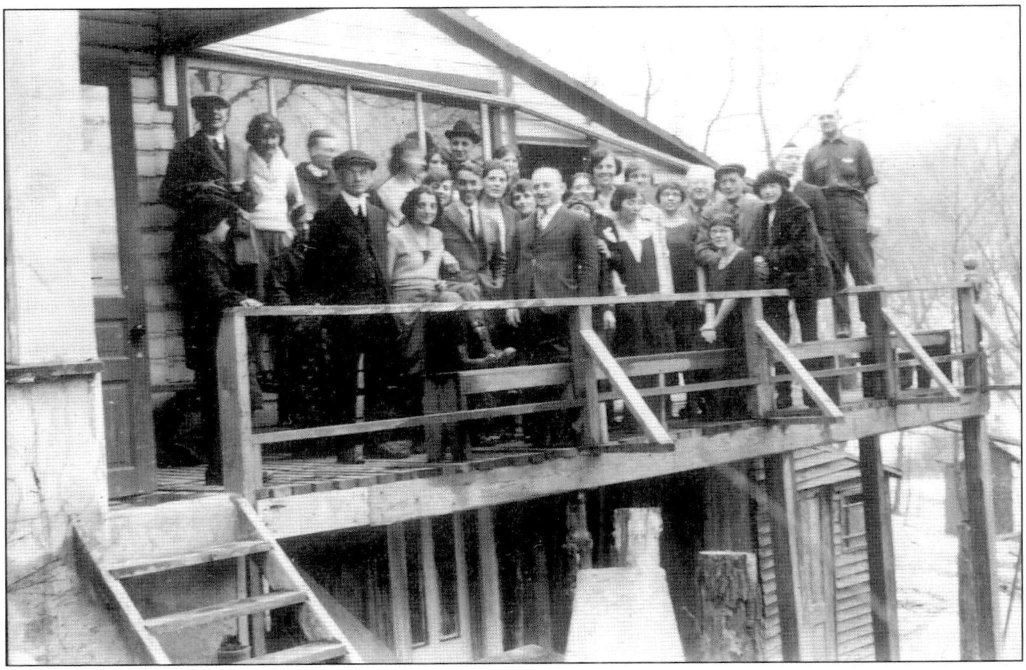

The "Palos Park Glee Club" enjoyed a day at the Palos camp. (February 25, 1923.)

HAZELHURST

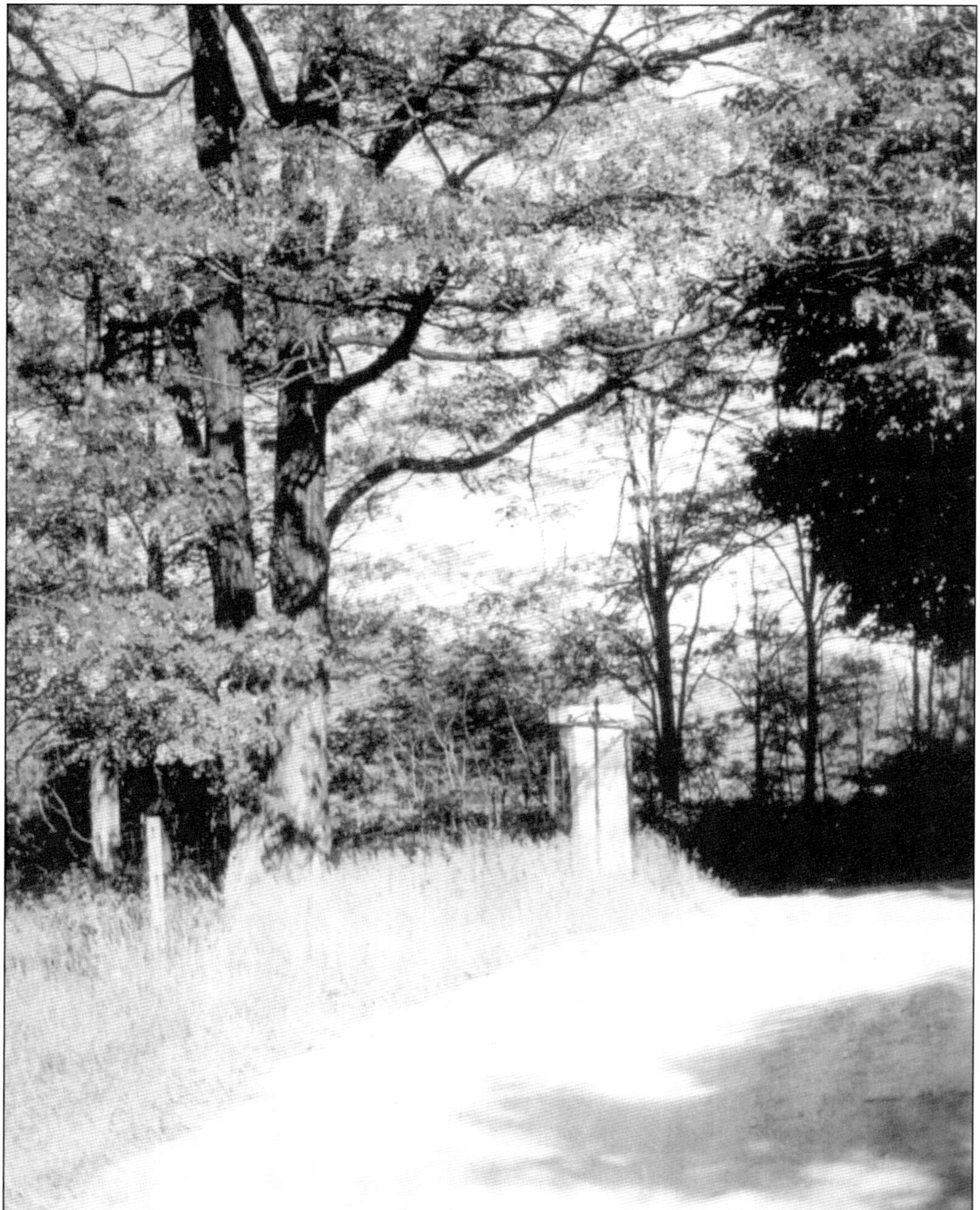

The entrance to Hazelhurst, near Harbert, Michigan, is marked by a small sign. The 60-acre property was purchased from the estate of William R. Hibbs on February 1, 1930, after the Tremont camp had been sold to the Indiana Dunes State Park.

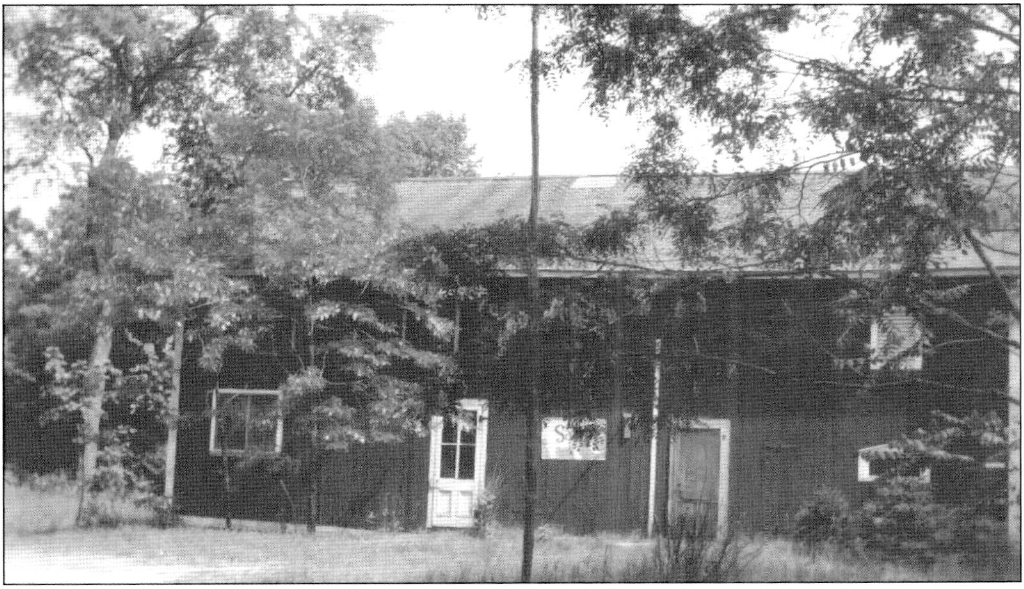

The barn is one of 11 structures that existed when the property was bought. About 20 cottages were brought up from the Tremont camp, and other new ones built. Now, there are 94 siteholders at the Hazelhurst camp. The barn is used today for events and shows.

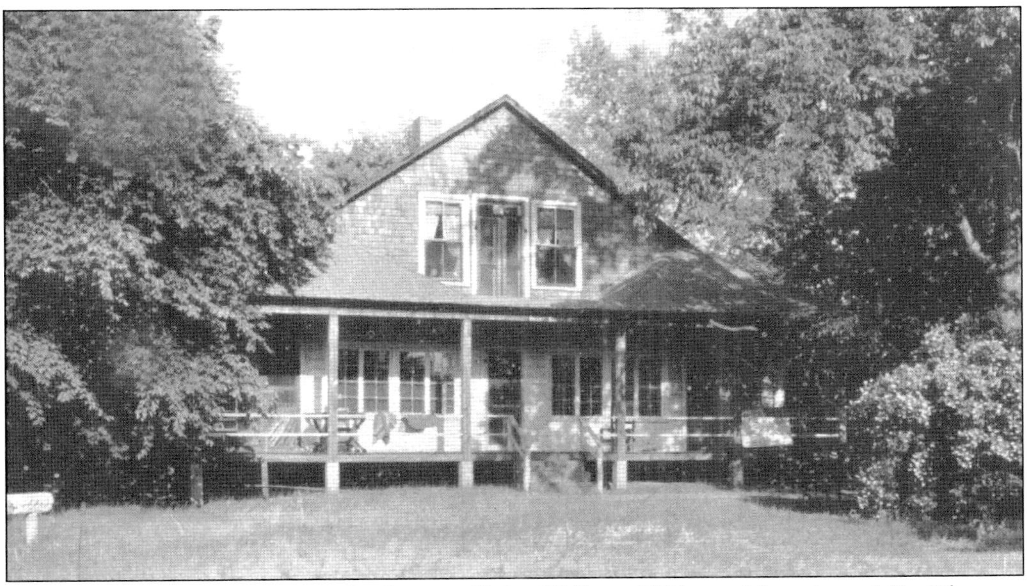

Buena Vista cottage was once the home of Mrs. William Hibbs and her sister, Miss Thomas, from whom the Hazelhurst property was originally purchased. The cottage was recently converted to a duplex which Prairie Club members can rent.

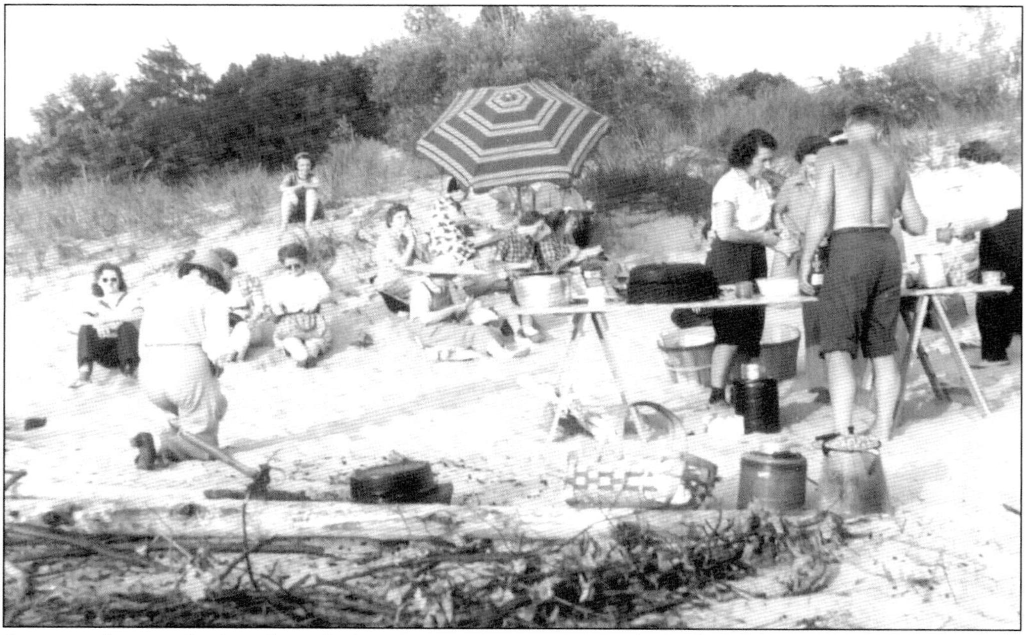

Summer fun on the beach includes picnics, swimming, and good conversation. (No date.)

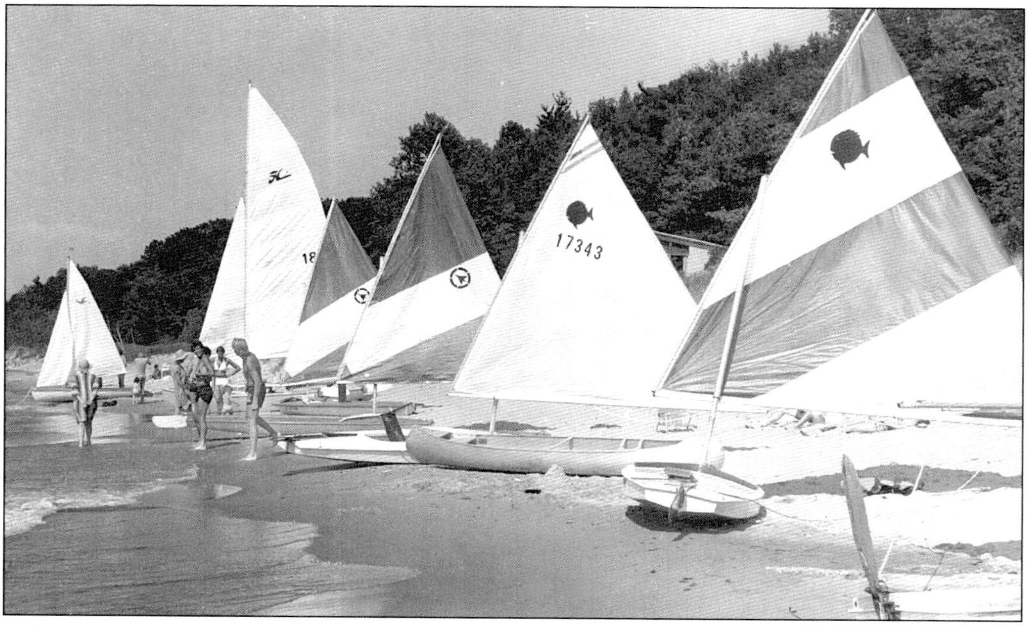

Sail boats, tethered to the edge of the shore, beckon with a promise of high spirited fun. (1978.)

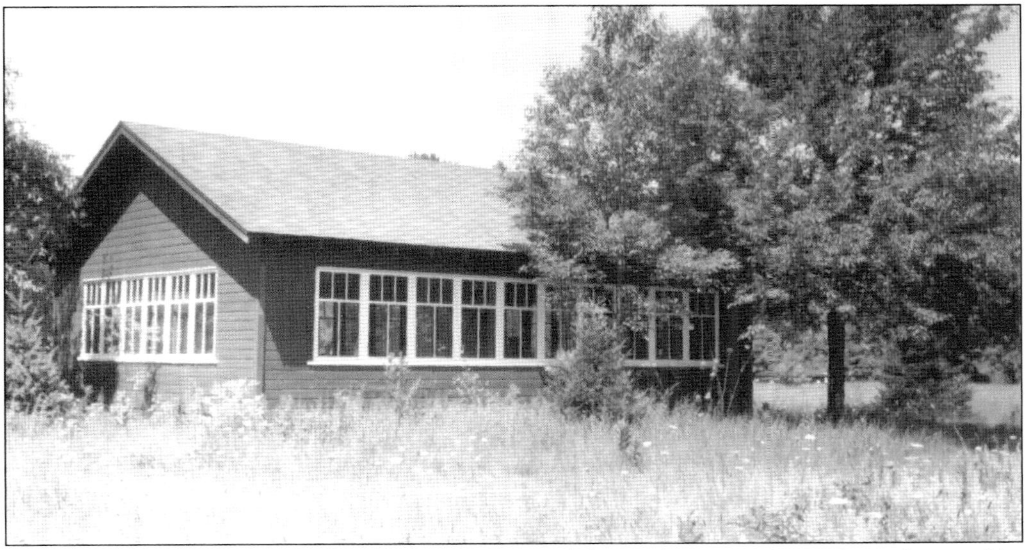

The Junior's clubhouse was built for young Prairie Club members in 1938, and was financed by the youths themselves. The clubhouse is still used by the youth today.

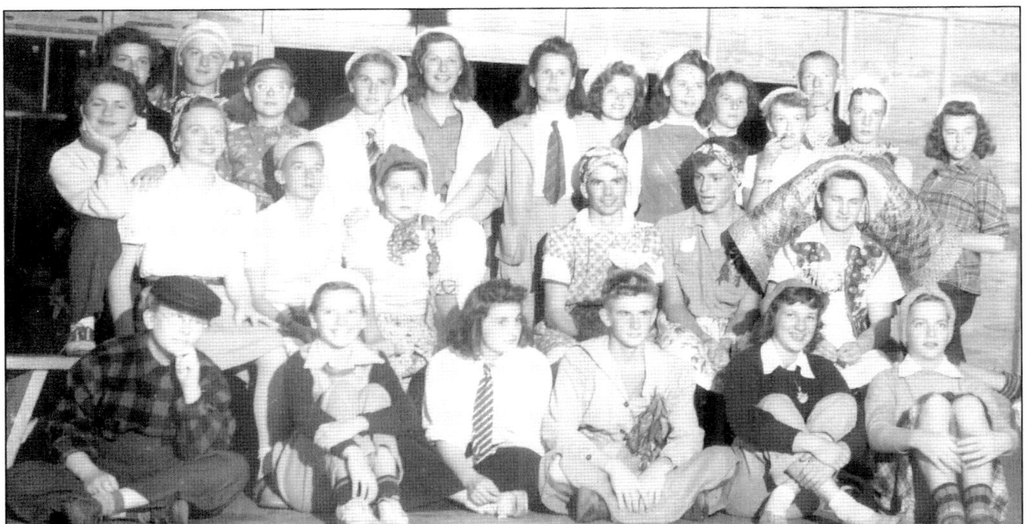

In this 1941 Turnabout Party at the Junior Clubhouse, boys wore girls' attire and vice versa. Pictured, from left to right, are as follows: (first row) Peggy Witte, Dottie Thale, Shirley Hunter (?), Warren North, Ginger Glessner, and Bob Simmons; (second row) Van Simmons, Dick Simmons, Dick James, Shiel Bishop, Bud Eltinge, and unidentified; (third row) unidentified, Eleanor Seels, Mickey Morphett, Dr. Hitz's niece, Betty Thale, Winnie Morphett (?), Carl Von Meding, and Dorothy Spurgin; (fourth row) unidentified, Bob Mitchell, Louise Eltinge, Janet Calkins, Jo Holden (?), and Carl Christ. (Photo courtesy of Dick Spurgin.)

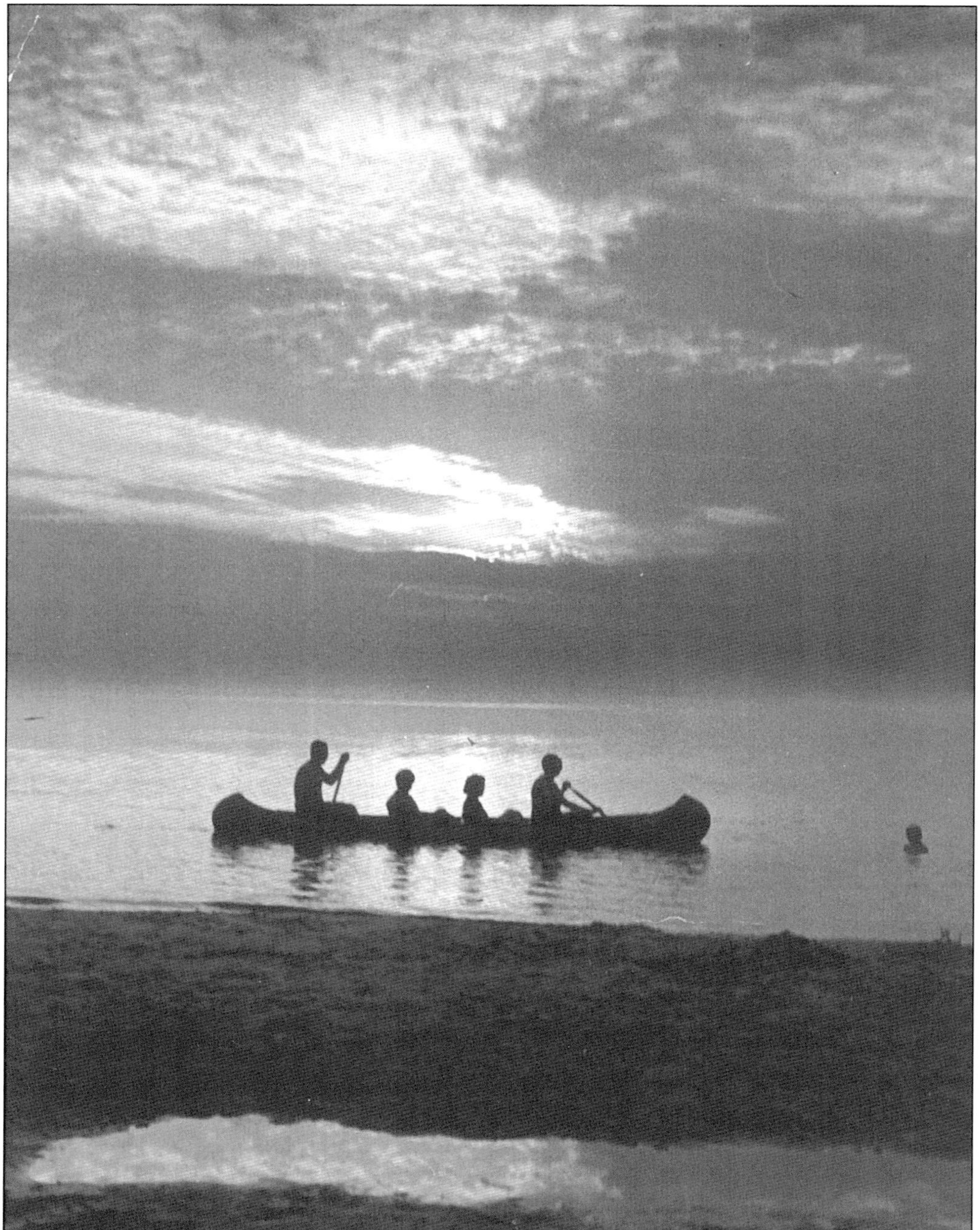

A sunset paddle on Lake Michigan brought the day to a peaceful close. (July 1943.)

Spring Grove

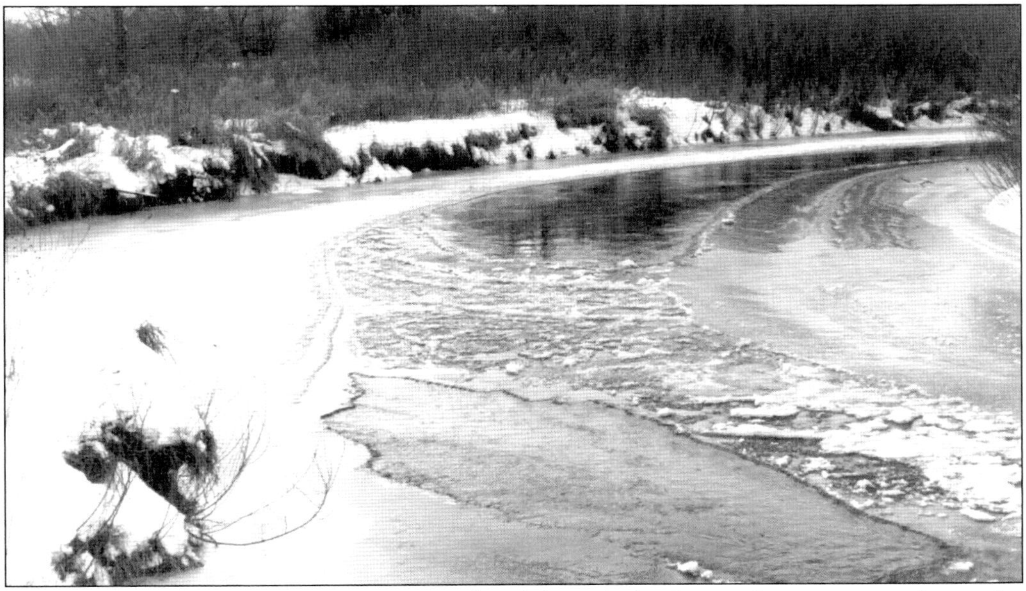

The Nippersink Creek winds its way around and through the Spring Grove camp and provides recreation as well as scenic views.

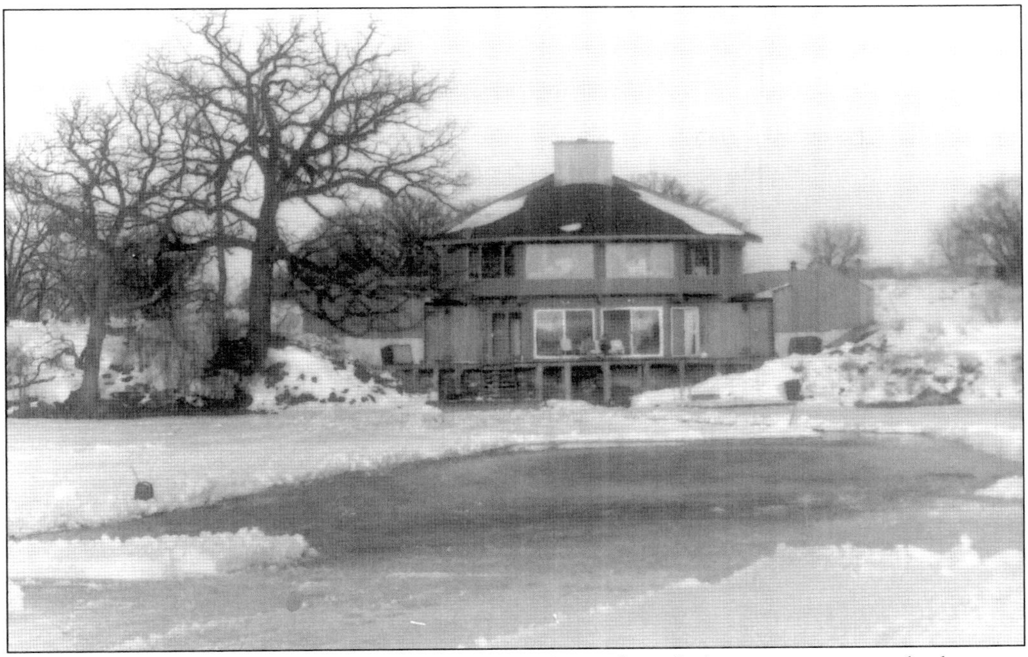

The lodge at Spring Grove was built in 1977, and includes a scenic overlook on a spring-fed pond.

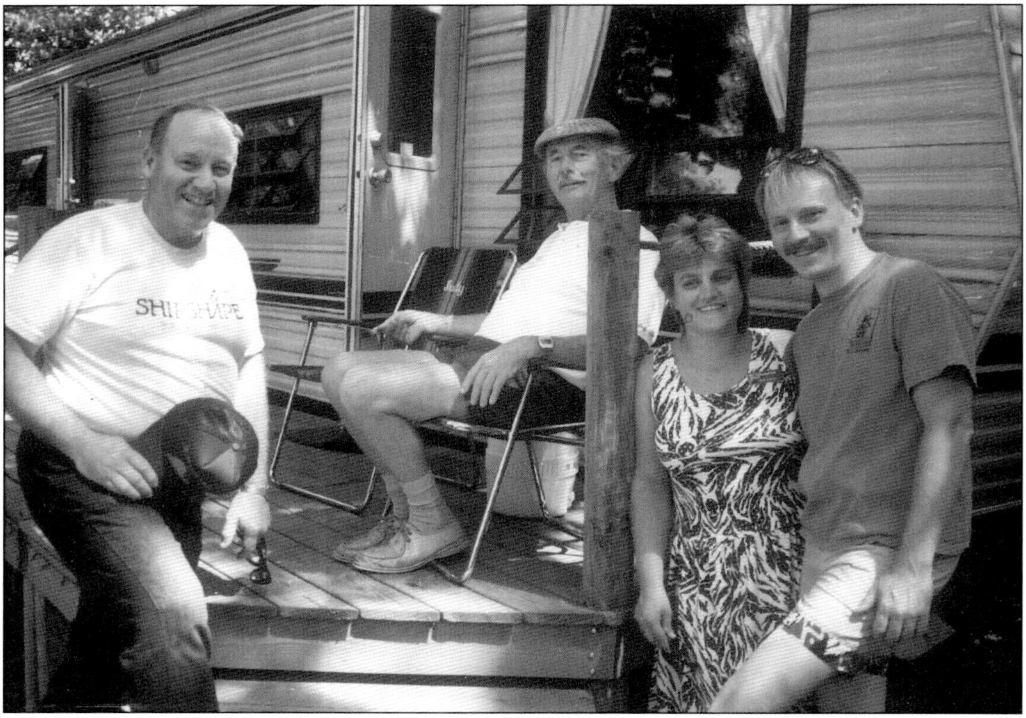

Camping sites are available at Spring Grove. Here, from left to right, are as follows: Chair Harold Kiehm and members Al Kleffner, Lorry, and Milt Davies pause outside Harold's trailer. (1988.)

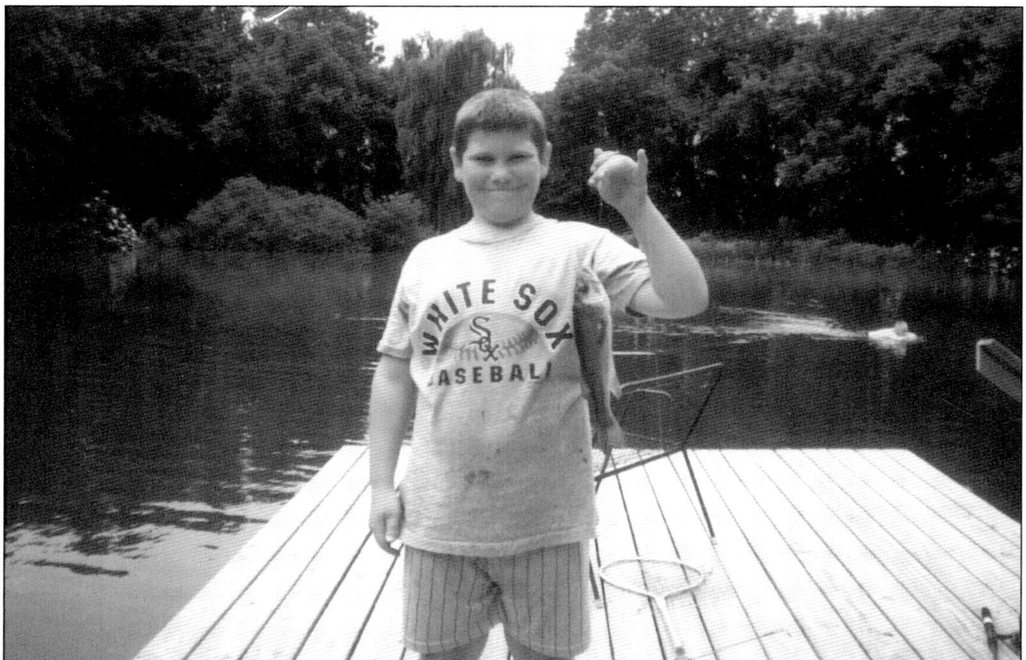

Fishing and swimming are great in the summer. Here, a young fisherman displays his catch.

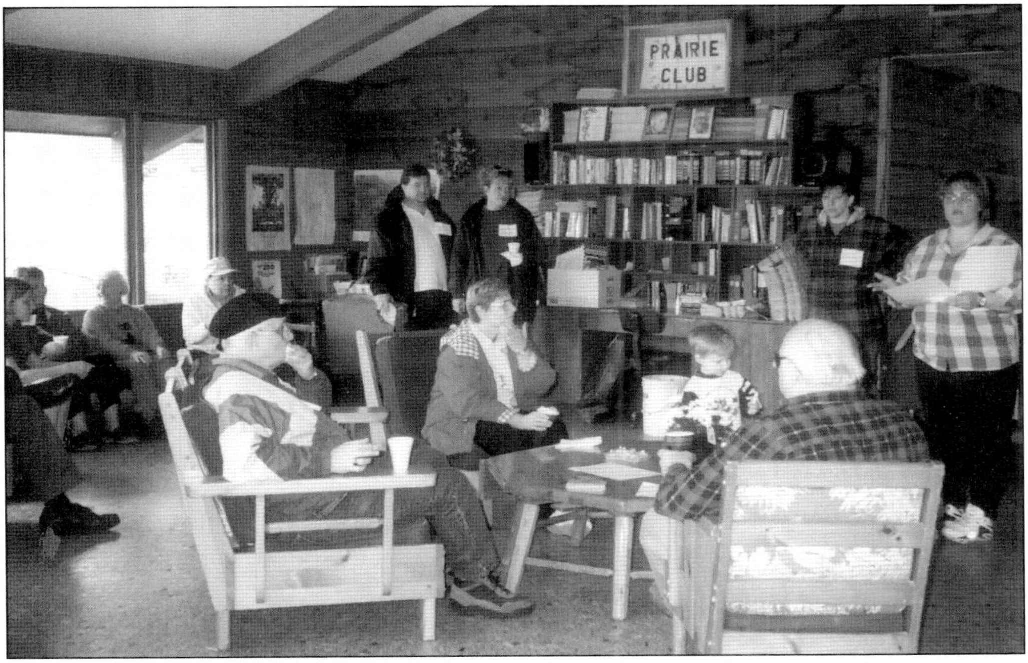

Inside the lodge, Prairie Club Executive Director Lorry Davies outlines the day's events.

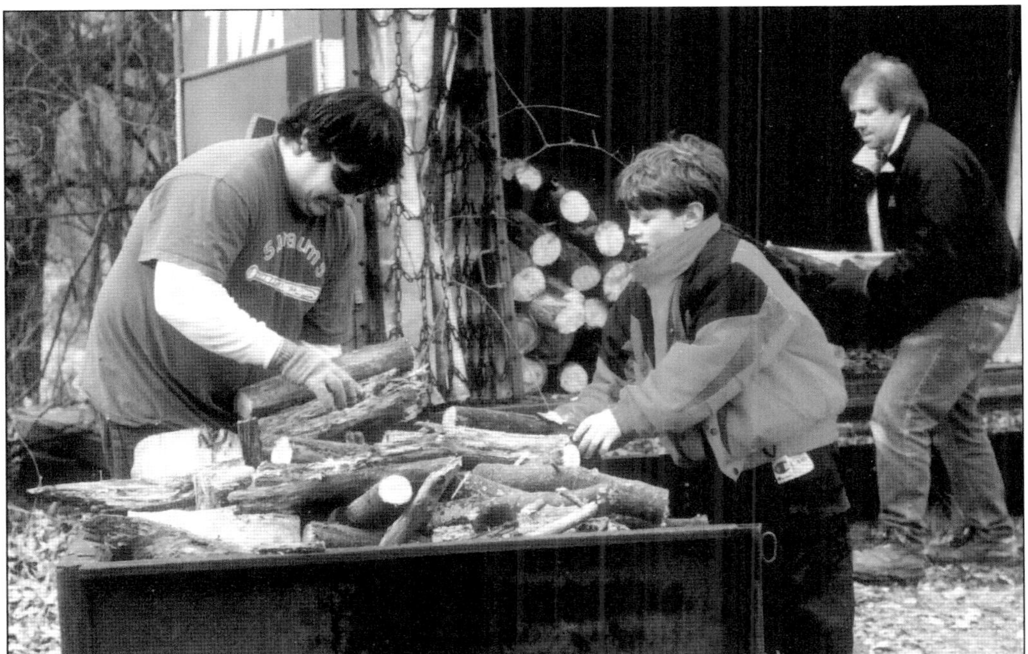

Work days are scheduled for each of the camps, and at Spring Grove, this includes gathering fire wood. Shown here, from left to right, are Pete Penkala, unidentified, and Vince Dembinski.

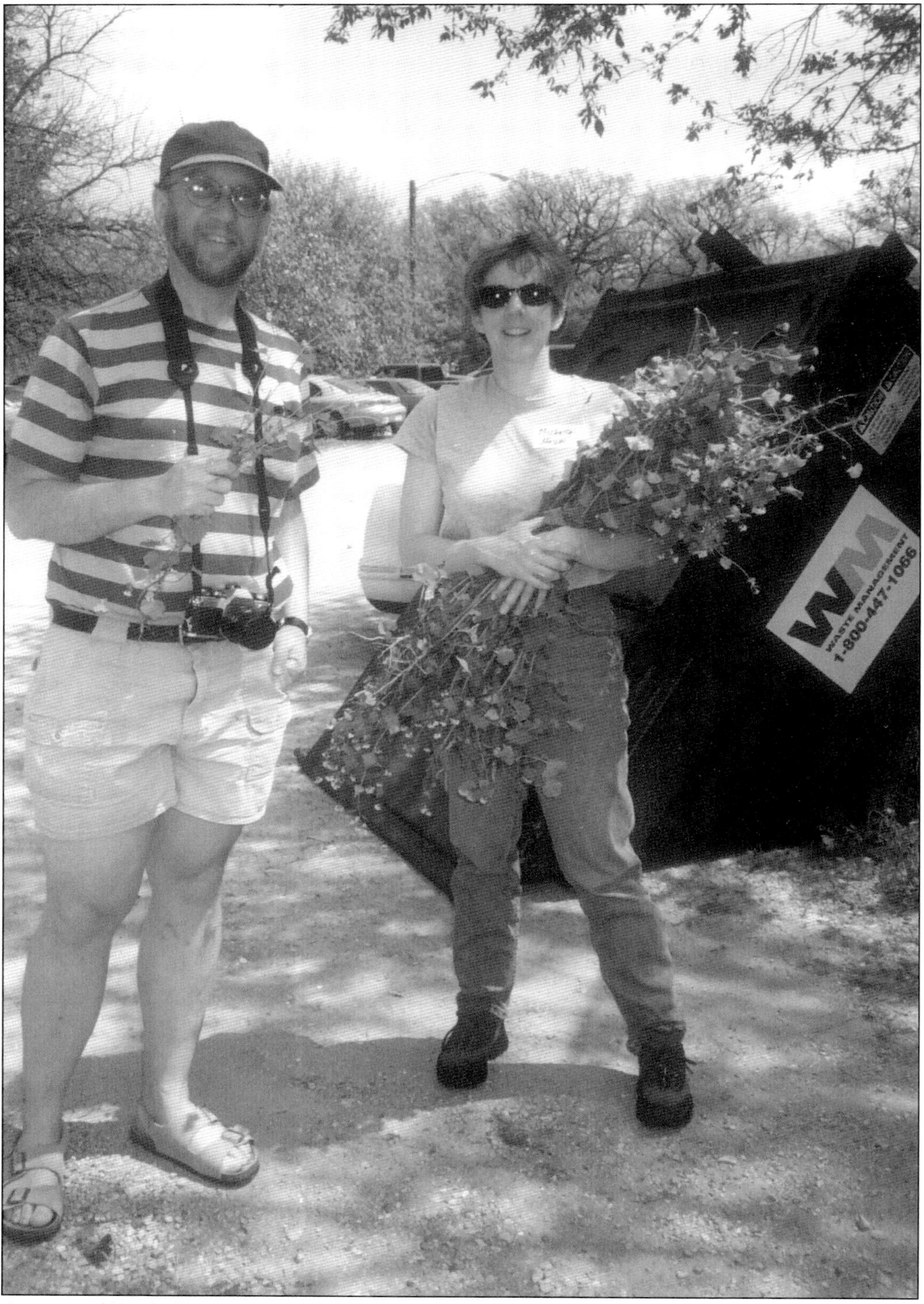

As part of Earth Day, Prairie Club members Glenn Kraus and Michelle Hayes help remove invasive garlic mustard. (1999.)

Eight

NATURE AND CONSERVATION

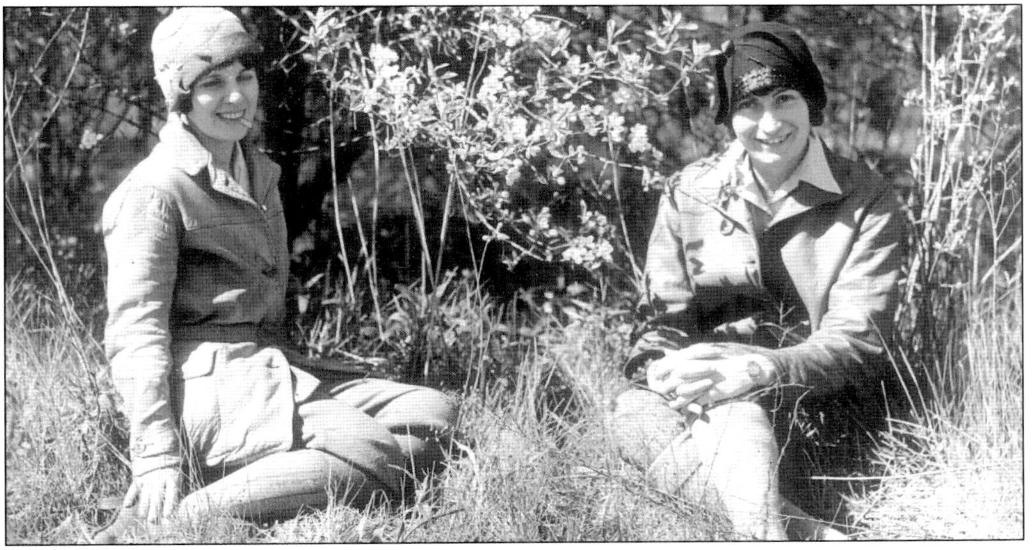

For Chicagoans, land has always been the currency of the community. Since the city was first platted, fortunes have been made and lost in real estate. For nature lovers, the price was often high. As the city pushed outwards, precious rural habitats were lost.

Conservation has been a core value for the Prairie Club since its inception. Even though the Chicago environs in the early 1900s were much more rural than today, Prairie Club members were particularly prescient. They foresaw a day when the oak savannahs were felled for timber, and prairie roses bloomed no more.

Anxious to preserve the natural world, the Prairie Club joined forces with other conservationist groups to lead and lobby. Members and friends of the Prairie Club included some of the nation's leading thinkers in ecology like Henry C. Cowles. Members Dwight Perkins and Jens Jensen were intimately involved in developing the Forest Preserve plans. These leaders found kindred spirits in their fellow Prairie Club members.

From the outset, each Prairie Club bulletin about the early Saturday Afternoon Walks exhorted: "In large parties, special care should be exercised to avoid doing damage to fences and cultivated fields. Flowers should not be gathered, nor limbs of trees or shrubs broken. Gates should be closed by the last member of the party."

A Conservation Committee was formally organized in 1913, and has remained active to this day. Some of the club's conservation efforts were dramatic, like the very public pageants in the Indiana Dunes, and some are more subtle, like the annual Earth Day activities or work days.

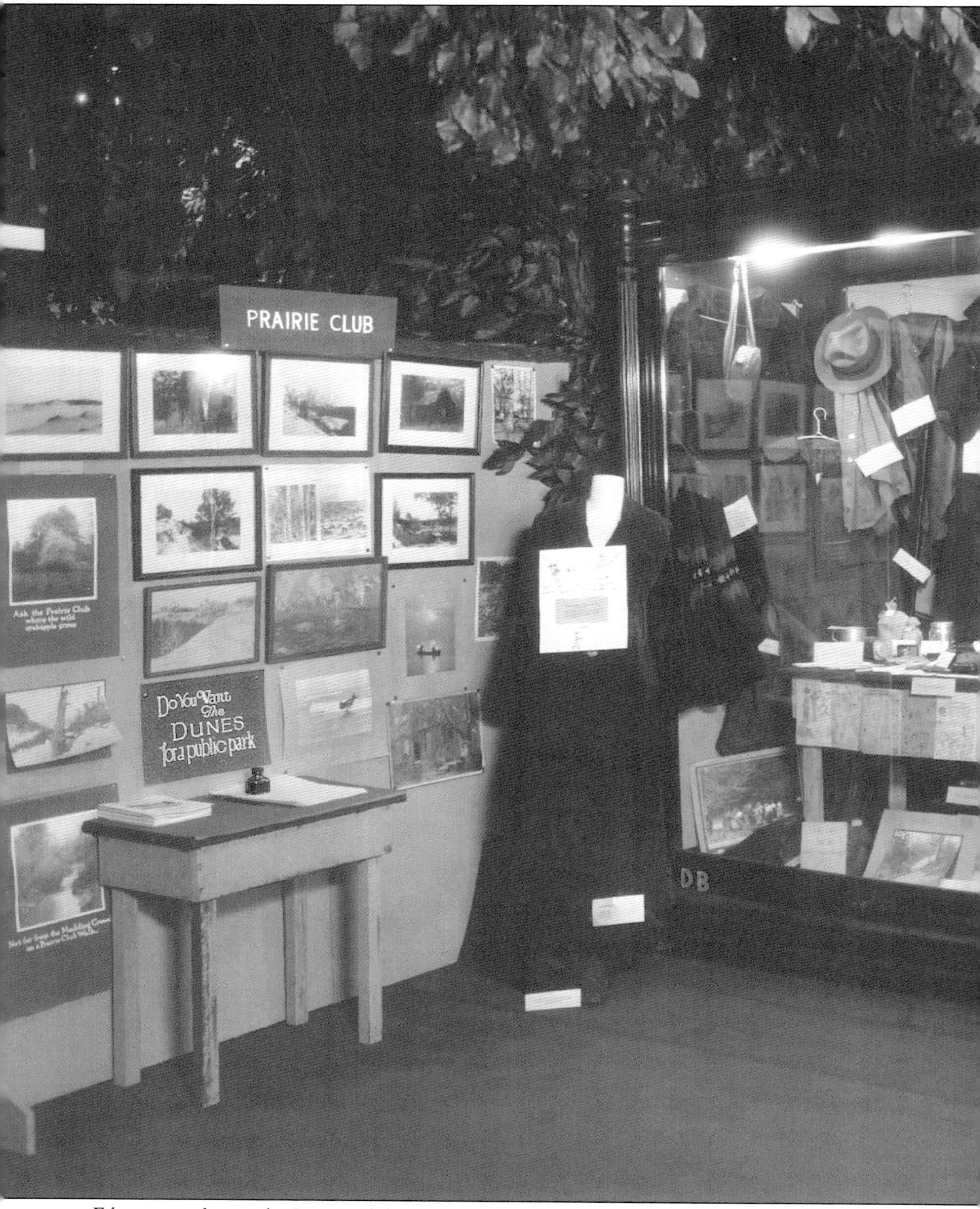

Education is key to the Prairie Club's mission. They help others appreciate and preserve the wonders

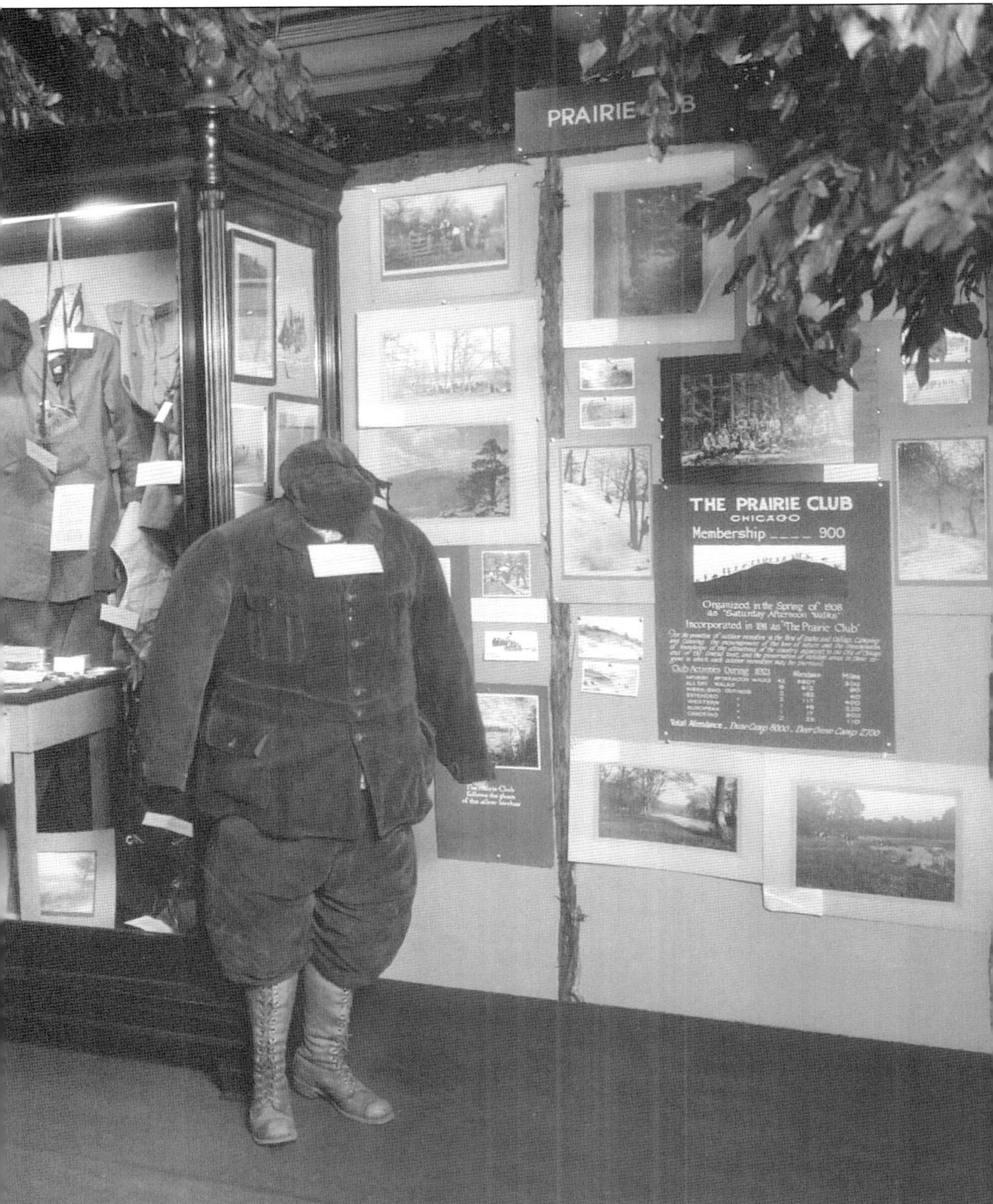

of nature through many activities, including walks and exhibits like this at Marshall Fields. (1922.)

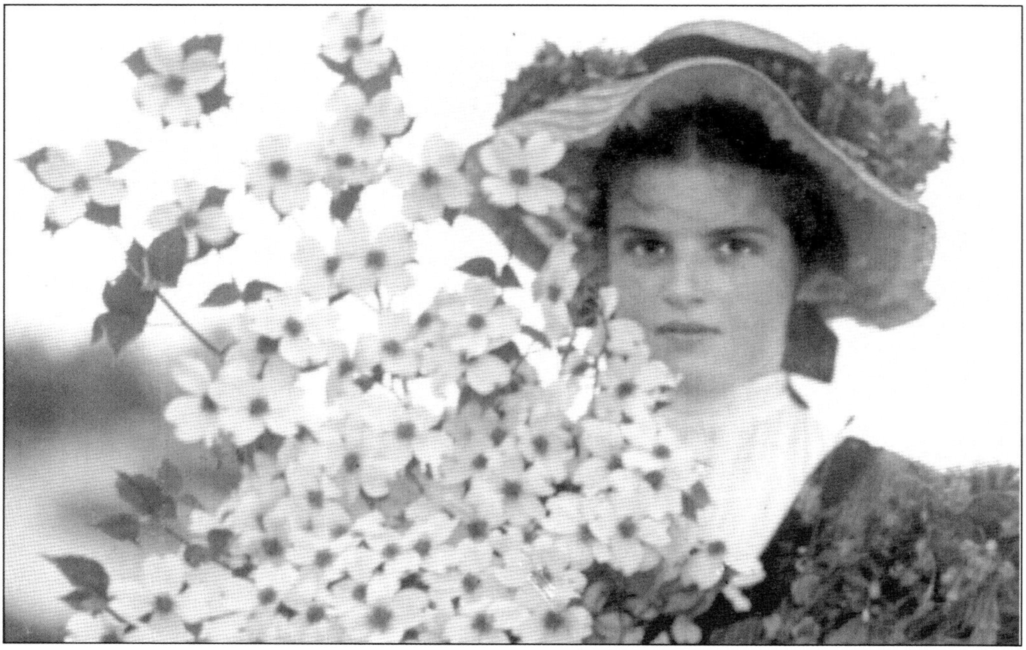

At the heart of it, Prairie Club members are nature lovers. This young lady with her basket of dogwood was lovely on Decoration Day at the Dunes. (May 31, 1909.)

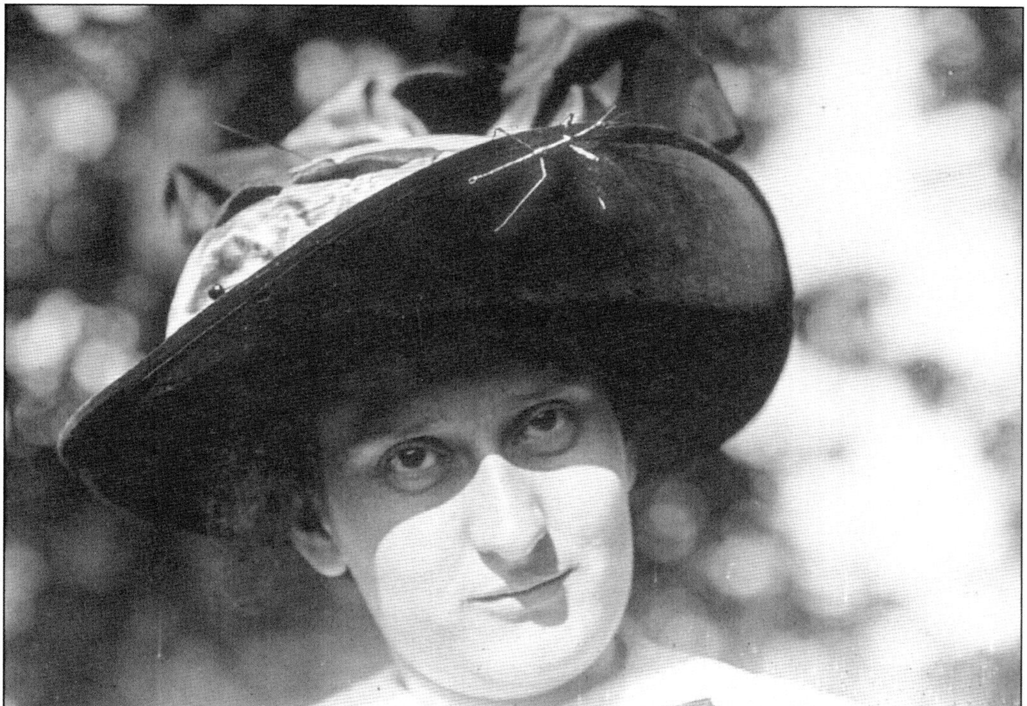

Who would be squeamish about a bug? Look carefully at the woman's hat. Fitting for the Prairie Club hike, a walking stick insect is perched on the upturned hat brim. (September 23, 1911.)

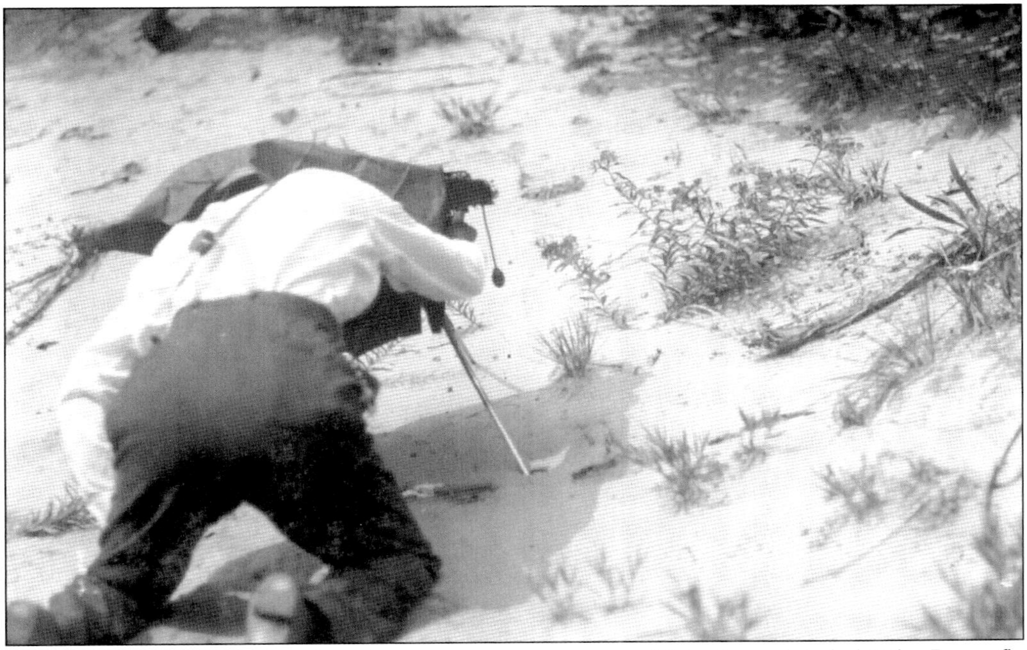

Of course, the only things taken from nature were pictures. This photo, labeled "The Butterfly Hunter," shows a photographer's pursuit of the winged insects near Furnessville, Indiana. (July 4, 1910.)

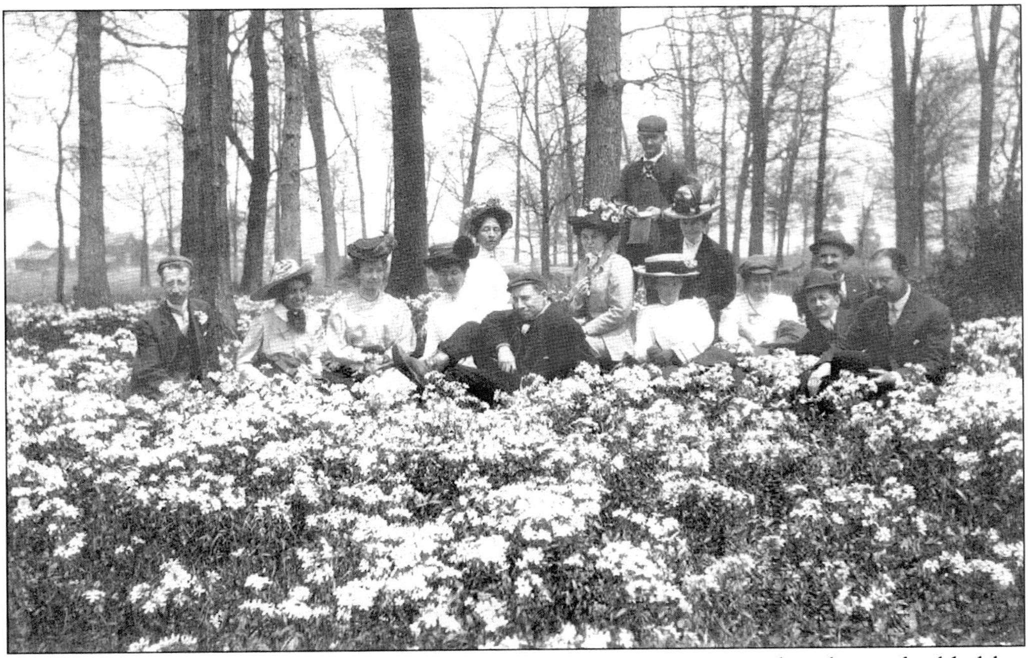

Sometimes it's hard to separate Prairie Club members from nature as in this photo of wild phlox seen near Mokena. (1910.)

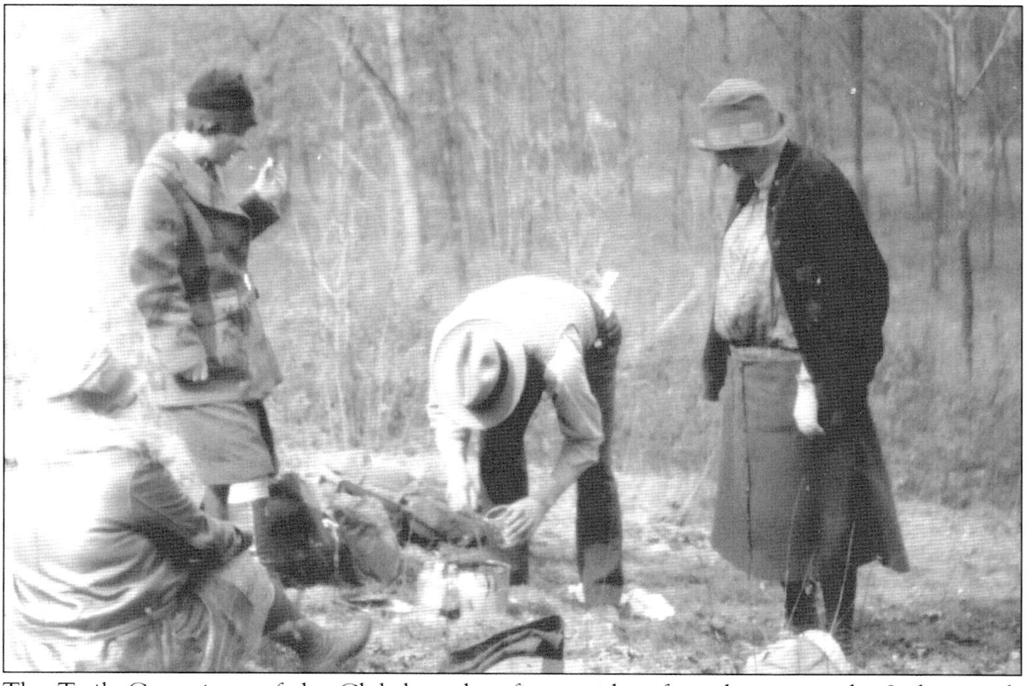

The Trails Committee of the Club hoped at first to identify and preserve the Indian trails around Chicago. Although this effort proved too difficult, the club was very instrumental in designing the forest preserve trails. Here, paint was mixed to mark trees. (1927.)

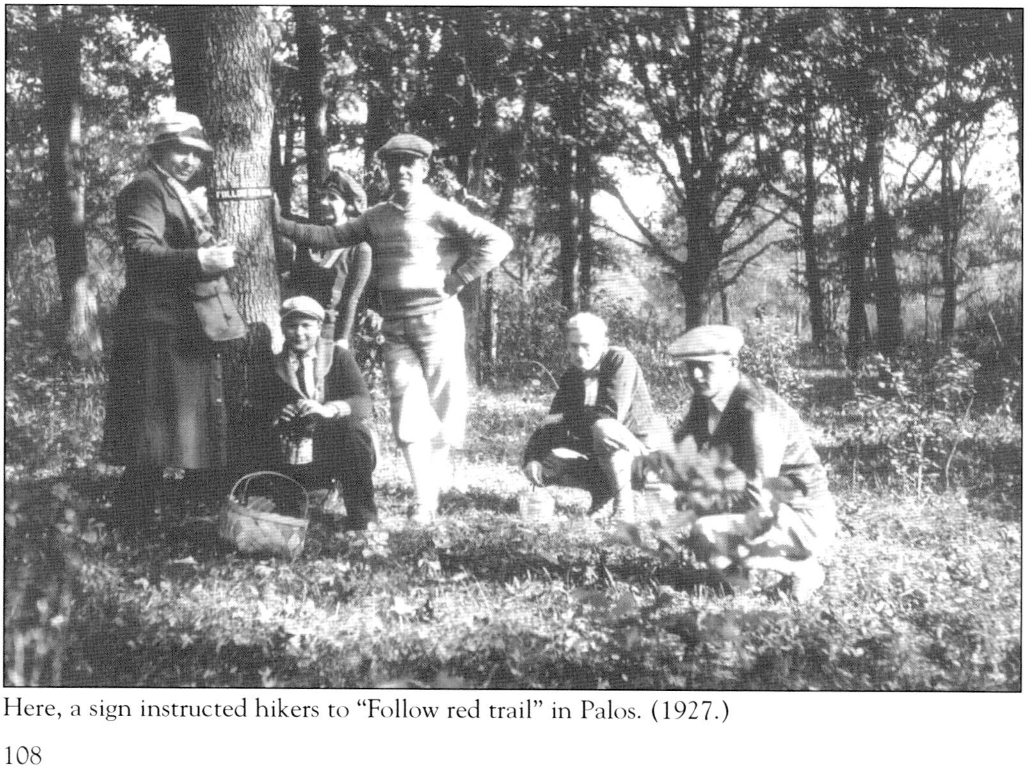

Here, a sign instructed hikers to "Follow red trail" in Palos. (1927.)

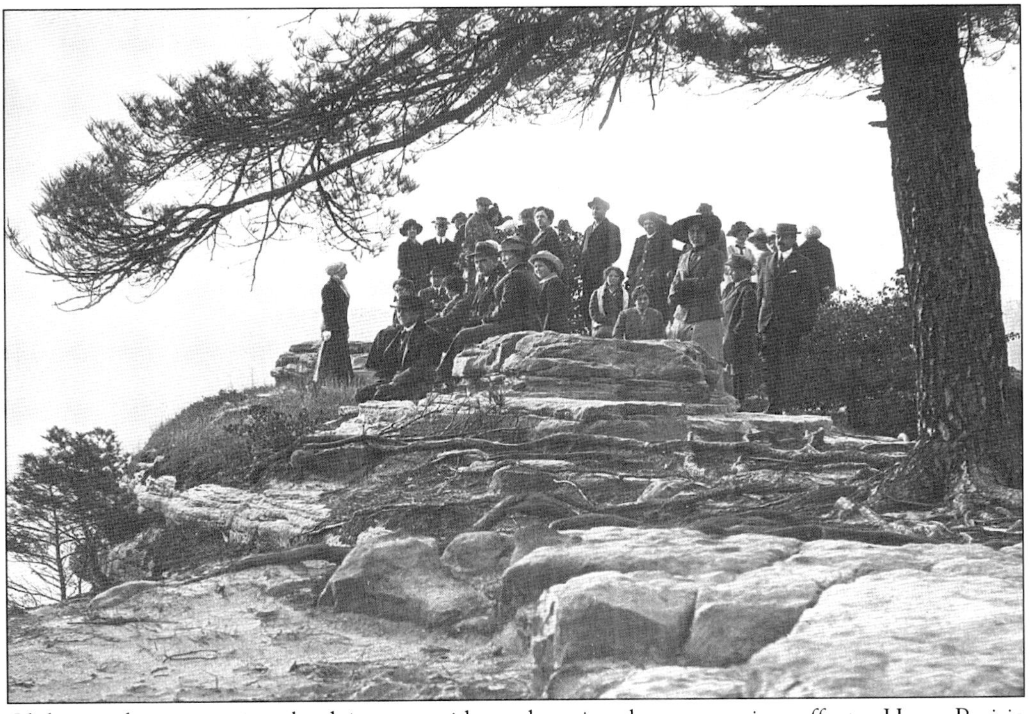

Club members were involved in statewide and national conservation efforts. Here, Prairie Club hikers paused for moment of reflection atop Starved Rock, now an Illinois State Park. (May 11, 1913.)

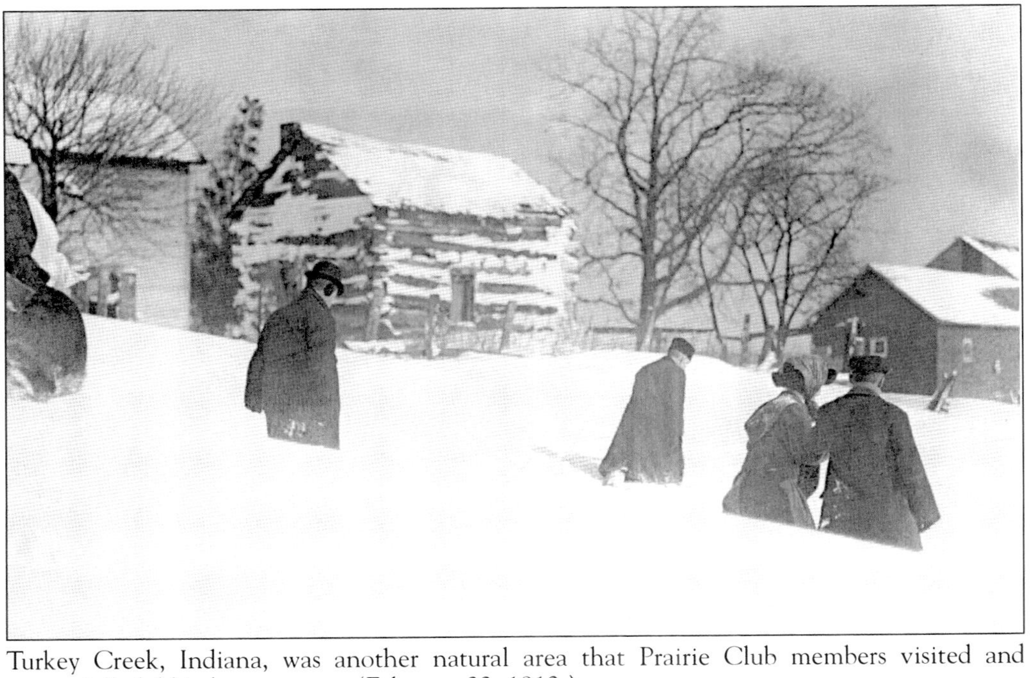

Turkey Creek, Indiana, was another natural area that Prairie Club members visited and successfully lobbied to preserve. (February 22, 1912.)

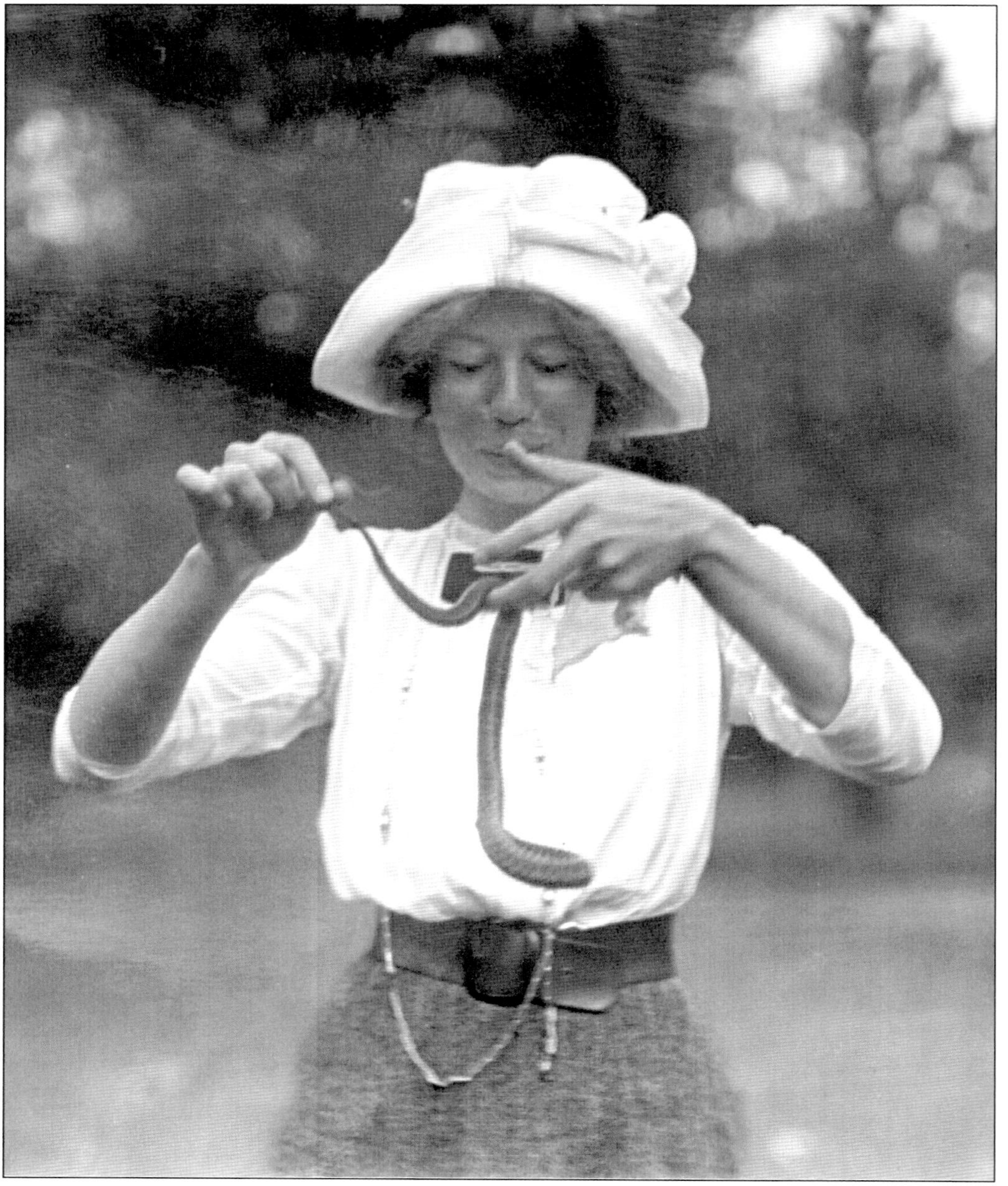

Snakes alive! With her elegant hat, this young lady was not afraid of a snake found on a walk along the Chicago River. (June 15, 1912.)

Eight

THAT'S ENTERTAINMENT!

All walk and no play does not a happy hiker make. In keeping with their goal to develop pursuits that celebrated nature, Prairie Club members enjoyed many outdoor activities. Winter sports included skiing and skating, summer meant swimming and boating, fall and spring included everything in between. Picnics, barbecues, square dancing, outdoor plays—any wholesome activity that encouraged fellowship and fun was fair game. With each generation, new and old traditions were made, all in the spirit of good, clean fun.

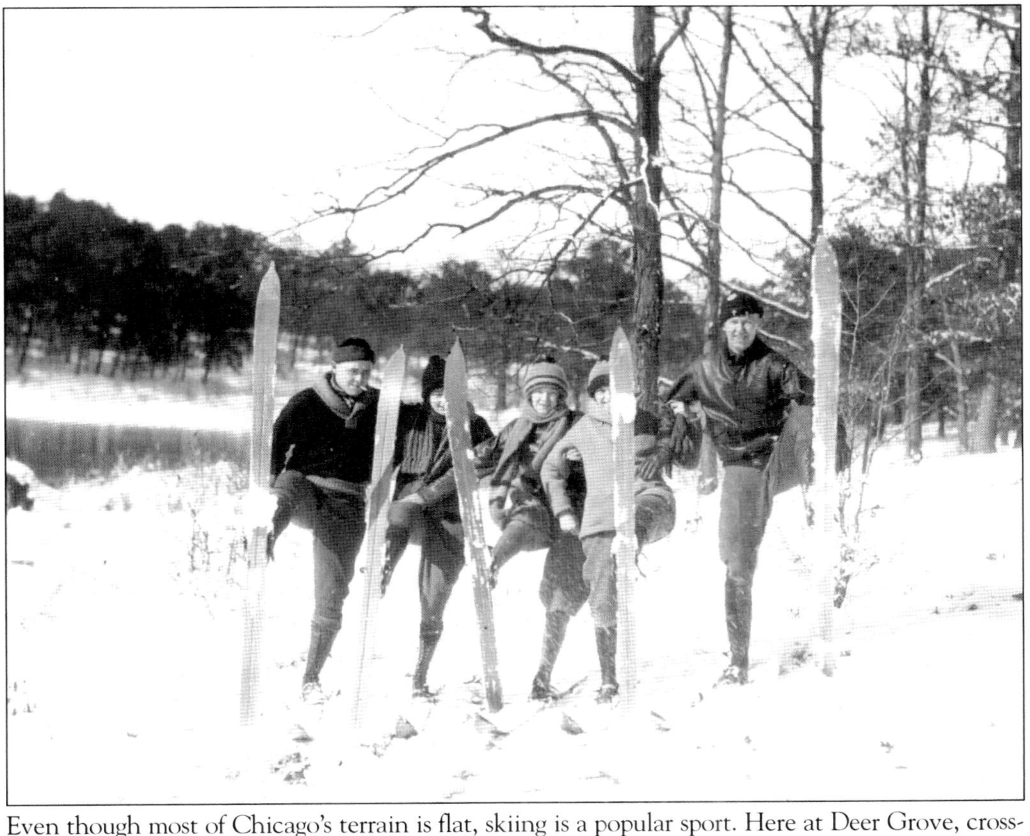

Even though most of Chicago's terrain is flat, skiing is a popular sport. Here at Deer Grove, cross-country skiing was a favorite, with a few hills providing some excitement. (November 8, 1925.)

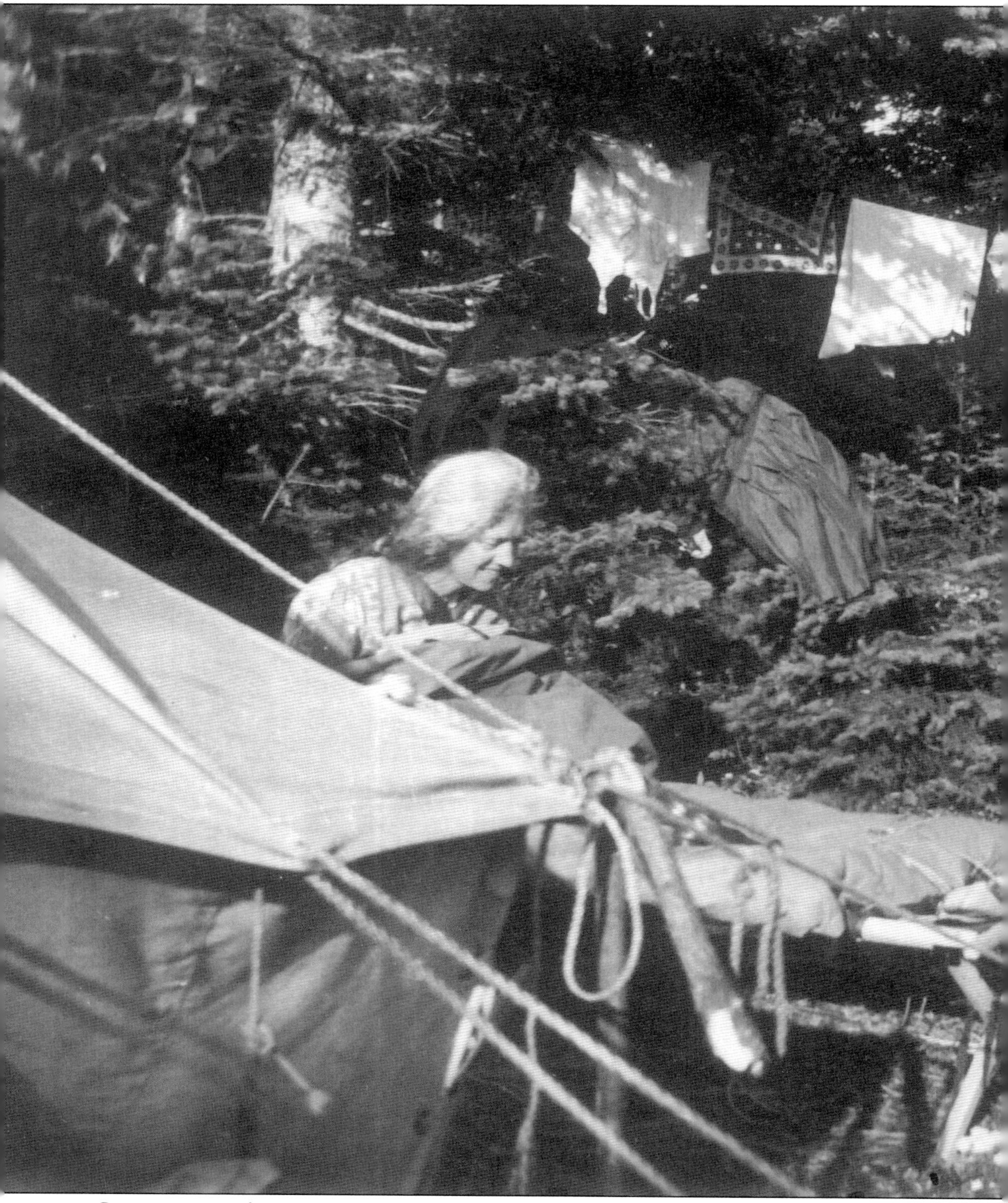

Camping was, of course, one of the favorite ways to enjoy the outdoors, even if it was a little hard to rise and shine in the mornings. These ladies keep sturdy boots near their beds, even as

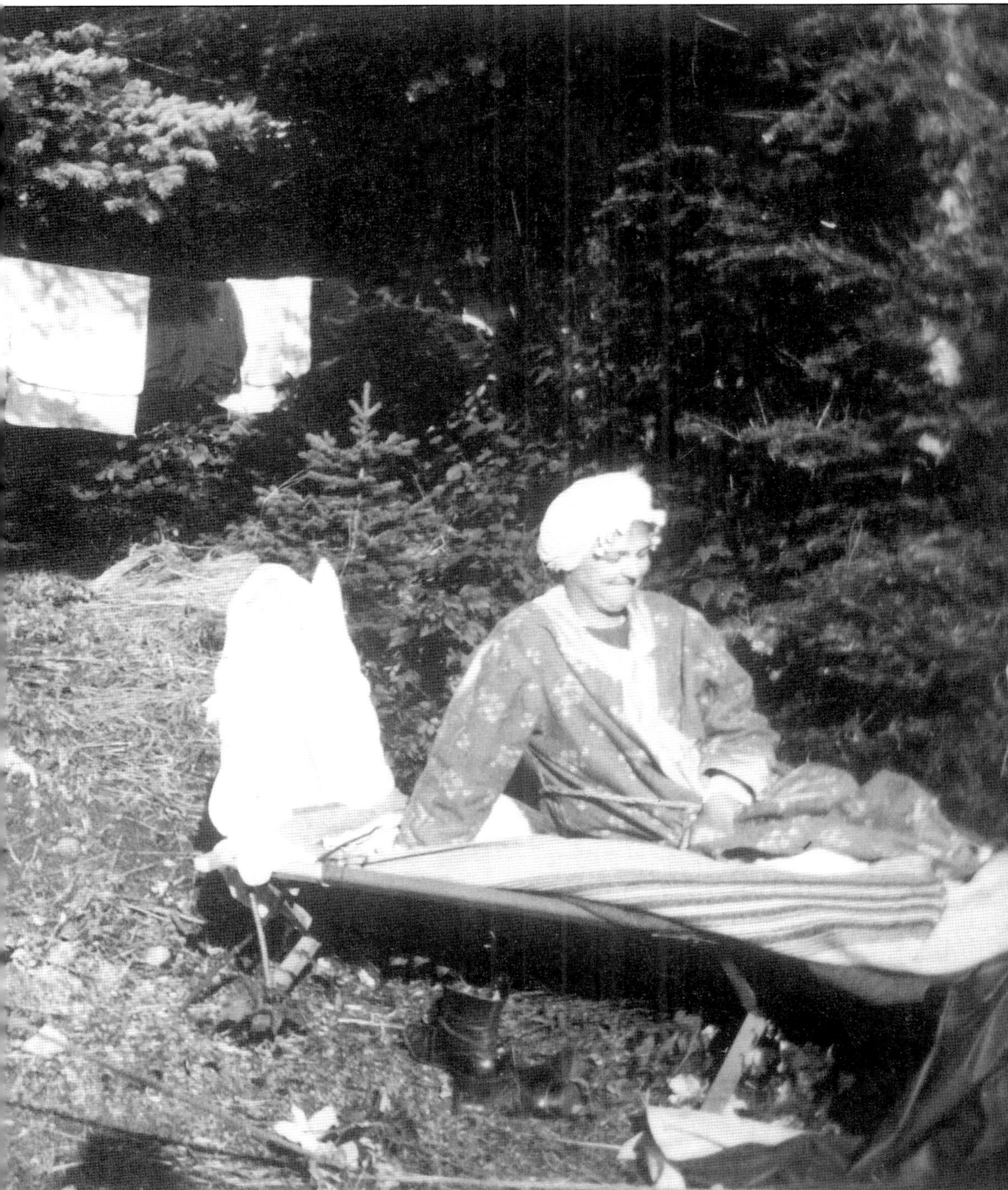

they wear the latest nightcaps and gowns. (1920.)

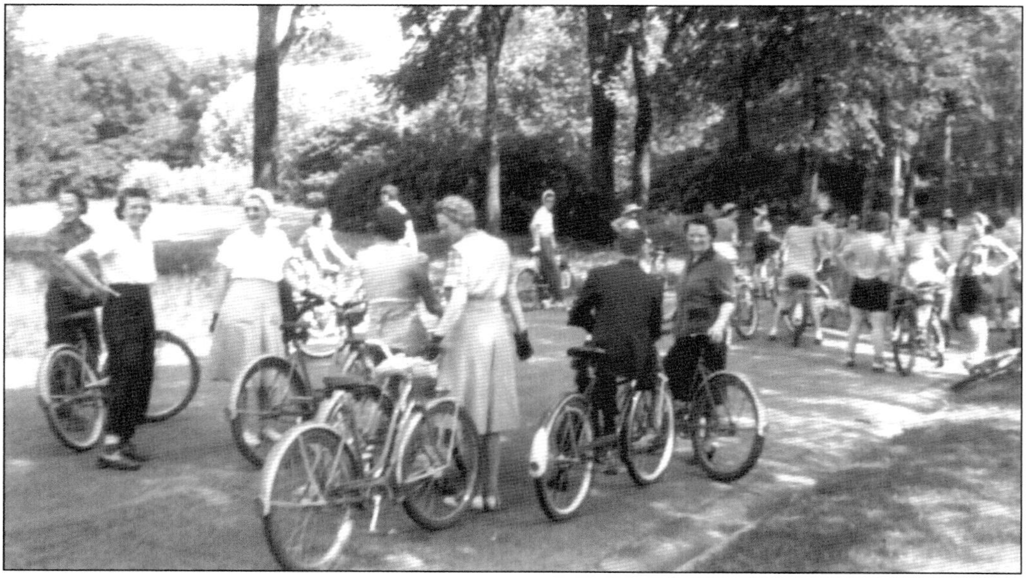

Bicycle trips became another popular means of people-powered transportation. (No date.)

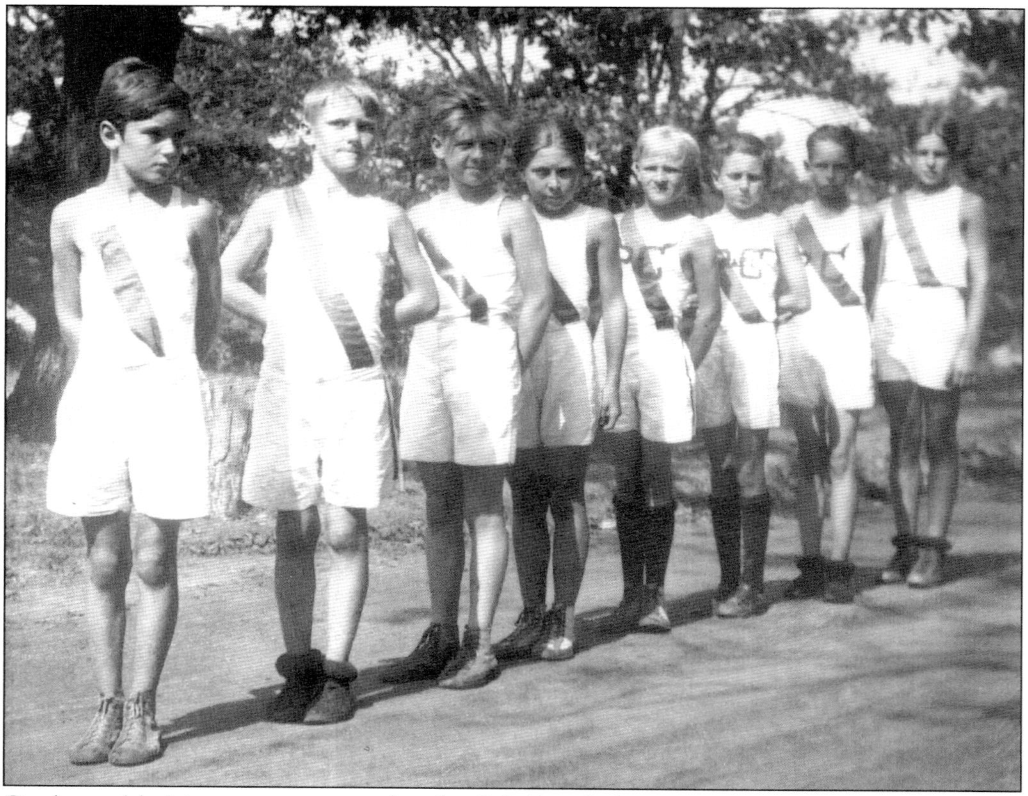

Outdoor athleticism was encouraged with a July Fourth foot race. (No date.)

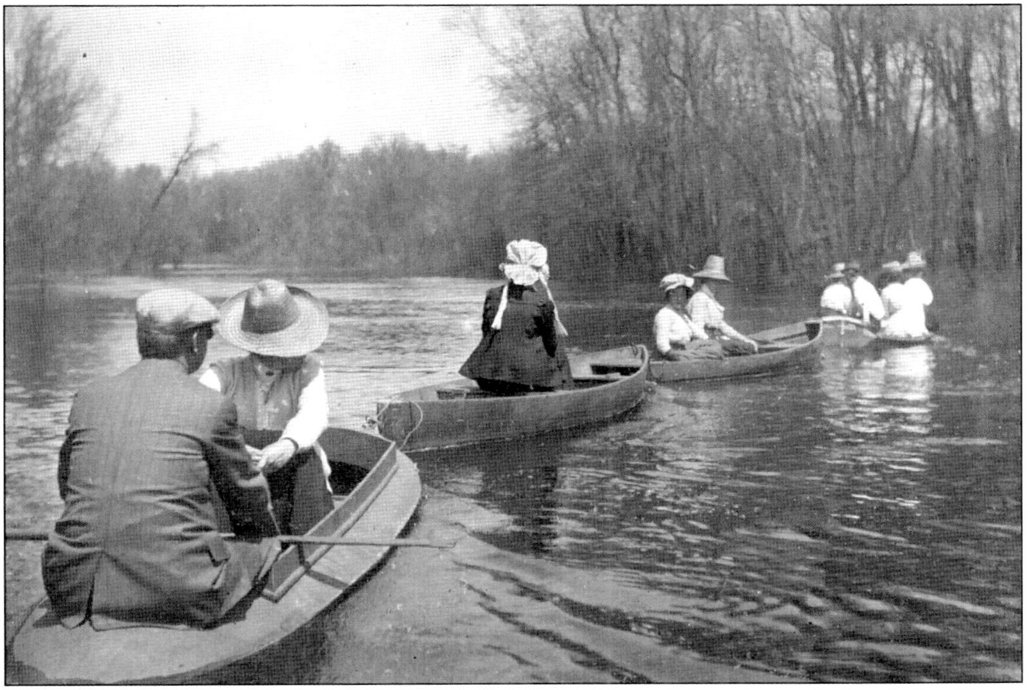

Canoeing was a favorite sport. Here *c.* 1911, hikers took their boats across the Kankakee River. Later, in the early 1920s, a club committee sponsored regular canoe outings.

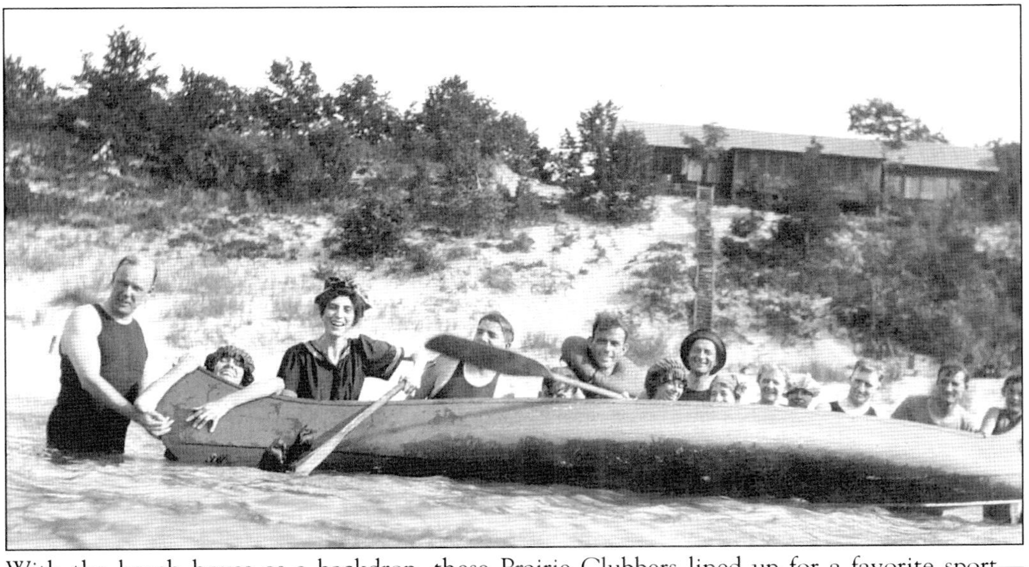

With the beach house as a backdrop, these Prairie Clubbers lined up for a favorite sport—canoeing. (1914.)

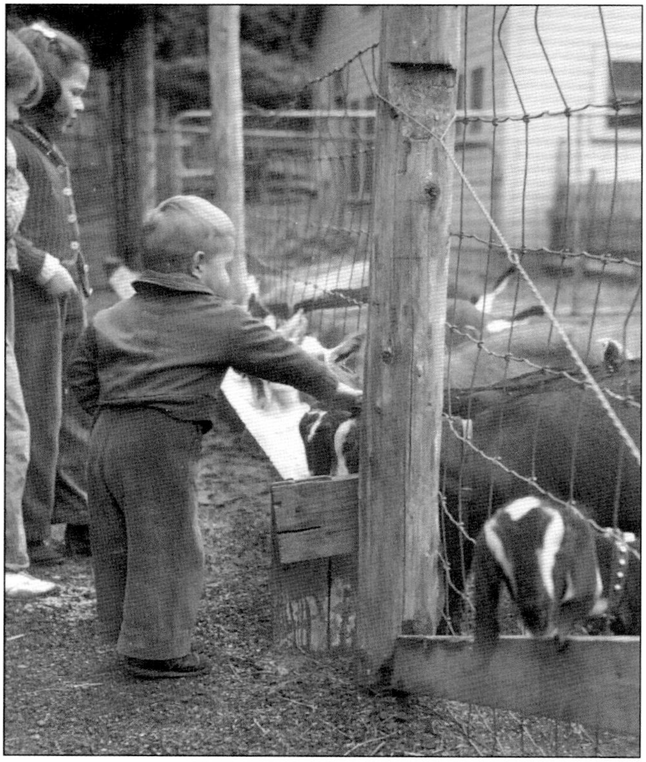

Encouraging a love of nature in youth is a Prairie Club ideal. Here, a young Otto Becker visits the goats at the nearby Michigan farm of poet Carl Sandburg. (1941.) (Photo coutesy of Otto Becker.)

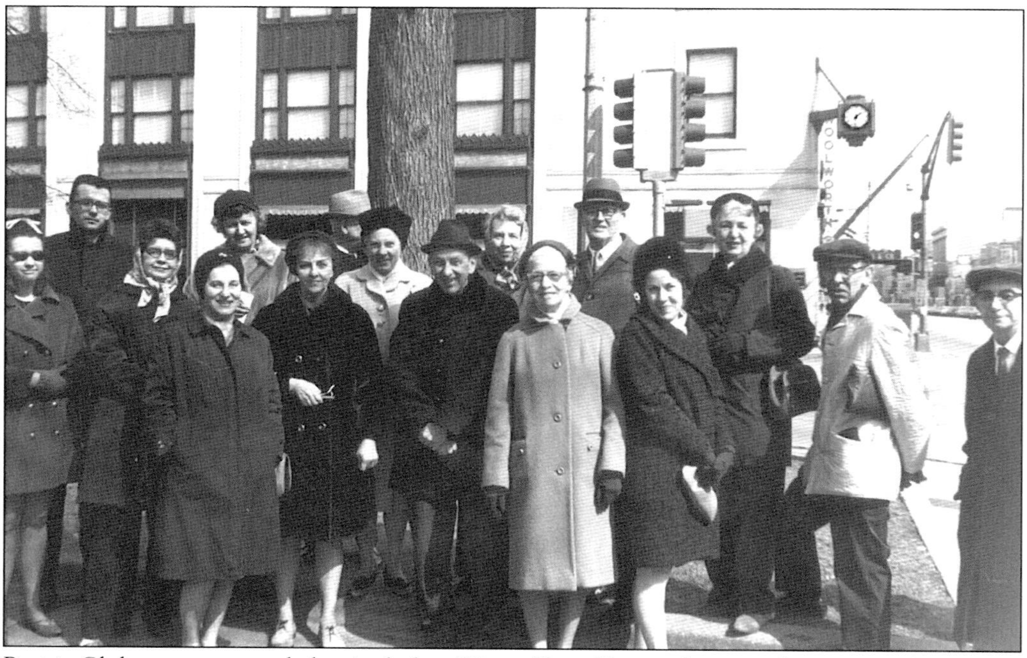

Prairie Club events expanded to include a "Know Your Chicago" event wherein members would visit various towns or sites near the city. Here, the group visits Oak Park. (No date.)

Song and music accompanied nearly all Prairie Club walks and events. This song book includes favorites like "The Prairie Club Tramping Song" and "If You Want to be a Dunebug." (1924.)

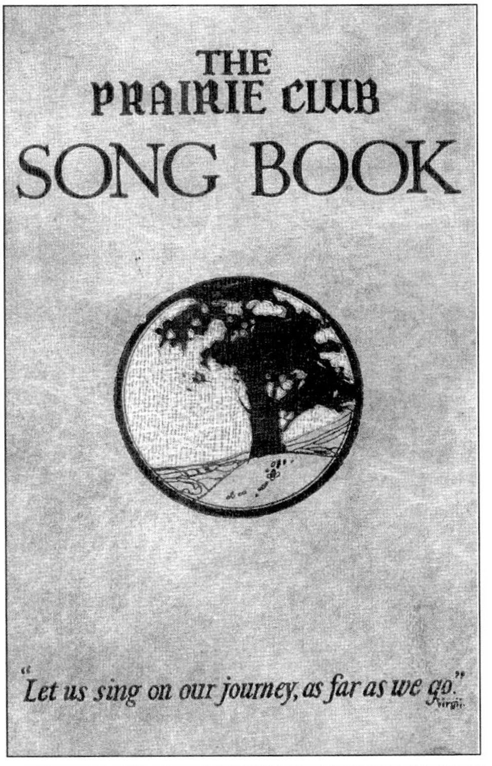

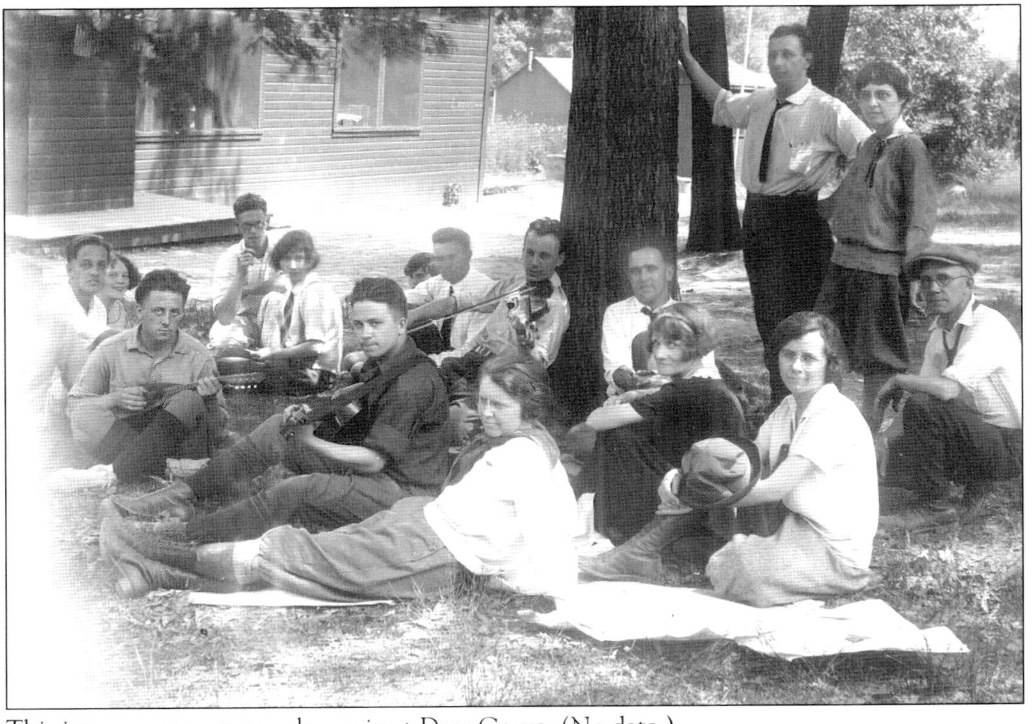

This impromptu group made music at Deer Grove. (No date.)

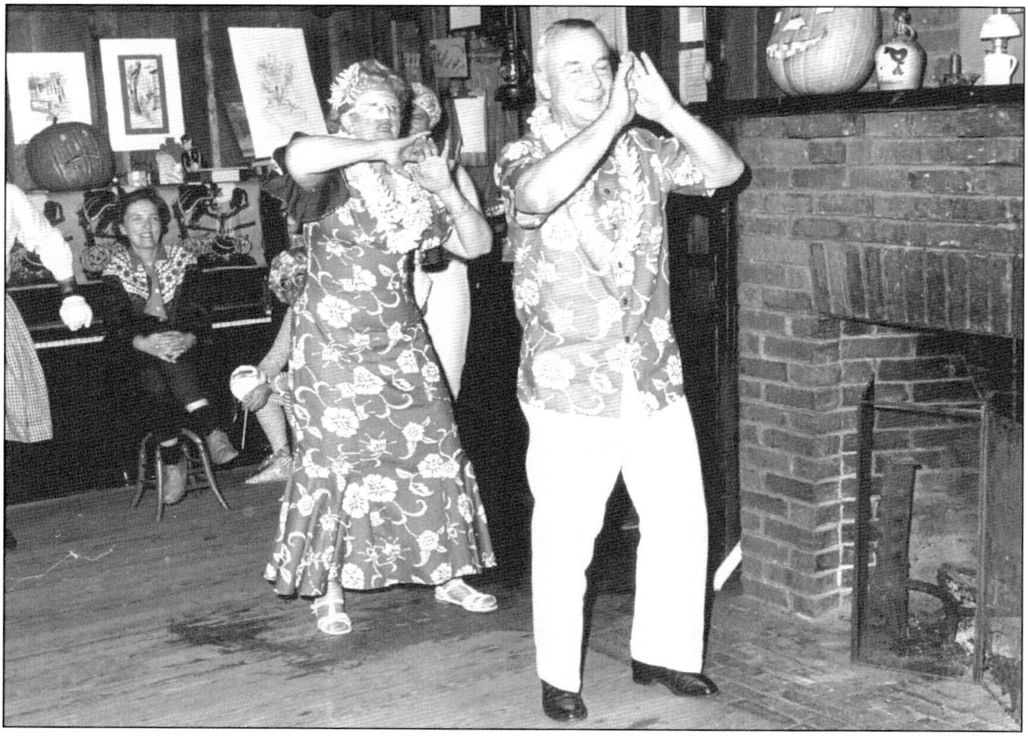

Dancing and decorated pumpkins were part of the fun at this Halloween party at the Tremont beach house in 1955.

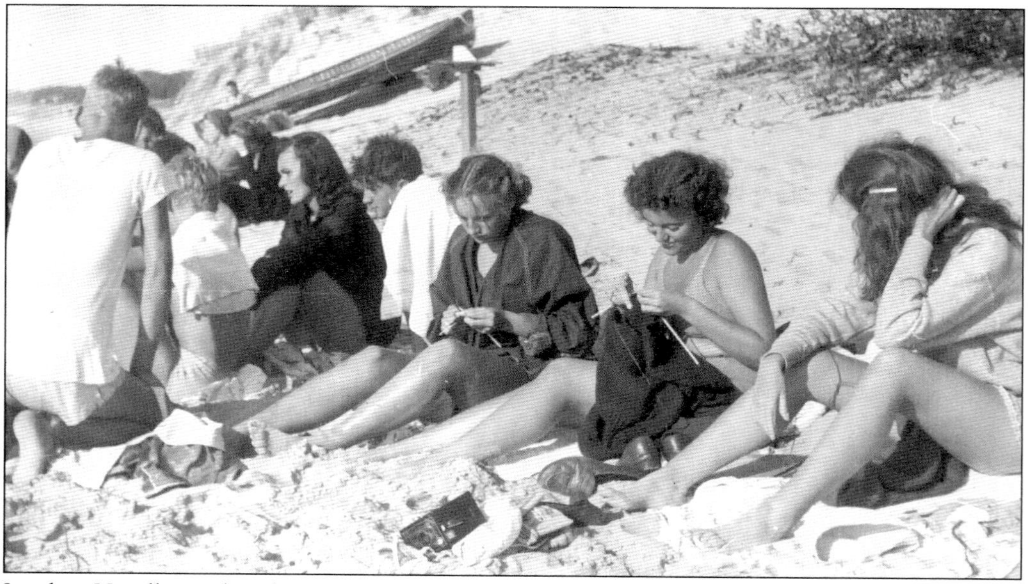

In this Hazelhurst beach scene, young men and women enjoyed conversation and some industrious knitting. Pictured, from left to right, are as follows: (back to camera) Bruce Herbert, Dick Spurgin, Joyce McMahon, John North, Isle Von Meding, Dorothy Spurgin, and Jane Lee Hughes. (1944.) (Photo courtesy of Dick Spurgin.)

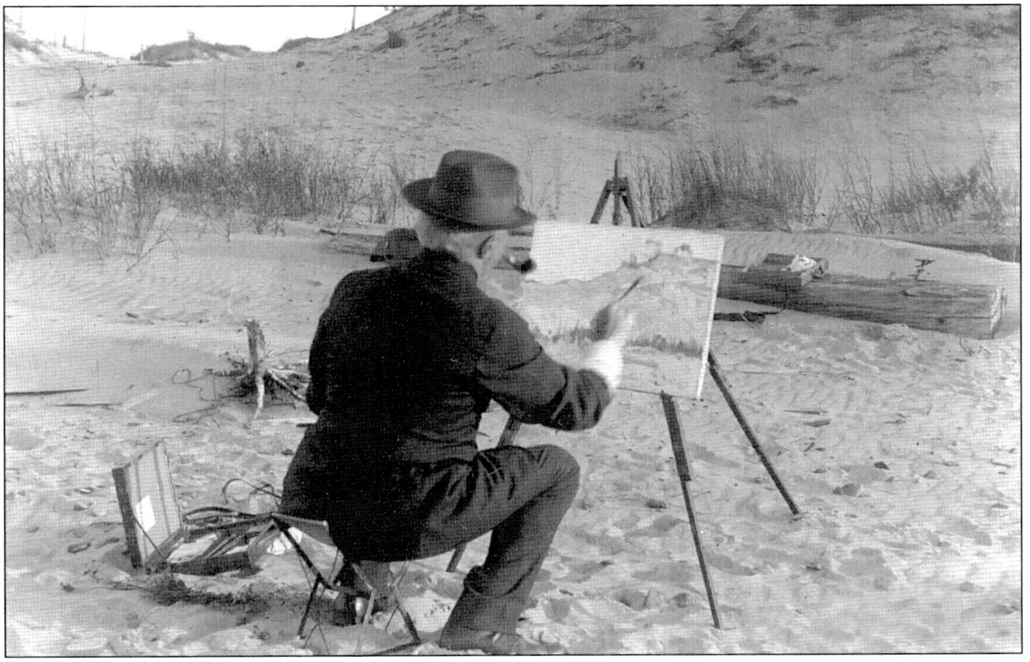

Many Prairie Club members had artistic inclinations, such as this painter in the Dunes in this photo dated October 19, 1913.

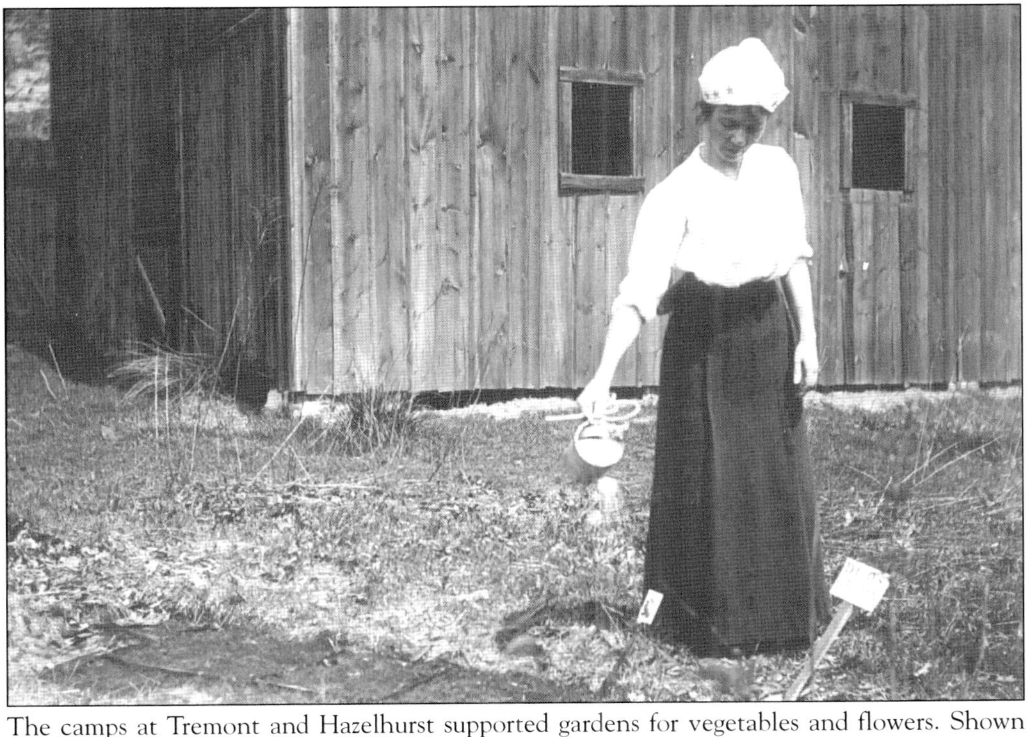

The camps at Tremont and Hazelhurst supported gardens for vegetables and flowers. Shown here, a Prairie Club member waters the garden at Tremont. (April 27, 1914.)

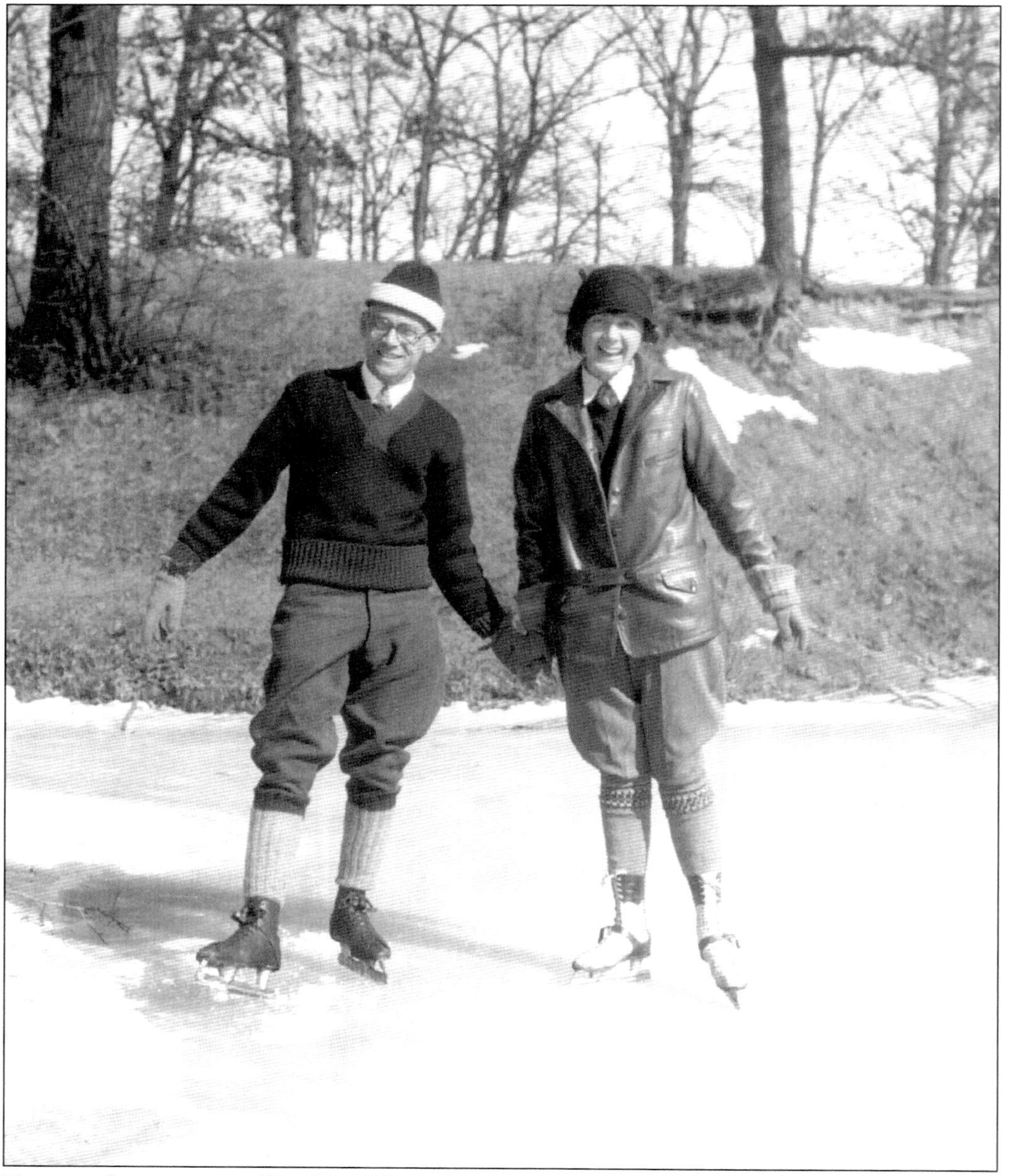

Notices of upcoming walks often exhorted, "Bring your skates." This couple enjoyed the sport at Deer Grove. (1928.)

Ten

PRAIRIE CLUB TODAY

More than 90 years young, the Prairie Club still honors its goals of conservation, education, and enjoyment of nature. Of course, the landscape has changed. Hikers today no longer struggle with awkward clothing, barbed wire, or wild terrain. Some of the camps exist only in memory and the pages of this book. Many of the threatened natural sites have, thankfully, been preserved.

But there is more to do. The 800 members of the Prairie Club are very active today in conservation and ecology issues. The club has just established a nonprofit Conservation and Education Fund to support worthy environmental efforts. A percentage of membership dues is given to groups protecting the rivers, parks, and prairies, and, of course, the Indiana Dunes.

On Saturday afternoons, no matter the weather, you will find them on the trail or path amidst the beauty of nature. Bring your sturdy boots and comfortable clothes and join the Prairie Club for a walk!

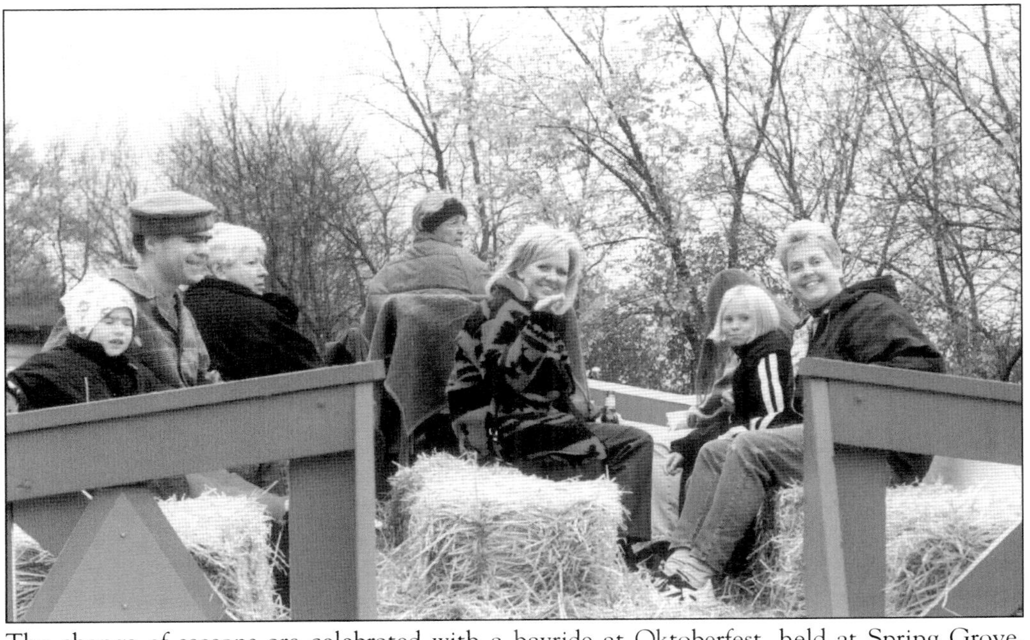

The change of seasons are celebrated with a hayride at Oktoberfest, held at Spring Grove. (October 1999.)

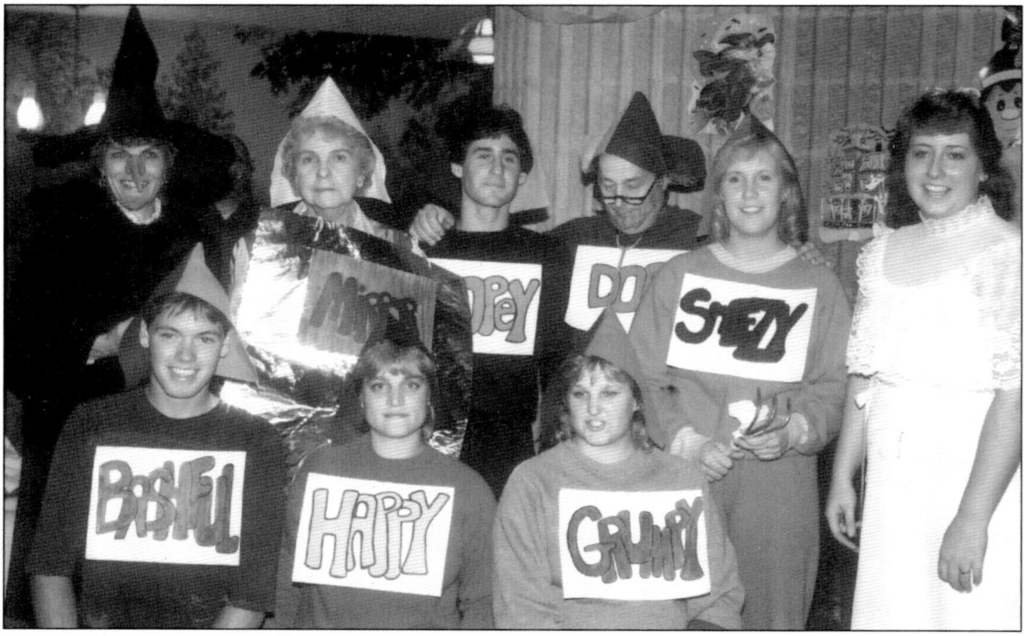

Prairie Club members still love costume parties. Here, the dwarfs and Snow White attend a Halloween Party. (1985.)

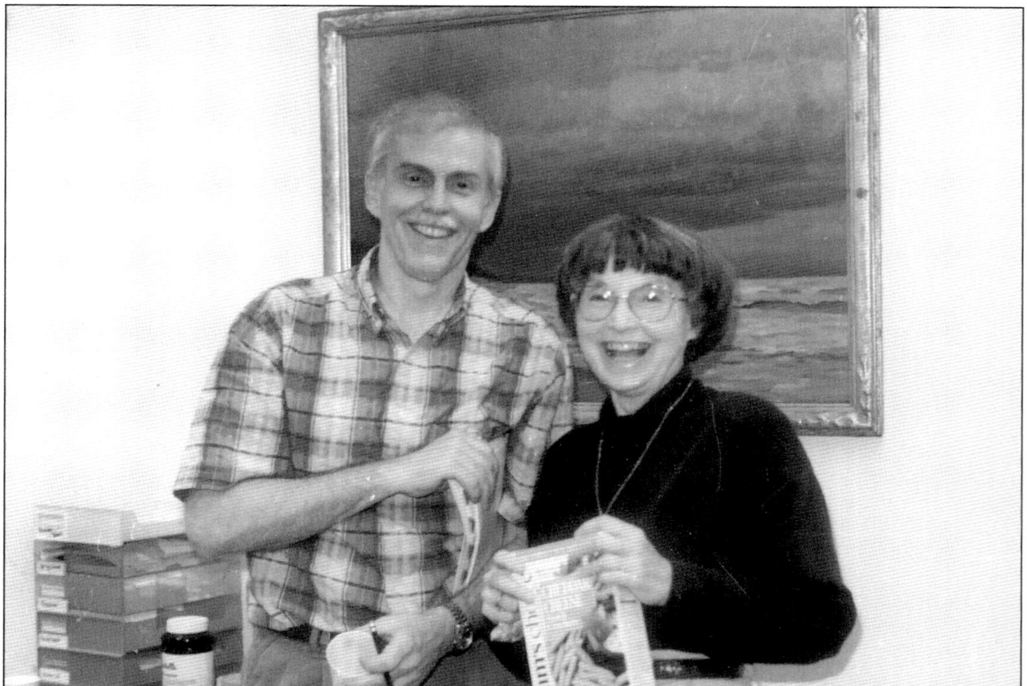

Standing in front of one of Frank V. Dudley's best known paintings in the Prairie Club office are past presidents Herb Carlson and Marlene Shales.

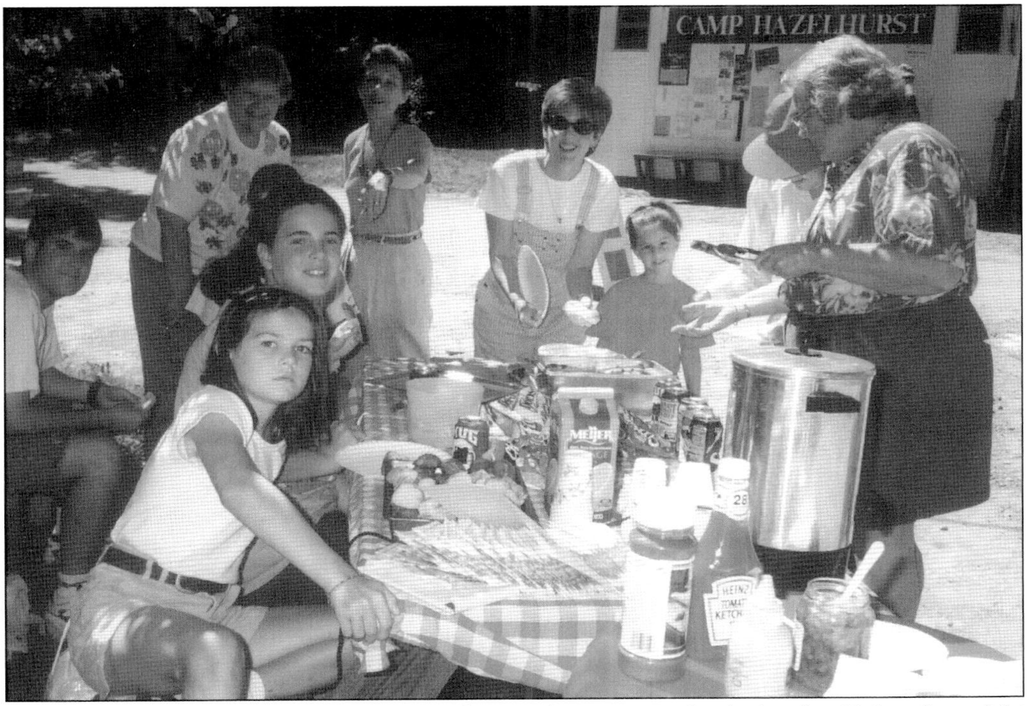

Every year, the Prairie Club sponsors a flea market to raise funds for the Helen Strezelcki Conservation scholarship. The Hazelhurst juniors are shown making refreshments. (1988.)

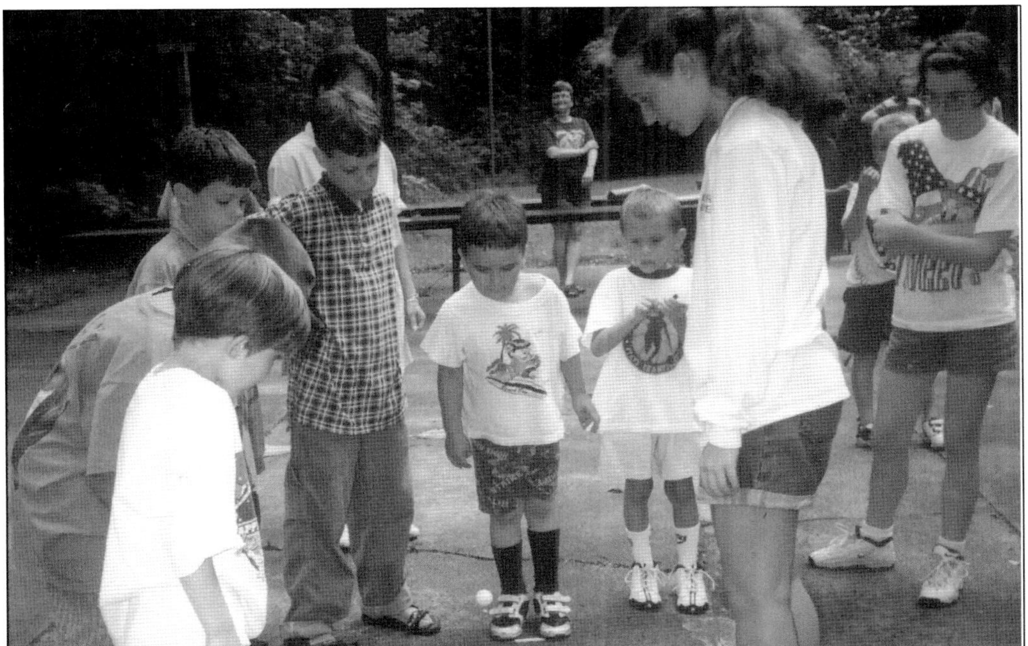

One of Chicago's favorite children's television shows, *Bozo the Clown*, featured "The Grand Prize Game," as played at Hazelhurst by these children.

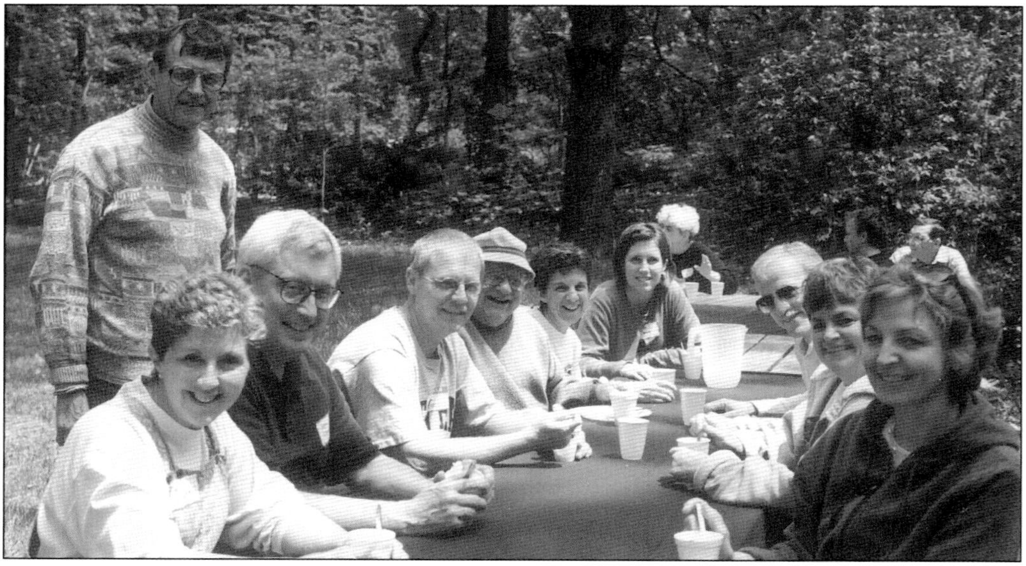

Picnics continue to be a favorite Prairie Club pastime. Here, Dick Spurgin (standing, left), Teri and John Clancy, Vic Charlson, Ben Rosen, Ellen Elrick, Katie Clancy, Margery and Tony Longo, Tom Longo, Doug Elrick, Julie Charlson, and Grazyna Wisniowska enjoy the outdoors.

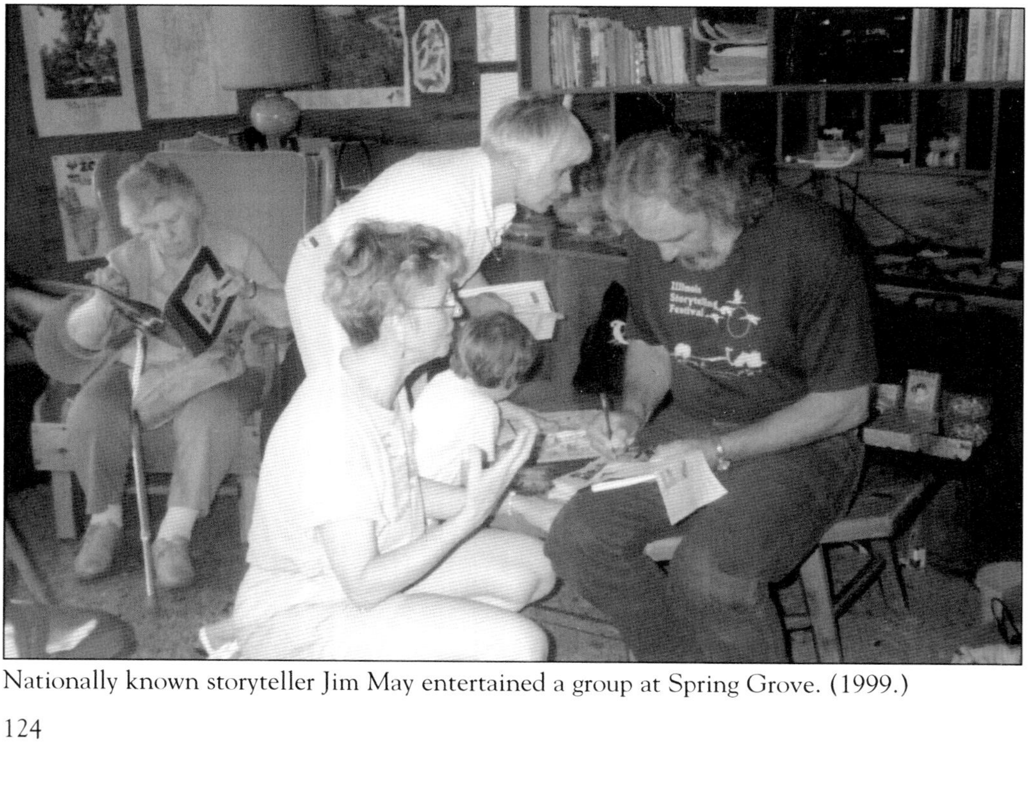

Nationally known storyteller Jim May entertained a group at Spring Grove. (1999.)

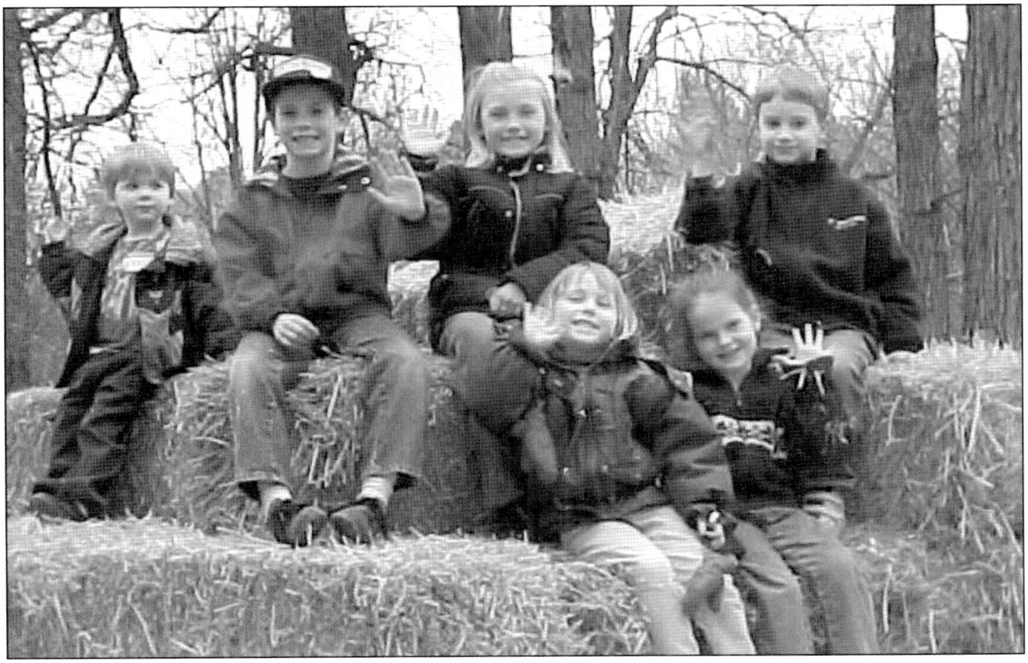

The children enjoyed climbing the haystack after the annual dinner at North Park Village Nature Center. (March 31, 2001.)

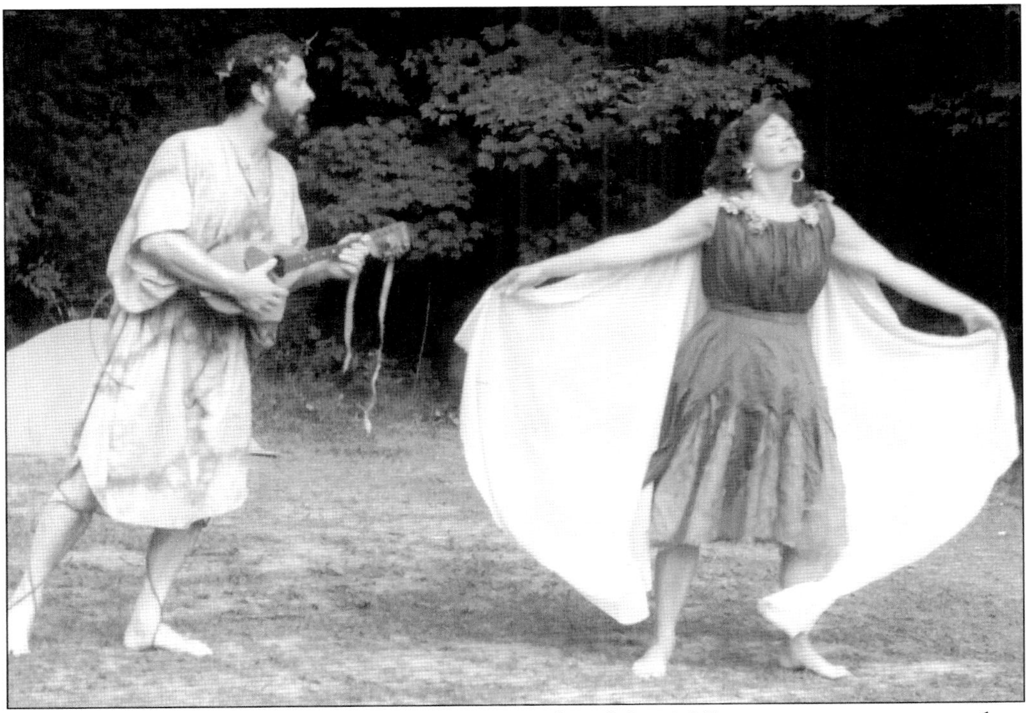

Capturing the spirit of the long ago masques, Ed and Jan Millermaier reenact an outdoor play. (1994.)

INDEX

CONTACT THE PRAIRIE CLUB AT:

533 W. North Ave., Suite 10
Elmhurst, IL 60126
Phone: (630) 516-1277

or via their website:

www.prairieclub.org

Photographs in the Prairie Club archives can be seen by contacting:

Westchester Public Library
100 West Indiana Avenue
Chesterton, Indiana 46304
Phone: (219) 921-0963
jane@wpl.lib.in.us.

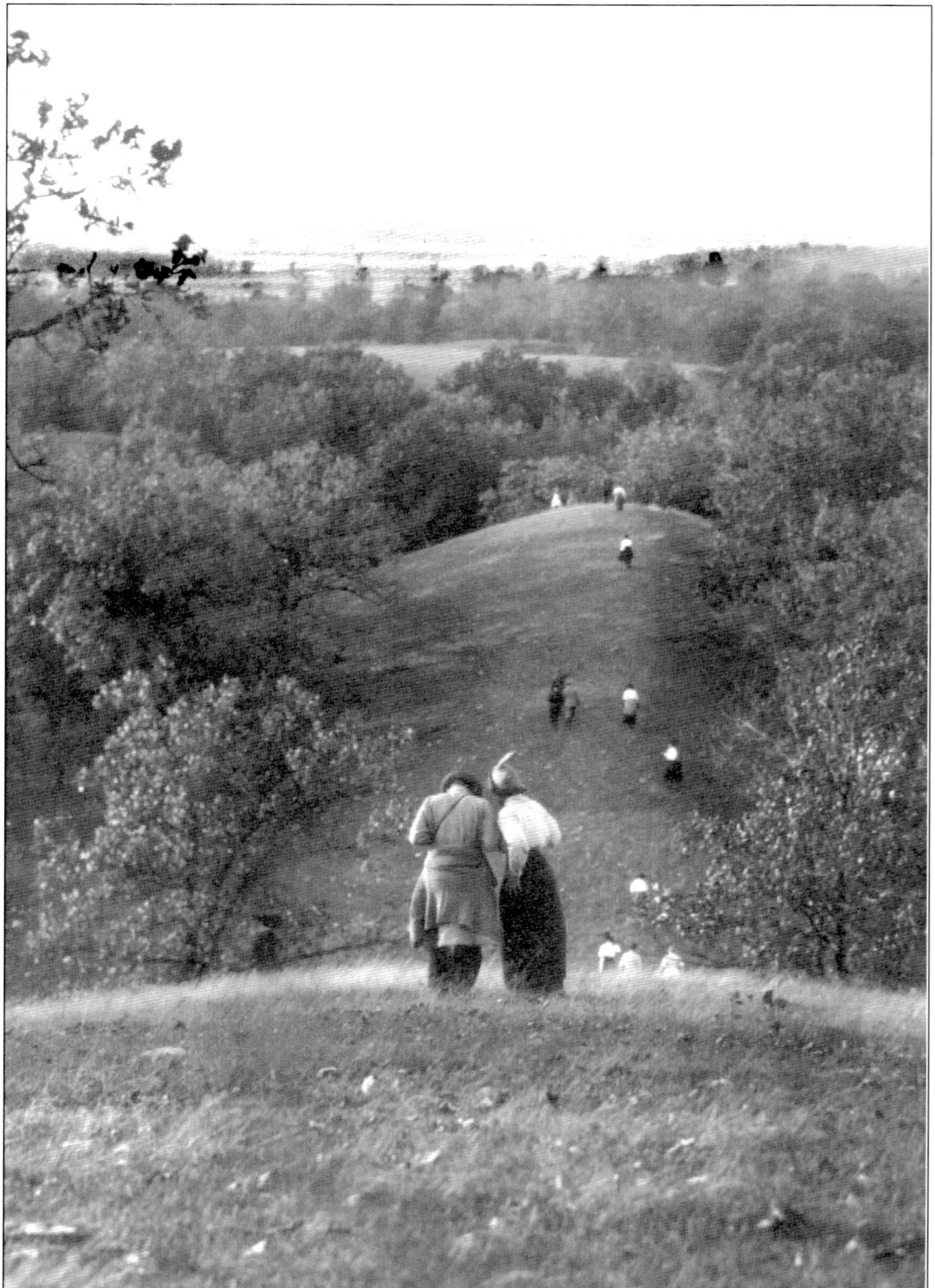

New friendships and a love of nature make for successful Prairie Club walks as on this longer hike from Lake Geneva to Burlington, Wisconsin. (November 12, 1913.)